PENGUIN BOOKS
# AARUSHI

Avirook Sen is a journalist. This is his second book.

# AARUSHI

## AVIROOK SEN

PENGUIN BOOKS

PENGUIN BOOKS

Published by the Penguin Group

Penguin Books India Pvt. Ltd, 7th Floor, Infinity Tower C, DLF Cyber City, Gurgaon 122 002, Haryana, India

Penguin Group (USA) Inc., 375 Hudson Street, New York, New York 10014, USA

Penguin Group (Canada), 90 Eglinton Avenue East, Suite 700, Toronto, Ontario, M4P 2Y3, Canada

Penguin Books Ltd, 80 Strand, London WC2R 0RL, England

Penguin Ireland, 25 St Stephen's Green, Dublin 2, Ireland (a division of Penguin Books Ltd)

Penguin Group (Australia), 707 Collins Street, Melbourne, Victoria 3008, Australia

Penguin Group (NZ), 67 Apollo Drive, Rosedale, Auckland 0632, New Zealand

Penguin Books (South Africa) (Pty) Ltd, Block D, Rosebank Office Park, 181 Jan Smuts Avenue, Parktown North, Johannesburg 2193, South Africa

Penguin Books Ltd, Registered Offices: 80 Strand, London WC2R 0RL, England

First published by Penguin Books India 2015

ISBN 9780143421214

Typeset in Sabon by Manipal Digital Systems, Manipal
Printed at Thomson Press India Ltd, New Delhi

A PENGUIN RANDOM HOUSE COMPANY

*For my mother, Gouri Sen (1935–2014)*

# Contents

# Cast of Characters

## The Family

Dr Rajesh Talwar, Dr Nupur Talwar: Successful dentists who lived in Noida. In their late forties. Both convicted for the 2008 murder of their only daughter Aarushi and their manservant Hemraj.

Dr Dinesh Talwar, Dr Vandana Talwar: Rajesh's elder brother and his wife.

Group Captain (retd) Bhalachandra Chitnis, his wife Lata: Nupur's parents. Live in the same housing complex as Rajesh and Nupur in an identical flat.

## The Friends

Ajay Chaddha: A businessman and close family friend.

Drs Praful and Anita Durrani: Close family friends, also live in Noida. They would go on holidays together with the Talwars. They employed Rajkumar, one of the suspects.

Vidushi Durrani, Fiza Jha: Aarushi's friends and schoolmates. Vidushi is Praful and Anita's daughter.

## The Judges

Preeti Singh: Ghaziabad magistrate who rejected the CBI's closure report and sent the case to trial.

Judge Shyam Lal: Trial judge in the CBI's fast-track court in Ghaziabad. Retired five days after delivering his judgement. Now practises law in Allahabad.

## The Lawyers

Tanveer Ahmed Mir: Delhi criminal lawyer. Came into the case a few months after the trial had begun. Remains the Talwars' lawyer in the appeal stage.

R.K. Saini: Public prosecutor for the CBI.

Satyaketu Singh, Manoj Sisodia: Ghaziabad lawyers retained by the Talwars.

Rebecca John: Senior advocate. Advised the Talwars from 2011. Appeared for the Talwars in the Allahabad High Court.

Harish Salve, U. Lalit, K.V. Vishwanathan: Appeared for the Talwars in the Supreme Court at various stages.

Sidharth Luthra: Additional Solicitor General. Appeared for the CBI in the Supreme Court.

## Other Suspects

Krishna: Rajesh Talwar's assistant at his dental clinic. Originally from Nepal. Lived with a relative in L-14 Jalvayu Vihar, a few houses away from the Talwars. Knew Hemraj well.

Rajkumar: Worked in the Durranis' home. Knew the Talwars very well because of the closeness between the families.

Vijay Mandal: Worked for Puneesh Tandon, the Talwars' neighbour. Lived in the garage below the Talwars' flat.

## The Investigators

Arun Kumar: Deputy inspector general who headed the first CBI team. Returned to his home state, Uttar Pradesh, in 2009.

A.G.L. Kaul: Additional superintendent of police. Became investigating officer after Kumar left. Reported to Superintendent of Police Neelabh Kishore.

Inspector Arvind Jaitley: Kaul's man Friday.

Vijay Shanker: CBI director when the case broke. Retired in July 2008.

Ashwani Kumar: Took over from Shanker. Handed over to A.P. Singh in late 2010.

## The Experts

Dr M.S. Dahiya: Deputy director, Forensic Science Laboratory, Gandhinagar. Reconstructed the crime; introduced the idea of 'dressing up' of the crime scene; believed the Talwars committed an honour killing and that Aarushi was engaged in intercourse when she was murdered.

Dr S.L. Vaya: Dahiya's former colleague. The behavioural scientist oversaw the scientific tests done on the Talwars and one of the servants. Believed that the Talwars were innocent.

Dr Sunil Dohare: Aarushi's post-mortem doctor. Made six changes to his original report over three years.

Dr Naresh Raj: Hemraj's post-mortem doctor. Claimed a surgical instrument may have been the murder weapon two years after his post-mortem report.

Dr B.K. Mohapatra: Forensic scientist at CFSL, the CBI's forensics department. Insisted that Hemraj's pillow cover was seized from Aarushi's room, suggesting Hemraj was killed there. Eventually admitted this wasn't the case.

**The Witnesses**

Bharti Mandal: The Talwars' temporary servant. It was her testimony that helped establish that the Talwars weren't locked in their flat from the outside but instead had locked the flat from the inside—and were therefore the killers.

Umesh Sharma: The Talwars' driver. Listed as a prosecution witness who was supposed to identify the golf club that allegedly delivered the fatal blows. He turned hostile, testifying for the Talwars, alleging he was beaten in the CBI office. Remains in the Talwars' employ.

K.K. Gautam: Retired deputy superintendent in Noida police. Was responsible for the discovery of Hemraj's body. His CBI testimony in 2008 claimed that Hemraj had visitors in his room. In 2010 his new testimony to the CBI denied the earlier statement. He established the honour killing motive in the trial court when he testified that the Talwars had asked him to manipulate the post-mortem report so that it didn't record rape. Post-retirement, he entered the field of education. He runs Invertis University in Bareilly.

# Timeline of Events

## 2008

16 May: Aarushi found murdered in her bed.
At noon her post-mortem by Dr Sunil Dohare records that a fatal blow was delivered to her head and that her throat was slit. 'Nothing abnormal' is detected in her sexual organs.

17 May: Hemraj's body found on the terrace, when the lock is broken at the behest of the former Noida policeman K.K. Gautam. Hemraj's body is in a state of decay.
At 9 p.m., Hemraj's post-mortem by Dr Naresh Raj is conducted. His wounds are very similar to Aarushi's.

23 May: Noida police arrest Rajesh Talwar for the double murder.

31 May: CBI takes over; Arun Kumar is the investigating officer.

12 June: Rajesh Talwar's assistant Krishna administered a narco analysis test.

13 June: Krishna arrested.

14 June:     CBI raids Krishna's room; recovers a khukri and a bloodstained pillow cover.

27 June:     Rajkumar arrested.

1 July:      K.K. Gautam gives his testimony to the CBI. He says that he had heard about the murders on the morning of 17 May when his eye doctor Sushil Choudhry (an acquaintance of the Talwars) asked him to accompany him to the Talwars' flat. Gautam observed three depressions on Hemraj's bed in the servant's room and three glasses, two with some liquor in them.

11 July:     Vijay Mandal arrested.

11 July:     Rajesh Talwar released.

31 July:     Vijay Shanker retires as director, CBI.

August       Arun Kumar readies to close the case with Krishna
(No exact    and Rajkumar as the suspects; Vijay Mandal would
dates):      be approver. CBI director Ashwani Kumar does not grant permission to make Mandal approver.

4 Sept:      Vijay Mandal released on bail as the CBI was unable to file a charge sheet against the three suspects in custody.

9 Sept:      Eight-member AIIMS panel of experts, including post-mortem doctors Sunil Dohare and Naresh Raj, submits report saying a khukri is the likely murder weapon.

12 Sept:     Krishna and Rajkumar released on bail.

6 Nov:       Hyderabad forensics laboratory CDFD sends report which says Hemraj's blood and DNA were found on the pillow cover seized from Krishna's room. Krishna lived in another flat in the same complex.

## 2009

7–8 Jan:     Rajesh and Nupur Talwar undergo brain-mapping test in FSL, Gandhinagar. Report says the test did not suggest their involvement in the crimes.

9 Sept: New CBI team headed by SP Neelabh Kishore takes over; Additional Superintendent A.G.L. Kaul is the investigating officer.

25 Sept: CBI sends an email to FSL, Gandhinagar, asking deputy director M.S. Dahiya to conduct a 'crime scene reconstruction'.

30 Sept: Dr Sunil Dohare, Aarushi's post-mortem doctor, changes his testimony telling the CBI that Aarushi's 'vaginal opening was prominently wide open and the cervix was visible'. He also says that he hadn't previously mentioned these facts in the post-mortem report because the 'findings were non-specific and very strange'. He tells the CBI that Dinesh Talwar asked him to speak to Dr T.D. Dogra of AIIMS on his cellphone as he went in for the post-mortem.

9 Oct: M.S. Dahiya is taken to the crime scene and holds discussions with Kaul in order to reconstruct the events of 15–16 May 2008.

12 Oct: Dr Naresh Raj, Hemraj's post-mortem doctor, changes his testimony and tells the CBI that a khukri could not have been the murder weapon; nature of injuries 'clearly point towards a surgically trained person' using a sharp-edged, light instrument.

13 Oct: CBI sends Dahiya a formal questionnaire and photographs of the crime scene.

26 Oct: Dahiya sends his report, suggesting that this was a case of honour killing, carried out by a father provoked by the misconduct of his child; that a golf club and surgical instrument were the likely murder weapons, both of which the Talwars had easy access to, and that the killers 'dressed up' the crime scene.

29 Oct: CBI asks Rajesh Talwar for the golf kit.

30 Oct:     Talwars hand over the entire golf kit to CBI.

**2010**

9 and       Nupur Talwar and Rajesh Talwar undergo narco
16 Feb:     analysis test in Gandhinagar. Scientists conclude
            they were not involved in the crimes.

May (third  Talwars called to Dehradun by Neelabh Kishore
week):      for questioning. Nupur Talwar mentions she and
            Ajay Chaddha had found a golf club in a loft while
            cleaning the flat some months after the incident.

24 May:     Story appears in the *Pioneer* quoting 'top-
            ranking' CBI sources who are all convinced the
            parents did it, using a golf club that was 'missing'.

28 May:     Dohare makes a further change saying that the wide
            opening of the vaginal canal and the absence of an
            even discharge indicate that Aarushi's private parts
            were manipulated and cleaned. He also says that a
            golf club could have been the murder weapon.

16 Apr:     K.K. Gautam now tells the CBI that he had heard
            of the murders on 16 May, when he received a
            call from Sushil Choudhry. He says Choudhry
            told him Aarushi may have been raped but he
            did not want this reported in the post-mortem.

1 June:     Ajay Chaddha writes to Kaul confirming that
            Nupur and he had found the club in the loft,
            examined it and put it back in the kit.

Nov:        CBI gets a new chief, Amar Pratap Singh; within
            a fortnight the decision to file a closure report is
            taken. Charges cannot be framed against any of
            the suspects because of a lack of evidence.

29 Dec:     CBI files closure report. Authored by Kaul, the
            report says sufficient evidence isn't available to
            prove Rajesh Talwar guilty.

## 2011

25 Jan:     Talwars protest against the closure report and demand a proper investigation. Rajesh Talwar attacked with a meat cleaver in the Ghaziabad court premises the same day.

9 Feb:      CBI special judicial magistrate Preeti Singh rejects the closure report and the Talwars' protest petition. Turns the closure report into a charge sheet and summons the Talwars to answer charges of murder and destruction of evidence. Nupur Talwar who was not one of the accused thus far becomes one.

27 Feb:     Preeti Singh rejects the Talwars' plea to excuse them from appearing in person.

Feb–Mar:    Talwars challenge the summoning in Allahabad High Court. They draw the court's attention to the November 2008 DNA report where there is direct evidence against Krishna. The CBI tells the court that this is a typographical error.

17 Mar:     CBI writes to CDFD, Hyderabad, suggesting there is a typo, asks for clarification.

18 Mar:     Court rejects the Talwars' plea, upholds the Ghaziabad magistrate's order. Says it is evident from photographs that there was a typo.

24 Mar:     CDFD sends a clarification, says there was a typo in the report. The Talwars prepare to approach the Supreme Court to quash Ghaziabad proceedings.

## 2012

9 Jan:      The Supreme Court rejects the Talwars' petition to quash the proceedings in Ghaziabad, but says Rajesh Talwar can remain on bail.

2 Mar:     The Supreme Court rejects the Talwars' petition to transfer the case out of Ghaziabad. Asks them to appear in the lower court.

11 Apr:    Ghaziabad court issues non-bailable arrest warrant against Nupur Talwar for not appearing before it.

30 Apr:    Nupur Talwar surrenders to court; arrested. Moves for bail.

25 May:    Additional Sessions Judge Shyam Lal frames charges of murder.

4 June:    Trial begins with deposition from the CBI witnesses.

29 Aug:    CBI witness and CFSL scientist B.K. Mohapatra forced to admit that Hemraj's pillow and pillow cover with his blood on it were not recovered from Aarushi's room—a crucial part of the CBI's argument that Hemraj was murdered in Aarushi's room. As the item is displayed, he reads out the original tag which says it was seized from Hemraj's room.

30 Aug:    K.K. Gautam testifies. Says Sushil Choudhry asked him to help omit the word 'rape' from the post-mortem report on behalf of the Talwars, implying an attempted cover-up.

3 & 4 Sept: Bharti Mandal, the Talwars' maid, testifies in trial court. Says the outermost door to the Talwars' flat didn't open. The inference that the flat was locked from the inside is drawn—meaning only the Talwars could have committed the crime. Bharti also tells the court that she has been taught to say this.

25 Sept:   Nupur Talwar released on bail by Supreme Court order.


**2013**

9 Apr:     M.S. Dahiya testifies. Says Aarushi and Hemraj were engaged in intercourse.

16 Apr:　　A.G.L. Kaul testifies. Describes graphically what, according to him, happened on the night of the murders. Admits breaking forensic lab seals without authority. CBI closes its evidence. The Talwars question why the CBI has dropped more than one hundred relied upon witnesses; seek the summoning of more than a dozen of them, without success.

14 May:　　Judge Shyam Lal passes an order against the Talwars for trying to delay the case by challenging his orders in higher courts. Moves on with the trial, allowing only seven of the 13 defence witnesses to testify.

June 20:　　Defence witnesses begin deposing.

7 Oct:　　The Talwars seek the Supreme Court's intervention in getting the CBI to comply with the Allahabad High Court order that grants the defence access to the raw data for all DNA testing done in the case. They want their own experts to assess the results. Court appears inclined to give them access.

8 Oct:　　The Supreme Court rules that the Talwars are trying to delay the case by seeking the information. CBI's Sidharth Luthra argues that the Talwars are trying to delay the case because Judge Shyam Lal retires in November.

24 Oct:　　Tanveer Ahmed Mir begins final arguments for the defence.

6 Nov:　　Judge Shyam Lal turns 60, retirement age.

25 Nov:　　Judge Shyam Lal finds Talwars guilty. They are taken to Dasna jail, and sentenced to life imprisonment the next day.

26 Nov:　　Judge Shyam Lal pronounces sentence; the Talwars prepare to go in appeal.

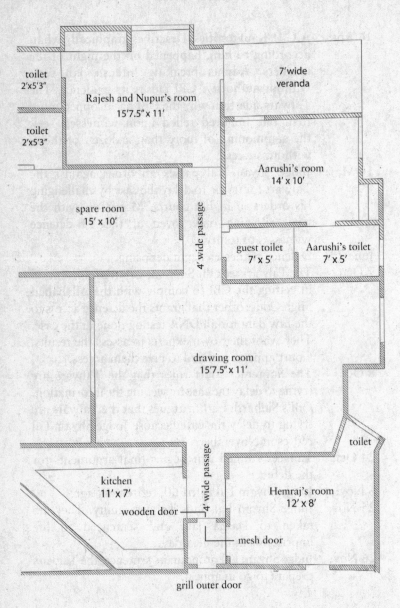

toilet
2'x5'3"

toilet
2'x5'3"

7'wide
veranda

Rajesh and Nupur's room
15'7.5" x 11'

Aarushi's room
14' x 10'

spare room
15' x 10'

4' wide passage

guest toilet
7' x 5'

Aarushi's toilet
7' x 5'

drawing room
15'7.5" x 11'

toilet

4' wide passage

kitchen
11' x 7'

wooden door

mesh door

Hemraj's room
12' x 8'

grill outer door

Layout of the Talwars' flat

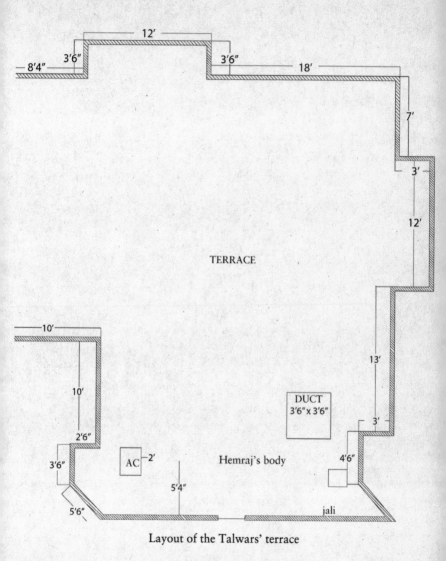

12'

3'6"          3'6"

8'4"                              18'

7'

3'

12'

TERRACE

10'

10'

2'6"

13'

DUCT
3'6" x 3'6"

3'

3'6"

AC   2'

Hemraj's body

4'6"

5'6"

5'4"

jali

Layout of the Talwars' terrace

# Introduction

Aarushi Talwar was murdered eight days before she was to turn fourteen. It was a macabre murder: a heavy blow had split her skull, a knife had sliced her neck. This was shocking but a day later, on 17 May 2008, the discovery of a second body made the incident a media event of staggering proportions. That the body belonged to the servant Hemraj and that there was a suggestion of sex between the 45-year-old and the teenager caught the public attention with every retelling. The local police claimed to have solved the case within a week, controversially blaming Aarushi's parents, Rajesh and Nupur Talwar. The resulting uproar led to the Central Bureau of Investigation (CBI) taking over the case in just over two weeks on 31 May. No substantial progress on the investigation was made for over a year, and a second CBI team took over in September 2009.

In December 2010, this team too said there was no evidence against the Talwars and sought the court's permission to close the case. The closure report, however, contained so many insinuations that, in February 2011, the magistrate rejected it and turned it into a charge sheet. She ordered that the Talwars stand trial. The trial began in June

2012, and lasted a year and a half. On 25 November 2013, the trial court found the Talwars guilty. They are now in Dasna jail in Uttar Pradesh. Their appeal is pending in the Allahabad High Court.

One of the measures of the popularity of a news story is how it compares with cricket ratings, which are usually very high. The Aarushi Talwar case got higher ratings than Indian Premier League games. The reason for this was not just the fact that the murders disturbed some kind of middle-class idyll, it was also that wafting through the story was the aroma of sex. The idea of the teenager and the servant engaged in coitus intrigued middle-class Indians. They wanted to know more.

I was out of the country working on my first book when the incident took place in 2008, and had very little interest in it. My involvement in reporting the story began with a phone call from Meenal Baghel, the fine writer and editor of the *Mumbai Mirror*, in May 2012. Meenal and I have known each other for more than 20 years, and she usually gets straight to the point. She said the Talwars' trial was to begin in a week. It made for a great narrative, and would I like to report it for her paper?

I took on the assignment.

I did not know the Talwars, or any of their friends or family. I began meeting the Talwars in court in 2012 just as frequently as I met officers and lawyers from the CBI. To make my work easier, I wanted a set of all documents related to the case, and this the Talwars readily gave me.

What I was clear about from the outset was this: my job was not to try and solve a crime. I was there to report on a trial. To me, this meant looking at the evidence for logic and authenticity; and perhaps finally answering a question quite different from the one I am still asked. It wasn't about who did it. The real question was whether there was convincing evidence that the Talwars did it. It was not for me to pass judgement, but equally, I felt it was my duty to examine the course of the investigation, read the documents that were in the public domain, access those that were not, and talk to people connected with the case. I did all of this in order to record facts, not to offer an opinion. Nor do I hold a brief for anyone connected with the case.

I can say with some confidence that I covered the trial proceedings with due diligence and have tried to tell the story accurately and faithfully. To that end, I resolved not to rely, for instance, on unnamed sources. All significant interviews in this book are on tape. The rest are recorded in carefully taken notes, or email exchanges between me and the interviewees. Public documents quoted are mentioned clearly. Although I believe I have done the best I can, and done it in good faith, I cannot rule out the possibility of errors in this book and would gladly correct them if they are pointed out.

Over the two and a half years that I worked on this book, I realized that the facts I gathered were also a commentary on the country we live in. When the astronaut Rakesh Sharma went to space in the early 1980s, the then prime minister, Indira Gandhi, asked him what India looked like from up there. Rakesh Sharma's response was memorable: *Saare jahan se achha* (better than all the world). This book is about what it looks like from the ground.

# Part One
## The Investigation

At about six in the morning on Friday, 16 May 2008, Bharti Mandal rang the doorbell at L-32 Jalvayu Vihar. This was her temporary workplace, and the home of the Talwars, Rajesh, Nupur and their teenage daughter Aarushi. A couple in their early forties, they were beginning to make a name for themselves as successful dentists. Aarushi, who was about to turn fourteen, was a star student at Delhi Public School, Noida.

The Talwars had moved to Jalvayu Vihar after Aarushi was born because Nupur's parents, the Chitnises, lived in the same complex in an identical flat. Like many middle-class working couples the Talwars needed the support of Aarushi's grandparents as they brought up their child. In a way, Aarushi had two homes in the same neighbourhood and this worked for everyone.

The Talwars weren't wealthy by Delhi's high standards. Their suburban housing complex was built in the early 1990s and originally intended for air force and naval officers, who received the land at a concession. It grew into a crowded middle-class settlement with four thousand flats and more than ten thousand residents, either paying rent or servicing that ubiquitous albatross around the neck of middle-income India, the home loan.

Jalvayu Vihar's pink apartment blocks were standard issue, its common areas just a little less tended to than its homes, which servants like Bharti swept and dusted. One of the thousands of invisible domestic workers who have flocked to Delhi and its suburbs from places as far as Malda, West Bengal, 2000 kilometres away, Bharti Mandal had come into the Talwars' lives only the previous week. Their regular maid, Kalpana, was on leave and had found Bharti as a replacement. She came in twice a day, once early in the morning and again in the evening. The Talwars' live-in servant, Hemraj, usually opened the door for her.

But on the morning of the 16th, when Bharti rang the doorbell situated next to the outer grill gate of the flat, no one responded. So she pressed the doorbell again and went to fetch the bucket and mop kept on the stairway to the terrace at the flat's entrance, thinking Hemraj would let her in shortly. But he didn't. Instead, Nupur Talwar appeared at the inner door of the flat.

To enter the Talwars' flat you had to get past three doors. The first was the iron grill door which opened on to a short passage. At the end of the passage was a pair of doors built into the same frame. Of these, the one on the outside was a mesh door. Behind it was a wooden door that led to the drawing room of the flat. The wooden door had a standard mortise lock—that is, it locked when the door was closed, and could only be opened from the inside or with a key. The mesh door had a two-way lock. It could also be bolted from the outside.

Nupur Talwar was woken by the repeated ringing of the doorbell. Letting the maid in was Hemraj's responsibility but that day he didn't seem to be around. When Nupur opened the innermost wooden door, she found the mesh door shut from the outside. She told Bharti that Hemraj may have gone to fetch milk and had probably bolted the door as he left. Bharti suggested that Nupur go to the balcony and throw down the keys in any case so that she could come back up and let herself in.

Meanwhile, Rajesh Talwar woke up. When he walked out of his bedroom he saw a bottle of Ballantine's Scotch whisky on the dining table. The family had retired at about 11.30 the previous night, and no one had had a drink. Alarmed, Rajesh asked Nupur what the bottle was doing on the dining table. The two of them then went towards Aarushi's room, found the door ajar, and entered.

The walls of the room were spattered with blood, but the soft toys on the bed including a large Bart Simpson were undisturbed. Aarushi lay on her bed covered in a white flannel blanket with a cheerful—and now completely incongruous—pattern of multicoloured rings on it. When Nupur Talwar lifted the light blanket they discovered that their only daughter's throat had been slit, and her skull, just above her forehead, crushed. Her pillow was soaked in blood which had dripped on to the mattress and the floor below. Her head had been partly covered by her favourite camouflage-print tote bag. Her mobile phone, which was always on the bedside table, was missing. It was a scene made more macabre by her untouched belongings: a few currency notes lying on a side table along with an iPod, its headphones attached as if someone had just taken them off, and the soft toys, which, with their button eyes, had seen everything.

Aarushi's head was hanging loose to one side, as if about to fall off. Even though he would have known his daughter was dead, Rajesh lifted her head and straightened it. At the time, he thought, she looked like a red doll. But he couldn't get himself to touch her face. In a daze, he walked in and out of the room, sitting on her bed and then getting up and banging his head violently against the wall.

In the meantime Bharti Mandal had climbed back up, pushed the outer grill gate open, and found the second mesh door bolted. She undid the latch and walked into the flat and found her employers hysterical. Bharti thought there had been a theft. 'Aunty threw her arms around me and started crying, when I asked her why are you crying so much, she said go inside and see what has happened. I went with Aunty and stood outside Aarushi's room.'

As she stood at Aarushi's door and took in the scene, not much except the slit throat of the teenager and the blanket that covered her body seems to have registered. In three statements to the investigators, the first of which was recorded the same day (the last on 11 June 2008), she could not recall, for instance, any details concerning the blood in the room.

When she had recovered from the shock, Bharti asked the Talwars whether she should inform the neighbours and security guards. They said yes. She hurried down to the Tandons' flat. Puneesh Tandon, who lived in the flat below, informed the security guard, who called the police. They arrived about an hour later. The first investigating officer (IO) on the case, Dataram Nanoria, of the Uttar Pradesh police, would interview Bharti later that day.

***

Just a week into her job, Bharti Mandal found herself at the centre of one of India's most bewildering murder mysteries—as its first witness. But as she left the flat that morning, she had no clue that she had seen only one half of a crime sliced in two. Concerned about where Hemraj may have gone that early in the morning, Nupur Talwar had called his cellphone when Bharti arrived. The call went through, and after a few seconds of silence, the person at the other end disconnected.

Whoever received and disconnected that call had Hemraj's phone. And Hemraj hadn't gone out on an errand—he had in fact been dead for several hours. The Talwars though had not yet found Hemraj's body and the fact that the call was received and cut off confirmed their suspicions that it was their servant who had killed Aarushi and fled.

The Talwars called the three couples closest to them: Nupur's parents, Group Captain (retd) Bhalachandra Chitnis and his wife Lata; Rajesh's brother Dr Dinesh Talwar and his wife Dr Vandana Talwar; and the Durranis, also dentists who shared a garage-turned-clinic with them in Jalvayu Vihar, and whose daughter, Vidushi, was one of Aarushi's closest friends.

The Chitnises got to the flat first—all they had to do was walk across a few rows of buildings. Group Captain Chitnis was silent in shock. When Puneesh Tandon arrived he saw the old man sitting in the drawing room, devastated, saying nothing. The Durranis and Dinesh and Vandana Talwar came at about 6.45 a.m. None of them could say much either. Vandana Talwar, an anaesthetist, took Aarushi's pulse, but the act was bereft of hope.

Within hours of the discovery of Aarushi's body, the flat was swarming with people. Policemen, the press, family, friends, curious strangers—everyone seemed to have descended upon the Talwars' home. And everyone seemed to be running amok. There was no effort on the part of the police to cordon off any area. Visitors conducted their own investigations. Two doctor friends of Rajesh, Rohit Kochar and Rajeev Varshney, arrived and chanced upon what they thought were bloodstains on the stairs leading up to the terrace, and on the lock of the terrace door.

They told the police and asked Rajesh for the keys to the terrace. In a daze, he went up a few steps, then turned back into the house. Hemraj had recently begun locking the terrace and Rajesh didn't seem to know where the keys were. The seniormost policeman on the scene, Mahesh Kumar Mishra, asked the constables to break the lock. But they couldn't find a locksmith. There was talk of getting the dog squad but the dogs were busy too. The prime minister of India was to visit Noida the next day, and everyone was busy. Rajesh and Nupur in the meantime walked around their flat in a state of shock. 'Find Hemraj' was their only coherent refrain. On the instructions of the police, Rajesh Talwar dictated an FIR, the first information report, in which he said he suspected Hemraj had committed the crime.

Meanwhile, there was morbid business to be taken care of. Aarushi's body had been taken for an autopsy. Dinesh Talwar and Rajesh's friend Ajay Chaddha reached the post-mortem house at nine. There was no doctor there, and the place was filthy. Chaddha went to fetch disinfectant and soap to get the post-mortem room cleaned. Dinesh Talwar worked his phone while the battered body of his niece lay in the open.

Dinesh called a doctor friend of his from his All India Institute of Medical Sciences (AIIMS) days. The friend called a Noida ophthalmologist, Dr Sushil Choudhry, who in turn called a patient of his—a recently retired Noida policeman called K.K. Gautam. Gautam was known to be an influential man; anyone who had any dealings with the police in Ghaziabad invariably had dealings with him. Gautam's interests went well beyond crime—he was involved in cricket administration and served as patron and president of Invertis University—and he loved the limelight. But he was a useful person to have on your side.

When his eye doctor requested him to see if he could have the post-mortem speeded up, Gautam made some calls without hesitation. Sometime after 11 a.m., Dr Sunil Dohare, the doctor who was to conduct the post-mortem, received a call from a superior saying 'some VIP person' had been murdered, and that he should hotfoot it to the post-mortem house.

According to Dohare, Dinesh Talwar also called up Dr T.D. Dogra, the head of department for forensic sciences at AIIMS. 'Why don't you speak to the doctor directly?' Dinesh Talwar told him and handed him the phone. Dr Dogra asked Dohare to take Aarushi's blood samples. The post-mortem doctor listened to Dr Dogra and assured him that 'whatever needed to be done would be done'.

Dohare completed his task sometime after 1 p.m. He inspected the wounds, found no injuries to Aarushi's private parts, wrote out a report saying 'nothing abnormal detected' in respect to her sexual organs. But he also took swabs of Aarushi's vagina and sent them to the pathologist at one of Noida's government hospitals to rule out sexual assault or rape.

That report came by the evening and said she was neither sexually assaulted nor raped.

The Talwars then readied themselves for the task of cremating their daughter's body. They left the house to the devices of whoever happened to be there: police personnel, media, friends. The house was in a mess, so a few women got together to get it swept and cleaned. All the while, the police looked on as the crime scene was wiped of possible clues. They did not find a locksmith that whole day or try to prise open the terrace door.

*** 

The next morning, the Talwars left for Haridwar to immerse Aarushi's ashes. But within minutes of setting out, they received a call from Dinesh Talwar, who was manning the flat in their absence: a body had been found on their terrace. Dazed, they returned. As Nupur waited outside the building with Aarushi's remains—Hindu custom forbids the re-entry of the ashes into the home—Rajesh made his way up the stairs.

K.K. Gautam was the man in command there. After making the phone calls the previous day, he had turned up at the autopsy centre to follow up on the post-mortem. The next day he had decided to drop by the Talwars' as a 'courtesy call', though to the media he appeared to be directing investigations.

When Gautam arrived at the flat on the morning of 17 May, Dinesh Talwar had complained to him that the bloodstained lock to the terrace door still hadn't been broken. Gautam noticed marks that suggested someone or something had been dragged across the terrace door. Though Aarushi's room had been a bloody scene, no one had noticed blood anywhere else in the apartment. There was no record of blood anywhere else inside the flat—except for traces on the bottle of Ballantine's whisky. Gautam knew every policeman on the scene and he was able to prevail upon them to break the lock on the terrace door.

Hemraj's putrefying body lay in the May sun to the left of the terrace door. It still had slippers on the feet. The corpse was partially covered by a cooler panel. A bed sheet had been hung on the other side, to prevent anyone from getting a clear sight of the body from Puneesh Tandon's adjacent terrace.

Rajesh Talwar was asked to identify the body, its face heavily swollen. Stunned by the revelation of a second murder in his home, he called Nupur to ask about Hemraj's T-shirt, and he looked at his hair. He confirmed to the police that it was Hemraj. The prime suspect had turned out to be a victim. So the question now was, who were the culprits?

For the Talwars, the week that followed was a blitz they would rather forget, but never will.

There were many factors that made the Aarushi murder big news: the gruesome crime had somehow located itself in an otherwise quiet middle-class neighbourhood. Aarushi's parents weren't celebrities, but were fairly well known in South Delhi circles; she went to a good school, was young and pretty. All in all there was an element of shock—'such things didn't happen to people like these'. The murder was newsworthy because it was exceptional.

But there was yet another factor at play. Those were boom years for the Indian media, the number of news channels had suddenly multiplied, and everyone was chasing market share. The easiest route to this was sensationalism.

The first headlines were straightforward. On 17 May, the Delhi tabloid *Mail Today* said: 'Schoolgirl Killed at Noida Home'; 'Finger of Suspicion Points at Missing Servant'. But even as that paper was being read that morning, Hemraj's body was discovered on the Talwars' terrace. Television had already covered the story non-stop the previous day; now the channels went berserk.

While the press intensified, the Noida police appeared to be doing very little. The only piece of overt investigation at the time involved a 15-year-old boy. Anmol Agarwal had been vying for Aarushi's affections and the two had exchanged several phone calls and texts in the days leading up to the murder. On the night of the murder, Anmol had tried calling Aarushi both on her mobile and on the landline, but had got no reply. He was thus the last person to try to contact Aarushi.

Anmol was picked up by the police, without the consent of his parents, on 22 May and put through a harrowing interrogation, where the police confronted him with the fact that he had exchanged 688 text messages with Aarushi and that he had tried to contact her on the fatal night. Anmol was frightened and he broke down and told the police that Aarushi had lots of boyfriends like him with whom she exchanged messages. When the police wondered if Aarushi was easy with her affections, Anmol readily agreed.

That day, the Talwars were also asked to come and identify a suspect. They followed a police vehicle in their car and were trailed all the way by a number of TV crews. Several kilometres on, they were suddenly asked to go home. They turned back and footage of this was captured. The next day, 23 May, the Noida police escorted Rajesh and Nupur Talwar to the police lines for questioning. At the police lines, Nupur and Rajesh were taken to different rooms. Rajesh was shown the footage from the previous day, which the police now claimed was proof that he was trying to flee. Shortly thereafter, under the heat and glare of the spotlights, Rajesh Talwar, dazed, dishevelled and screaming that he had been framed, was arrested for the murder of his daughter and servant.

Gurdarshan Singh, inspector general of police (IGP), Meerut range, held a triumphant press conference the same day where he claimed the case had been solved. According to him, 'Shruti'—this is what he kept calling Aarushi, though that was not even her nickname—had found out about Rajesh's extramarital affair with her best friend's mother, Anita Durrani, and had decided to have an affair of her own—with the manservant Hemraj.

According to Singh's theory, Rajesh got home after 11 that night and found Hemraj in Aarushi's room in an 'objectionable but not compromising' position (Singh presumably couldn't go further as the post-mortem and the pathology report hadn't shown up any sign of sexual activity). The sequence of events was this: Rajesh Talwar takes Hemraj to the terrace, kills him, comes back down, has a few swigs of Ballantine's Finest, and then kills his daughter to protect the honour of the family. And the murder weapons? A hammer and a scalpel. The non-recovery of which, according to the IGP, was a 'big thing'.

That there had been virtually no investigation did not stop Singh. Nor did the fact that the girl he was calling 'characterless' would have turned fourteen the day after his press conference.

The Indian Premier League, with its mixture of glamour and games, had enthralled the country every evening in its debut season, but on 23 May more people watched Gurdarshan Singh tell his tale of murder and debauchery than Punjab playing Hyderabad. In ratings terms, this was astounding.

There was an expected—and justifiable—uproar after the press conference. The Union Women and Child Development

Minister Renuka Choudhury's charge that the police had flouted Press Council guidelines and her outrage over the slander of the dead teenager and her family forced Gurdarshan Singh to make a small change to his theory, which he otherwise stuck to. He now said that Hemraj was merely comforting a distressed Aarushi.

The press now turned wild, revelling in the story of the adulterous father and the sexually precocious daughter. The next day, the *Times of India*'s front page said: 'Dad Killed Aarushi: Cops'. 'Couldn't Tolerate Her Objection to His Extramarital Affair with Fellow Dentist'. Acres of space was devoted over four pages inside. Some of the more notable headlines were: 'Attack Showed Clinical Precision and Planning' and 'Dr Death and the House of Horror'.

Television completely swallowed the line that the case had been 'cracked'. On 25 May Zee News ran a fictional reconstruction of the police version of events of the night of 15–16 May that crossed over from news to lurid entertainment without any difficulty at all. Zee wasn't the only television channel doing this. As the journalist Vir Sanghvi observed in his widely read column 'Counterpoint', a television anchor actually went on air after dipping his hands in red paint.

Meanwhile, the Noida police leaked almost all of Aarushi's personal communications, her text messages to friends, her social media pages, and an email to her father which they felt was particularly incriminating. In it, Aarushi had apologized to her dad for something he didn't approve of. It wasn't clear what she was apologizing for, but it was evident from the 'LOLZ' (laughing out loud) at the end of the mail that it couldn't have been something earth-shattering. But the police built a story of loose moral behaviour around it, which fit in with Gurdarshan Singh's assessment that she was 'characterless'. It also buttressed the theory that her relations with her father were strained. Why send an email if you live under the same roof? One commentator pointed out that when Gandhi was about Aarushi's age, he too had written a letter to his father. A far more explicit one, in which he had admitted to stealing money, smoking and eating meat.

The news television coverage had inspired India's undisputed queen of the 'family drama', Ekta Kapoor, to base an episode of her hit serial *Kahani Ghar Ghar Ki* on the murders. Star Plus lapped up the idea. The National Commission for Protection of Child Rights (NCPCR) objected, and asked the Union minister for information and broadcasting, Priya Ranjan Dasmunsi, to step in. Dasmunsi spoke to channel officials personally, extracting an assurance that the episode would not be aired.

The *Hindustan Times* reported that his ministry had already issued notices to some television channels over their coverage of the double murders, and Dasmunsi told students at the Indian Institute of Mass Communication, Delhi: 'Unhealthy competition among media companies is threatening all journalistic norms and values.'

The police had advised the Talwars not to speak to the media, but Nupur Talwar went ahead and on 25 May gave an interview to the English news channel NDTV. The television interview was meant to counter Gurdarshan Singh and his narrative of the Talwars' deviance. The decision to do the interview was preceded by conflicting advice from friends, well-wishers and lawyers. So far, there had been no mention of Nupur Talwar's involvement in the crime, just the odd question about what she might have been doing while her daughter was being slaughtered. It was Rajesh who was arrested. But the circumstances of the crime—parents in the room adjoining the scene of their daughter's murder—cast her as a defendant.

She put herself on the stand, so to speak, before the largest jury imaginable. A jury she couldn't see, but one that could watch her as closely as it wished. What she said would be important, of course, but how she behaved—her conduct—that is what would settle matters.

Just as Gurdarshan Singh's press conference provided the first chapter of the prosecution's narrative, over the years to follow, Nupur Talwar's interview, intended to compete with that narrative, ended up complementing it.

Nupur Talwar's face showed many of the signs of stress that one would expect from the sleepless nights that had followed her daughter's murder and her husband's arrest. There were moments when she looked close to breaking down, but she did not, could not—or would not—cry.

The effect this had on the audience can still be seen in the comments sections of any story related to the murders. The overwhelming sentiment is that Nupur Talwar was cold, emotionless, a fake.

From the investigations through the trial, Nupur Talwar's 'coldness' was probably the one factor that weighed down the Talwars' case the most. The second unspoken factor that played consistently against the Talwars was their 'poshness', especially Nupur's. The Talwars may have lived in a middle-class environment, but it was easy for those who met her or saw her on television to place her a few notches higher.

Not every viewer was anti-Talwar. The case polarized—and continues to—people. Aarushi's classmates held a march protesting her character assassination. A host of prominent people also voiced their outrage. The NCPCR issued a notice to the UP police asking it to explain the basis of the allegations against the child victim. It seemed to me the case was taking a political turn.

Uttar Pradesh was ruled at the time by the Bahujan Samaj Party (BSP), and Chief Minister Mayawati's relations with the Congress-led United Progressive Alliance (UPA) at the Centre were strained. Law and order is a state subject. Mayawati, to whom the Noida police was ultimately answerable, objected strongly to the notice from a central body. 'More heinous crimes are being committed in Congress-ruled states', the

*Hindustan Times* quoted her as saying. She was tentative about the investigation, however, saying it wouldn't be 'dignified' to reveal some of the 'grave' facts that her force had unearthed.

Mayawati floated the idea of transferring the case to the CBI. A branch of the CBI investigates 'special crimes', and the state government can initiate the process by sending a request to the department of personnel and training (under the Prime Minister's Office, PMO) at the Centre. Mayawati said she had made several requests in the recent past that had been turned down. In this case, the Union home minister (who technically does not oversee the CBI) weighed in to say there was no need for a CBI investigation.

Perhaps it was about exacting a price from the fiery UP chief minister. Mayawati was being asked to say, in some way, that she had lost faith in her police force, and required the Centre to help out. This would, of course, be used against her politically, and she was well aware of this.

But by the following week the voices against Gurdarshan Singh only grew louder, sharper. Sanghvi wrote:

> Most worrying of all is the IGP's obsession with sex. Every possible motive leads back to sex. First, there was the extraordinary statement that Rajesh Talwar found his daughter in an objectionable position with Hemraj, the servant. As Aarushi and Hemraj are dead, and Rajesh Talwar denies the incident how could the IGP possibly have known about the incident? Then there's the suggestion that Rajesh Talwar was having an affair with a colleague and that his daughter objected; off the record, the police have painted the parents as orgy goers and wife swappers. And now, the cops are claiming that the father was motivated by Aarushi's relations with various boyfriends.

This is not a sex crime. So why is the Noida police going on and on about sex, ruining the reputations of the dead and the living without a shred of evidence?

My guess is that they are not just incompetent, they are also sex starved. Perhaps the IGP needs professional help.

On 1 June 2008 Mayawati was forced to transfer Gurdarshan Singh and two of his subordinates and hand over the case to the CBI. But even this was handled politically: the chief minister said she had transferred the officers not for botching up the probe, but because her government did not want to be accused of causing problems for the CBI or of projecting that the line the UP police had taken was correct.

The lines of politics were redrawing the lines of investigation. Within days of the CBI taking over, headlines such as 'Noida Police Theory Trashed' began appearing in the press. Those who held the view that the UP police was in serious error may have had good reason to do so, but for the average media consumer, it looked less like investigation, more like politics.

The Talwars neither approached nor knew any of the politicians who publicly or otherwise intervened, but an impression was formed that they must have had an inside line to them. Why else would such powerful people speak up on their behalf, transfer officers, and so on?

A rumour that Nupur Talwar was Mayawati's dentist began circulating in the cesspool of chatter in Delhi's upper circles. Nupur assisted her senior Dr Sidharth Mehta at his Khan Market clinic, and he did indeed treat Mayawati. But she had never even seen the chief minister, whose appointments were specially fixed and never during regular clinic hours.

Earlier in the investigation the UP police had found on Rajesh the prominent lawyer Pinaki Misra's visiting card.

This was seen as a sign of guilt. Who else but the guilty would carry a hotshot lawyer's card around? It went even further. Misra was interested in the case, and expressed outrage at the Talwars' victimization. So now a rumour gained ground that Misra was Nupur Talwar's uncle. In no time, this became the 'truth'. In fact, Pinaki Misra was Rajesh Talwar's patient. But he wasn't Nupur's uncle.

What were people thinking? A *Hindustan Times*-C-Fore survey published on 1 June polled people in six major Indian cities and found that 41 per cent now 'feared' being harmed by friends or family. But two-thirds, or 66 per cent, thought the police would never find the killers.

Another survey in the same publication in the second week of June gives us an idea of what people thought of the media coverage. Nine out of ten people felt the media was 'obsessed' by the case. Three-fourths of the respondents said they were following the coverage very closely. Three-fourths also felt that the media had already pronounced Rajesh Talwar guilty; 64 per cent felt that the coverage would bias both the investigation and the courts.

Inside a month of the murders, with an investigation that wasn't worth a cheap magnifying glass, the damage had been done. Rajesh Talwar passed multiple lie detector tests. But the public didn't believe him. It preferred to believe the policemen and the press instead.

The planting of stories in the media didn't stop even after the CBI had taken over the case. Perhaps the most scurrilous story that was put in circulation was one meant to cement the Talwars' image as orgy-goers. The story went that on the night of the murders the couple took part in a major orgy. Mumbai's *Mid-Day*, in the last week of June, quoted unnamed sources saying that a wife-swapping ring which was under investigation since February that year had led them to the Talwars in Sector 25. The report quoted sources as saying neighbours of the Talwars felt that they were in some sort of 'club', and that when the members of the club met Aarushi would be locked in the room while the club's activities were arranged around the flat.

Zee News ran it; so did Headlines Today, Aaj Tak and *Mail Today*. The story claimed the CBI as the source, and was based on the 'information' that Rajesh Talwar had booked a dozen rooms at a Delhi hotel and the couple spent three or four hours there. It went on to say that Hemraj was blackmailing Aarushi. There was not one line of confirmation from the CBI, the hotel or its staff. The Talwars were never asked for a version.

This was in early July 2008; Rajesh Talwar was still in jail. Nupur wrote to Arun Kumar, in charge of the CBI team, in despair. The CBI issued an official denial. And the channels? Not a word of the story was recanted. No apology was offered.

*** 

Vijay Shanker, the CBI director, had been watching the circus keenly, and he was horrified. When the case was handed over to his agency, he told me, he felt duty-bound to bring some sanity back: 'If the CBI doesn't investigate this, who will?'

As the head of the CBI team that took over from the UP police, Arun Kumar's first job was to make an inventory of the investigative blunders that had occurred over the two weeks since the incident. He immediately noted something that any experienced investigator would. This was the delay in the discovery of the second body. As the UP police fumbled along, Hemraj's body lay for a whole day on the roof, just one locked door away from discovery.

Kumar thought it was impossible that the murderer(s) would make the assumption that the police would not find the body on the first day. 'No killer would think that, especially when the body was in the same building,' he said. The Talwars, an educated, intelligent couple, were the least likely people to make this assumption, he thought. It was simply too risky. There was no way they could have prevented every policeman on the scene from looking behind the bloodstained terrace door. In fact, Mahesh Mishra, the superintendent of police (SP) who arrived on the scene on the morning of 16 May, had left instructions with subordinates to break the lock.

Yet the UP police announced that the Talwars had tried to hide the body. Kumar found this claim illogical. He also learned that Krishna Thadarai, the Talwars' clinic employee who lived just a few apartments away in the same block, in L-14 Jalvayu Vihar, had been picked up by the UP police on the first day. Hemraj was assumed missing, and the police thought that Krishna, a fellow Nepali who also worked for the Talwars and knew Hemraj well, perhaps knew his whereabouts.

Krishna was a 22-year-old who had come to India from his village in western Nepal about ten years ago for medical treatment, but had stayed back. He was keen to educate himself and had just appeared for his 12th grade exams from an open school. He had been working for Rajesh Talwar for two years.

The young Nepali was confined and questioned for about ten days by the Noida police, who shifted him from station to station in the area, as hapless relatives tried to reach him with food. The confinement was illegal, and investigators never mention it, but this is just how the system works for his class of people. Arun Kumar had watched Gurdarshan Singh's press conference, and something struck him as he read Krishna's account in the case diary: 'The version given by Singh was exactly what Krishna had told the police, almost verbatim.'

It was Krishna who had successfully seeded the idea in the police that Rajesh Talwar was an adulterer and debauch, who was having an affair with his friend and colleague Dr Anita Durrani; that Aarushi was anguished when she discovered this and sought comfort in Hemraj's arms; that Rajesh was deeply suspicious of Hemraj.

Then there were details which had been extracted from the Talwars' routine: that on Tuesdays and Saturdays, when Nupur Talwar went to work in Dr Sidharth Mehta's Khan Market clinic, Dr Durrani and Dr Talwar would close the Noida clinic early and head for the L-32 flat. (They did this because they often went together to pick up Aarushi and Dr Durrani's daughter Vidushi from school; this was Nupur's responsibility on other days.)

Krishna also said he was always told to take the day off early on those days, and that he never actually saw Talwar and Durrani together. When asked about this, he said that Hemraj had seen the two in the Talwars' flat. Arun Kumar wryly noted that, with Hemraj dead, this was an unverified piece of hearsay.

As Arun Kumar went through the case diary in the first week of June, what became clear to him was that the theory floated by the UP police wasn't a result of any investigation. It was what one man had told them, sans corroboration.

In the meantime, the CBI and forensic teams from the CBI's forensic lab, Central Forensic Science Laboratory (CFSL), began collecting whatever evidence was left at the crime scene. In a statement made to CBI investigators on 1 July 2008, K.K. Gautam said he had done a 'formal inspection' of Hemraj's room and that he had concluded from the depressions on the mattress that three people may have sat on it. He had also observed three glasses, two of them containing some amounts of liquor, and a bottle of whisky which was a quarter full. He had inspected the toilet too and deduced that more than one person had recently used it. His statement suggested the presence of outsiders

on the night of the murders. Kumar decided that Krishna
would need to be interrogated again.

***

The first court-authorized narco analysis test in India was
done at the Sabarmati jail in Gujarat in 1989 by a young
behavioural scientist named Dr S.L. Vaya. At the time police
liberally, but completely illegally, injected sodium pentothal
(or truth serum) into suspects. Dr Vaya felt that a valuable
investigative tool such as this needed to be legitimized, and
administered by professionals. 'There was no lab to speak
of at the time, so I used to carry equipment around in a box.
The first procedure was done in jail that way,' she said, 'but
I insisted on consent and a court sanction.'

Soon, police forces from all over the country began using
her team's services at the Forensic Science Laboratory (FSL),
Gandhinagar, and other labs like it. FSL Gandhinagar was
highly regarded and charged a high fee for the procedure,
Rs 50,000 per subject. This became a steady revenue stream
for the institution.

The lab is reasonably well equipped today. The narco
room looks like a hospital operation theatre where the
patient lies down and is brought to a trance state with
carefully measured injections of the truth serum. The sodium
pentothal injection has two effects on a human being: it
produces a sense of serenity and well-being; it also makes
them talk—and reveal information without fear. Scientists
say this is the most humane way of eliciting information
from suspects, filling gaps in an investigation.

Alongside this, brain-mapping is done in a soundproof
room where the subject sits behind a one-way glass window
(the scientists outside can look in), with electrodes attached
to various parts of the body. The procedure is non-invasive:
an earpiece gives audio cues, while a screen provides the

text and is used to show the subject photographs. The machine looks for waves of different frequencies, each band indicating how the brain has processed the cue. There are pre- and post-test interviews, relevant parts of which find their way into the final report.

Dr Vaya was a respected veteran in her field by 2008. The CBI had turned to her lab in the other notorious crime from Noida, the Nithari killings. In December 2006, skeletal remains of women and children were found in a drain behind Moninder Singh Pandher's house in the Nithari village of Noida. Pandher and his servant Surinder Koli were accused of raping, killing, dismembering and disposing of 17 children, including ten girls. That case had opened up when Koli revealed in his narco test details such as how he would find out the names of his victims from the loudspeaker announcements during evening prayers asking for information on missing children. Koli was convicted but his death sentence was later commuted.

The polygraph or lie detector test consists of a customary pre-test interview, after which subjects are familiarized with the equipment and given sitting instructions. A number of tubes and wires are then attached to them. These record physiological responses to questions read that must be categorically answered in 'yes' or 'no' terms. The questions come every 25 seconds.

The questions are straightforward. As the subject answers questions, every physiological change in the subject, whether it is in respiration, pulse rate, blood pressure or even skin reflex—through electrodes attached to fingers—is recorded. A comparison with his normal physiological performance guides the examiner to an opinion on whether or not the subject is telling the truth.

The Supreme Court has judged that the forcible use of such scientific tests is a violation of fundamental rights. Even when the tests were conducted with consent, the court has said that the subject is not in control of his responses so the results are inadmissible. 'However, any information or material that is subsequently discovered with the help of voluntary administered test results can be admitted, in accordance with Section 27 of the Evidence Act.' This meant that if a suspect revealed something during the test like, say, where he had kept Hemraj's phone after the murder, the test and his narration would not be admissible as evidence; but the police could, based on what he had said, recover the phone and then present it as evidence which would be admissible in a court of law.

Bibha Rani Ray, then director of the CFSL, conducted the polygraph test on Krishna. She and other behavioural scientists concluded that he was being deceptive and manipulative. He was intelligent and very keen on shifting blame. He was also 'loyal to no one'.

Within days the results of Krishna's lie detector tests were confirmed by narco analysis at Bangalore during which he spilled details of the crime and the weapon used. Among other things, Krishna said that he and two other servants in the area, Rajkumar and Vijay Mandal, were present in the Talwars' flat with Hemraj at midnight; he witnessed Rajkumar committing the crime; and Rajesh Talwar had nothing to do with the murders. According to the scientists conducting the test, Krishna's answers were out of sequence and filled with attempts at deception. This is why the CBI also admitted that there was some evidence of the servants' involvement when they filed the closure report; however, this was too little to go by.

Days later, on 18 June, the CBI sought, and got, an extension of Krishna's custody. The CBI presented before the magistrate the case diary in which it recorded that Krishna had confessed to the crimes, that a khukri had been used and that he could recover Aarushi's mobile phone. Remand was granted, and the CBI raided the servants' quarters of

L-14 Jalvayu Vihar. Vijay Kumar and Anuj Arya of the CBI were both a part of this raid. The recoveries included a khukri with specks of blood on it and a bloodstained purple pillow cover.

In the following three weeks, Rajkumar and Vijay Mandal were also taken into custody. Rajkumar was employed by the Durranis. He was a little younger than Krishna and everyone who knew him, including his employers, remarked about his good looks and easy manner. He got along well with the Durranis and the Talwars. The cellphone handset he used had originally belonged to Aarushi, who had passed it on to her friend Vidushi, who in turn had handed it down to Rajkumar.

The Durranis found it hard to believe he was involved in the crime when he was arrested. But when the results of his scientific tests came in, R.K. Saini, the CBI counsel, showed the results to them saying, *'Dekhiye kaise nevley paale the aap logon ne'* (Look at the sort of mongoose you've had as a pet).

Vijay Mandal worked for Puneesh Tandon and lived in the garage below. He was also in his early twenties and had had a troubled childhood; his lasting memories were the severe beatings he got at the hands of his parents. He left home to find employment, but his anger problems meant he couldn't hold down jobs.

Rajkumar's scientific tests were similar in their fundamentals to Krishna's, but had many differences. He said they watched TV and listened to Nepali songs; Krishna got drunk on the terrace; and there was a fight between Hemraj and Krishna in which Hemraj admonished him, *'Awaaz se sab jag jayenge'* (The noise will wake up everyone). Then Aarushi was murdered.

At the lab, Dr Vaya's report records, Rajkumar was fidgety and uncooperative. He was confronted with the story that Krishna had put out about him ten days earlier at the Bangalore laboratory. In constant fear of being implicated, he asked the scientists at one point: '*Main isme phas to nahin jaoonga?*' (I won't get trapped in this?)

In Dr Vaya's assessment, Rajkumar was capable of withstanding long hours of interrogation and determined to protect himself. So despite his narrative, culled from interviews and tests in the lab, Dr Vaya felt Rajkumar was unlikely to confess.

Vijay Mandal's scientific tests in Mumbai also revealed that all three of them were present with Hemraj in the Talwars' flat at midnight and that there was a struggle with Aarushi; he also spoke of his fear when he realized Aarushi was dead.

The most important point of convergence was their independent admissions that *they were with Hemraj* late that night.

The problem was that Krishna said Rajkumar committed the murders, and Rajkumar said Krishna committed the murders. Outside of the tests, when questioned by the police, all three claimed alibis: each said he was asleep, at home, and not at the Talwars' flat. Vijay Mandal in fact had his employer give the alibi that he was in bed by 9.30 p.m.

In a conversation with me after the trial, Bibha Rani Ray remembered that it had become fairly clear to her that the servants had some sort of 'infatuation or lust for the girl'. She said she could not tell for certain that all three servants were present at the crime scene, but that 'Someone was there, not necessarily all three, but someone was there. They all had easy access to the house.'

\*\*\*

It emerged that Rajesh had scolded Krishna publicly for a poorly made dental cast a few days earlier. The assistant felt humiliated and was simmering with rage and had told

Hemraj that he would sort his employer out. But as a motive for murder, this was disproportionately weak.

Vaya told Arun Kumar that there was enough material in tests done on Krishna and Rajkumar for the CBI to investigate and frame charges even without a confession. They would just have to work hard on the investigation.

There was a press outcry over Krishna being forced to take his narco tests. The media asked if the 'confessions' the CBI claimed to have from the servants would pass muster in court. (They wouldn't: the only kind of confession that is legitimate is one where a magistrate records a suspect's story under Section 164 of the Code of Criminal Procedure, CrPC. This wasn't anywhere close to happening.) Krishna's family had also approached the National Human Rights Commission, saying he was forced to undergo invasive narco analysis and a confession was beaten out of him.

Arun Kumar's team made some attempts to find incriminating evidence such as the cellphones of the victims, but these were unsuccessful. Kumar turned his attention to the weakest link: the tests on Vijay Mandal pointed to his being part of the crime scene, but as a witness rather than as a perpetrator. Kumar felt he could extract a statement under Section 164 from Mandal which would form the basis of the charge sheet against Krishna and Rajkumar. Mandal would get off lighter if he agreed. Kumar felt this was his best chance.

Most Indian investigators work towards getting a confession rather than investigating the case. It is the easiest way to get a conviction in court—and the laziest.

***

Given the nature of the media involvement, Vijay Shanker would get a number of direct inquiries about the case, even though it was being investigated by a subordinate.

He told Arun Kumar to hold a press conference to clear things up.

'I remember that there would be twenty cameras outside the CBI office,' Vijay Shanker told me later. 'And you know these poor television reporters, they would have to stand out in the heat all day. So I told Arun, these people come every day, why don't you tell them about the progress, how you're going about it. Whatever you can say. What you can't say, you can't say.'

On 11 July 2008, with the servants and Rajesh Talwar still in custody, Arun Kumar held a press conference. The media sought a lot of answers, and Kumar wasn't able to provide all of them—he could not, he said, say who committed the crimes. But on the basis of the investigations till then, the CBI had found no incriminating evidence against Rajesh Talwar. Two polygraph tests were done on him and while the results of the first were 'inconclusive' (a technical term that means the interpreting scientist cannot draw conclusions, not a sign of guilt) the second test made it clear that the dentist was not being deceptive on any count. The CBI sought Rajesh Talwar's release.

Arun Kumar also said that the scientific tests on the servants had opened up a new line of investigation: Krishna, Rajkumar and Vijay Mandal were suspects. With no reason for the agency to keep Rajesh Talwar in custody, the CBI applied for his release. Fifty days after he was arrested Rajesh Talwar walked out of prison.

***

Rajesh Talwar would later speak about those days to me and other journalists. Of the nights he spent on the floor, covering his face with a stinking sheet to keep the mosquitoes away. Of the rudimentary dental chair the jail authorities allowed him to eventually set up, where the few hours of work with patients helped him keep his tenuous hold on sanity.

But of all his experiences from that time, one incident haunts him most. While he was in custody he would be taken to court for his plea for bail. All undertrials who were to make their appearance in court that day would be handcuffed and bundled into the same vehicle. This was uncomfortable enough, but on this particular day, the police handcuffed Rajesh and Krishna together. Rajesh said he wept and pleaded with the policemen: 'Don't do this, this man has killed my daughter!' Krishna didn't respond at all. All the police said was, 'We have only one pair of handcuffs.'

\*\*\*

On the evening of 15 May, the Talwars' driver Umesh had come up to the flat to deposit the car keys at 9.30 p.m. This made him the last person to have seen all four people in the house alive. The Talwars were preparing for dinner when he left. That evening Aarushi's parents had a surprise for her. She would turn fourteen in a few days, and the digital camera Rajesh had bought online had arrived. Rajesh had ordered an extra special camera—while Aarushi's friends all had 5 megapixel cameras, this one was 10 megapixels. The excited father wanted to hide the camera from Aarushi, and told Nupur about it. She said she wouldn't be able to keep this little secret and the two decided to give her the camera that night.

Just as her parents had hoped, Aarushi was thrilled. She spent the rest of the evening with Rajesh and Nupur, taking pictures of her parents and herself, keeping the ones she liked, deleting the ones she didn't. She complained that her cellphone was giving her trouble, and there was some talk of getting her a new handset. What we know is that her phone was turned off.

There could be a reason for this. There were two boys, Anmol Agarwal and Sankalp Arora, who had a crush on her and would speak with her regularly. Anmol was in her grade; Sankalp was a bit older. She had earlier had a crush on Sankalp but was now becoming a little interested in Anmol though she worried about his love for partying. In any case, these were matters that were confusing to her more than anyone else and she probably didn't want to deal with all of that this evening. She was more excited about her camera.

Sankalp tried to contact her several times that evening, but Aarushi's phone was switched off, and no one was picking up the landline. At school that morning, there had been talk of a bunch of them going out for a movie and lunch to one of the malls, plans that did not materialize. Aarushi wasn't very keen—possibly because Sankalp would be there too—and told her friends, 'I may not be there physically, but I'll be there mentally.' She was, however, looking forward to the bash Rajesh had organized for her on the 18th, a grand 1000-rupee-a-plate affair at the Superstar restaurant, to which many of her friends, including Anmol, had already been invited.

The Talwars ate their dinner happily that evening, and at around eleven went to their bedrooms. Hemraj had served himself his dinner too, but he never ate it, as his post-mortem later showed. Rajesh had a few things to do before retiring. He needed to confirm whether the American Dentistry Association had received a payment he had made for a fellowship, but the Internet connection was slow. He asked Nupur to go to Aarushi's room and switch the router off and on. Nupur remembers entering Aarushi's room, and seeing her daughter reading. What she cannot remember is whether she locked the door from the outside as she usually did. Neither was she sure where she kept the keys to Aarushi's door that night (they would usually be kept in the parents' bedroom). After the murder, the keys were found in the drawing room.

Shortly thereafter, Nupur fell asleep. Rajesh was on the phone till a little after 11.30 p.m.; Nupur's brother had called. When Rajesh was done, he too fell asleep.

Half an hour later Anmol Agarwal, having failed to reach Aarushi on her cellphone, tried one of the Talwars' landlines—one that he usually spoke to Aarushi on. The handset and its base were kept in the parents' bedroom, with its ringer volume turned down at night. Anmol's call, a little after midnight, went unanswered.

*** 

Nupur Chitnis and Rajesh Talwar had met as students in Delhi's Maulana Azad Medical College in the mid-1980s. They fell in love and were married in an unusual ceremony in 1989. Rajesh was of Punjabi stock, Nupur was Maharashtrian, so two pandits came and struck a compromise. They got married at midday instead of the customary morning or evening. Aarushi arrived on 24 May 1994, after five years of trying to conceive, and, to Rajesh, her gender was irrelevant. He doted on her.

Rajesh's dad was a prominent Delhi doctor, and Rajesh remembers his childhood as being happy. He had a few problems adjusting to school early on, but then settled down to become a very good student. His elder brother Dinesh was a constant protective presence.

Bhalachandra Chitnis, Nupur Talwar's dad, was an air force officer. His postings took him to various places. Nupur grew up as a reserved and collected little girl—qualities that would remain. Chitnis did a stint in London, when Nupur was about six, and remembers a spell when his wife Lata was away in India, and it was just him and Nupur. 'Even at that age, she was extremely considerate. She would never ask for anything. And I don't remember seeing her cry unless she was physically hurt.'

Because of her father's transfers, Nupur went to various schools. 'She was always very straight-talking, and insisted on correctness. If the teacher said "matchbox", for instance, she would say it was "a box of matches". When they said "have a glass of water", she would reply "I'll have a drink of water",' remembers her father. One could call this childish or pedantic, or both, but it showed a certain assertiveness—a trait for which she was both admired and respected within the family. The other little girls all wanted to be like Nupur. When Aarushi's body was discovered and Rajesh was lost and helpless, banging his head against the wall, it was Nupur who informed their friends.

Any reasonable background check on the Talwars tells you that they were a snug, happy unit. This is the opinion of all those who know them. These are the people who don't authoritatively describe them as depraved and degenerate. Aarushi has left behind a fair amount of proof of what her life was like with her parents. A Mother's Day card to Nupur four days before she was murdered says: 'Mom . . . what should I say. . . You are the B.E.S.T. . . . We have had a gazillion fights, a million "I will never talk to you". But after all u r the one who will always be there for me.'

The ease of communication in the family can be seen by the way that Aarushi, who was often dropped or picked up from school by the rotund Rajesh, teasingly threatened her father that she would forbid him from coming to her school unless he went to the gym and shed some pounds like the other dads. She would write, in school essays and cards to her parents, about humorous and happy things that happened in the family when she was an infant. Like the time Nupur slipped on the stairs while carrying her: 'My father just took me with him and forgot my mom . . . Then we found that my mom had a broken leg and I was fine with not even a scratch!!!' There were parties and holidays with friends like the Durranis. Trips to Kasauli and Manali and a memorable one to Singapore and Malaysia a year before her death.

Her demands from Santa on her last Christmas distils who she was:

Dear Santa,
Merry Christmas to you. I know you will be tired from running here and there giving children what they wanted but I want something totally different. I want the well-being of my family. I want no harm to reach them. Please fulfill my wish. My second wish is that I want my parents to always be with me and my friends too!!

My third wish is a bit silly—I WANT A DOG. Not from you but from my parents. I wish they agree!!!
Merry Christmas.

'He didn't fulfil even one of her wishes, did he . . . ?' Rajesh asked plaintively as he and Nupur recounted their memories to me in their flat in Delhi.

The Talwars had reason to be proud of their daughter. 'She was always in the first three in her class, first, second or third . . . Below that was too much to handle for her,' Nupur said.

In an essay about her schooldays, Aarushi berated herself for slipping from 92 per cent in one year to 89 in the next. She got her precious scholar badges every year, and having done so consistently well over three years, she was awarded a blue scholar blazer by the school.

She was intensely proud of this, but Nupur said, 'She never used to wear it . . . She'd say she wanted to be like everybody else.'

Yes, there were boys. But having a boyfriend at thirteen or fourteen did not mean physical intimacy; that was something Aarushi's schedule did not allow in any case, going from school straight to her grandparents', and then to her own home when her parents returned home for the day. Having a boyfriend was, instead, a gauge of popularity, something played out in polls and other means on social media networks. It wasn't as if the parents didn't know about the boys. They were protective—Rajesh a little more so—and often insisted that she went out with her friends in the company of at least one adult, but there were times they gave in. She would go through the highs and lows of puppy love like any other teenager from the same milieu, but her biggest, most serious crush, Nupur told me smiling, was on Johnny Depp.

'We had a tree growing outside, a big tree. So she used to call it Johnny Depp. And every night it would be "Good night Johnny Depp". This was a ritual in our house. In school she was asked to write about her room, so she wrote that she had this tree and she called it Johnny Depp, and her teacher sent it to every class to be read out . . . She must have been in class six or seven.'

We were sitting in the drawing room of the Talwars' South Delhi flat. Nupur across from me, Rajesh to my right, Aarushi on every wall. It was 24 November 2013, the day before the court judgement, and our conversation was subdued. I had interviewed the Talwars many times and was having trouble thinking of new questions to ask.

I chose to just listen. In the past, Nupur usually spoke when she had a point to make, and she seemed to relish the tough questions. I remembered asking her earlier about the strain the murders might have put on her relationship with her husband. Did it ever cross her mind that he might have done it? She'd looked me in the eye and said that if she had even a decimal point of a doubt, she would have led the way to prosecute Rajesh. Her daughter had been murdered, what possible reason could there be to protect her killer?

Nupur would always look people in the eye—and this troubled some—but today, I found her looking away a lot. Rajesh went through his usual cycle of indignation and despair—his pitch would rise as he spoke of injustice, he was often close to tears, and then he would become quiet and stare blankly, perhaps at a future that was bewilderingly real and inconceivable all at once.

They seemed to know that a guilty verdict was coming, that for now the fight was over. It was the only time Nupur let her guard down in front of me. In the silences during that conversation, I could almost hear her counting her losses. It was the first time I saw her weep.

As I read the press, it seemed to me the CBI had made the Talwars out to be killers as sharp as their scalpels. Geniuses of a kind. Daring, clever, and almost successful. But I felt that if they were guilty, their genius lay not in the execution of the murders or the meticulousness of the alleged cover-up. It lay in keeping up, for five years, the impossible pretence that they were innocent. It lay in sticking together as a couple. This was a broken family—its most vibrant, beautiful part had been lost. But the two people left in it genuinely loved each other. That was true whether they were guilty or not.

'Just three days ago I was going through her things, small small things she'd written. On the 11th she had written a Mother's Day card . . . She never believed in buying cards. She'd make, draw, write. She'd do it for everyone, Nana, Nani.

'In fact I found a small diary, two–three pages only. One her *hisaab*, like chips, Kurkure, she had her account of what she had spent. Her pocket money was Rs 200, which never included phone and clothes. She used to say "phone and clothes yours".' Both parents laughed at that memory, as if it were a private joke.

'One place she's written, "Mom doesn't know . . . but I didn't feel like drinking milk that day, I threw it in the pot . . ."

'I was reading it and thinking "she doesn't know still . . .
threw it in the pot . . ."'

Nupur Talwar trailed off, and looked down, overcome
by emotion at the thought of this childish deception. Rajesh
began to weep. 'It's very very painful what they are doing to
her . . . I'm not saying because it's my child. I'm saying because
she was a good soul. All children are good souls . . . But you
know, she never demanded anything or threw a tantrum.
Never. Not even once.'

Nupur recovered her composure. 'I remember one
Christmas, 2006 or 2007, we decided to buy her an iPod.
We told her, you have to go to Nani's house, we have to
go to the other flat to see what work is going on. I think
she thought that there was something suspicious, but
she said okay, I'll go. We came back, we kept the packet
somewhere. Next day we gave it to her. She was so excited,
and she finally said, "I have a big stomach ache, so I have
to tell you something." I said, what? She said, "I knew you
had gone to get something for me. So I even saw what you
had got for me."'

Nupur was smiling again. 'So she did this whole drama
about being excited about it . . . And then Rajesh one
anniversary told her, come let's go buy Mom earrings. So
she told me that Dad wants to buy you earrings . . . she said
she couldn't keep the gift a secret.

'You know, she may have been on Facebook, Orkut
whatever, but there was an innocence about her. They've
made her out to be secretive, hiding things . . . she was never
like that.

'They've made her out to be a 35-year-old. I remember,
when I got bail and I was coming out, there was a jailor, he
says I never say this to anyone but I am going to say you're
not going to come back. Then he says, *Sunne mein aya aap
ki bitiya tees saal ki thi.*"' (We heard that your daughter is
30 years old.)

'Hmm u hate me . . . I noe ma fault m such a frekin slut . . . I noe.' The same girl who wrote to Santa also wrote this. It was a reply to her thwarted teenage suitor, Sankalp Arora. Sankalp had found out about Aarushi's intention to 'break up' with him on social media. Trawling through her Facebook and Orkut accounts, the police found many such messages from Aarushi. Sankalp was persistent: his messages are filled with 'ooo jaanu, lubh you, muah muah'—the kind of language that at a certain age may seem the best form of expression.

Aarushi had many male admirers. There was Ishan, there was Arnav, there was Sankalp after him, and Anmol after Sankalp. She indulged them in the way a 14-year-old would. A glimpse into her Orkut world is telling.

'Which is the best couple in 8th?' The polling numbers were out on Orkut under 'kool 10th studentz of DPS'. The forum wasn't restricted to just 10th graders; 'popular' girls and boys from other classes found a place too.

So along with Utkarsh–Vanita, Vaibhav–Surabhi, Dhruv–Avani and sundry other 'couples' is Aarushi–Arnav, who got a healthy 38 per cent of the vote. But that wasn't all: Aarushi's name was linked with Sankalp as well in the same poll (18 per cent).

That bit of ambiguity tells its own story. Was there a procession of boys courting Aarushi? Was she, therefore, 'fast'? Or was she just what every other kid that age, in her environment, wanted to be—well known and popular? Pretty, bright and well spoken, Aarushi made all the polls. There was even one just about her: 'who is d perfect person for Aarushi?' 21 per cent of her friends voted Sankalp, 18 per cent Arnav.

A friend of Aarushi's wrote back to express surprise (if tinged with a little adolescent excitement) about 'Sanki' being linked to her, saying she had voted for Arnav. Aarushi's response:

'Ahem . . . hello delete this thing rite away . . . lol.'

The most important part of that message is the one that the more prurient among the older generation will miss, and those of Aarushi's age will get instantly: it's the LOL. Laugh out loud. This is just a bit of juvenile fun. And Aarushi wasn't the only one indulging in it.

Now that they are young adults, Aarushi's friends look at these messages and smile, they understand what was going on, and that none of it was sinister. Rajeshwari, a friend of Aarushi's, blogged: 'Didn't we all have these streaks in us when we were fourteen? How abnormal is it for an urban, public school-educated fourteen-year-old of the twenty-first century to own a cellphone, use it to text a friend of the opposite gender and put up a few harmless pictures of a birthday party on a social networking website?' And was it a crime to have a 'boyfriend'? And isn't the meaning of boyfriend at thirteen a fair order removed from what it is at thirty?

Mixed in with the so-called adult stuff on the social networks that Aarushi was part of was a lot of pure childishness. Like a chain mail that said the reader would be kissed by the love of their life if they forwarded the mail to ten other people, and cursed in love if they didn't. This was, and largely remains, the online life of the teenager. And through all the boys and polls and chain mails, she remained focused on her studies. Her friend Vidushi said, 'Of all of us at that age, Aarushi probably had the firmest sense of right and wrong.'

That, though, was not the way the police saw it. They took things literally, and in their eyes Aarushi's 'character' painted itself. One message from Sankalp made reference to a 'booze party' in the future. This was then tied to an email Aarushi had sent to Rajesh which had no connection to alcohol, but contained an apology: 'I wnt do it again.' The mail ended with the daughter making up with her parents, telling them how much she loved them. And in fact, it had to do with her going out with some friends unaccompanied by an adult.

This is not what the investigators understood it to be. They would not bother with the cards and letters that were in the scrapbooks of the Talwars. They preferred looking at Facebook and Orkut.

The pictures Aarushi deleted on the night she died became a cause for suspicion. Why would she do that? The simple explanation that kids with digital cameras often do this was not enough. The police could have mined the data card to possibly recover the pictures, but the lab it was sent to wasn't equipped to do this.

Vidushi had talked about a 'sleepover' at Aarushi's place planned for the 19th. What was a sleepover? Did adults also participate? Why not? Again, the explanation that kids that age wanted to be left alone in each other's company—and that there were no boys—wasn't good enough. Every answer the Talwars gave was held against them, just as much as the answers they did not have.

The police, looking at Aarushi's bedroom door during the investigation, wondered: What type of parents kept their child locked up? Aarushi's casual remark to her friends about physically not being there for the outing the following day was now treated by the UP police as a premonition. What would make her say something like this on the day she would be murdered?

The police were alarmed by the language in the social media exchanges. For kids in their early teens, profanities such as slut or bitch are of no consequences; they are merely words in a world where language is increasingly sexualized. The threshold for the use of such adult words has lowered; film censors permit more and more sexual words in films without certifying them as 'Adults only'. For my generation, such language is alternatively alarming or indecipherable. The police is even more removed from their casual usage. It thus seized upon the profanities (real or imagined) and the mention of sleepover and the use of phrases containing multiple 'partners' as something more sinister than the kids themselves ever intended.

One afternoon during the trial, I met three of Aarushi's friends at the Durranis' home in Noida, not far from where the Talwars lived. Their apartment was not unlike the Talwars' with simple seating in the drawing room, where a desert cooler whirred. Vidushi Durrani had been like a sister to Aarushi. The two other girls were Manini Mathur and Fiza Jha. Fiza's mother Masooma also joined the conversation. The girls were now nineteen, and in college, each pursuing a professional degree. As her mother looked on, Fiza, poised and articulate, told me about their growing-up years.

'None of us really had a "boyfriend". But we could spend hours talking to a boy. I sometimes wonder now what it is we talked about. It's almost silly. We could be on the phone while watching some television show, not saying anything at all, for hours. We really didn't know what a relationship was.'

Those were the early days of social media, and platforms like Orkut were unsophisticated by today's standards. But the kids were drawn to them nevertheless—there was a thrill in being able to have a connected group. Juvenile activities, such as voting which was the best 'couple' in their class, or just exchanging 'endorsements', were fun.

Vidushi and Aarushi were close enough for them to share passwords. Because of this Vidushi had a harrowing time explaining to the police why Aarushi had 'threatened' her with an 'I'll kill you'. 'It was just a prank, I posed as her and posted something, and she got mad at me, in the way that you do when someone plays a prank,' said Vidushi.

Of the lot of them, Aarushi was the most protected, they said—and always the one with the greatest sense of responsibility, of right and wrong. 'That's how she was,' said Vidushi, 'even when we played with dolls as kids.'

Fiza and Aarushi went to dance classes together. They loved music. Got joy from trivial things. Aarushi and a few other friends would reward themselves with an ear-piercing each time they achieved a milestone. They talked about boys, what with Aarushi being so popular, but it wasn't anything different from what they might have read in a young-adult novel.

But did the same girls speak the kind of language that was found on Aarushi's profiles?

A round of mild laughter rippled through the room. Masooma Jha spoke: 'I couldn't imagine this when we were growing up, my parents would be horrified! And when I discovered the way these kids spoke, I wasn't that happy either. But that's how it was, I understood that it didn't mean my child had been corrupted. Or that she had changed into someone loose. They were still kids. Our kids, and they'd be fine.' The thing about language is that it catches on in groups: members begin to express themselves in a similar way. 'At that age, we never thought about appropriateness when among friends, maybe we should have, but we didn't. It didn't make any of us a worse person though,' said Fiza.

This nuance was well beyond the comprehension of the constabulary, to whom using the word 'slut' about oneself was confessing one's promiscuous nature.

When I brought up the question of sex, everyone laughed. 'Believe me, if one of us was, all of us would know.'

That the question had come up in their dear friend's context made everyone serious. 'Specially not Aarushi. It's unimaginable, she was the best of us in many ways.'

Vidushi and Aarushi used to spend a lot of time together beyond school hours and on holidays, so I asked her whether she knew Hemraj. Of course she did. She thought of him as someone old, quiet and benign, never felt even a hint of a threat. They never really interacted that much. But if she or Aarushi ever wanted anything—a glass of water, or coffee, say—he'd always bring it to them. It was almost as if he was there, but not quite. It may sound politically incorrect, but they never really noticed Hemraj.

Just as we have a new generation of kids with their own language and behaviour, we also have, almost unnoticed, a new generation of servants. The old manservant or cook or maid who is 'part of the family' is well and truly a thing of the past. The mobility of the middle class, smaller family units and smaller living spaces have ensured this. In India's metros and their suburbs the demand and supply of this cheap labour seems to have found some kind of equilibrium. Those in such jobs are usually at least informally organized—there is a network which provides information about vacancies and better pay. On the employer's side there is enough of a supply of domestic help that they can be tried and replaced with ease. There could be temporary discomfort, but the servant is someone fairly easily replaced.

All this adds up to shorter service spans, which doesn't leave much of a chance for the help to become part of the family, leading to, in some ways, an 'invisibilization' of the individual. That is what Vidushi Durrani meant when she said they never 'noticed' Hemraj. In 2008 when he was asked to identify Hemraj's corpse, its face puffed up, a storm raging through his own head, the same thought had crossed Rajesh Talwar's mind. He had called Nupur to ask if Hemraj owned a T-shirt with 'New York' printed on it; all the while he was thinking that he had 'never noticed Hemraj'.

As I spoke to Aarushi's friends, I realized the staggering order of improbability of a consensual liaison between Hemraj and Aarushi. For is it possible to have a relationship with someone who is invisible?

Yam Prasad Banjade—or Hemraj—had come to work for the Talwars seven months before he was murdered. He was born in 1963, according to his passport, but he was probably much older. Originally from Agrakanchi in Nepal,

Hemraj had come to India seeking work in the 1980s. 'Yamraj' would have been closer to his name, but you can hardly address someone as 'the lord of death', so Hemraj stuck.

The Talwars remember him as mild-mannered, if a little moody at times. But his conduct with everyone—from the Talwars to their servants—left no room for complaint. His job was cook and factotum rolled into one, and he was proficient at it. Those who knew him, like Aarushi's grandparents, said he treated her like a grandchild.

Hemraj had arrived at the Talwars' through the Nepali servants' network, and he was friendly with Rajesh's assistant Krishna and the Durranis' manservant Rajkumar. When he came to live with the Talwars, he also got to know Vijay Mandal, Puneesh Tandon's employee.

For their part, the Talwars tried to make Hemraj comfortable: they gave him the servant's room within the flat, appointing it with a television and a desert cooler. Hemraj, as far as they knew, was a teetotaller, so Rajesh Talwar's bar was safe.

Information on Hemraj was thin. He had a wife and grandchildren back home; he hadn't been with the Talwars long enough for them to really get to know him. Rohini Gupta was a former employer who could speak authoritatively about him, as he had worked for her and her businessman husband at their South Delhi home for a decade and a half. Gupta, now in her sixties and divorced, had two girls of her own. 'I can say one thing: I'd vouch for his character one hundred per cent. We never ever had any situation. In fact, he was extremely protective. If in a fit of anger I wanted to whack the children, he would always intervene. He'd always stop us. And we lived in a joint family, there weren't just my two girls, there were six others. We never had a trust issue with him.' In fact, she added, her ex-husband was a man with a volatile temper; yet he never, in all the time that

Hemraj worked for them, ever raised his hand against the servant.

Hemraj did, however, 'like a drink every once in a while' she said. 'We had to be careful about the beer bottle count in the refrigerator, and keep an eye on the liquor stock in the bar. That's all. But we were okay with this—he had been very loyal to the family.'

Hemraj left her employ to put his feet up, said Gupta. 'He told me that he'd been able to construct a pucca house and had enough savings to get by. Also, he was getting old, he was becoming hard of hearing. He just wanted to retire.' Hemraj returned to the Guptas four or five years later. He had run out of money because of a health problem in the family and was looking for work. Rohini Gupta and her husband had divorced by then, and the circumstances in that household had changed but Hemraj was told he could always come back if he didn't find employment elsewhere. Shortly thereafter, he informed them that he'd got a job with the Talwars in Noida.

The myth about Hemraj being a teetotaller had been around since the murders. Since he was not a drinker himself, he was less likely to host a booze party in his room: this was the CBI's logic for later dismissing the possibility that Hemraj's friends had visited him and then killed Aarushi and him. Hemraj's post-mortem report didn't throw up any traces of alcohol. He hadn't had a drink the night he was killed, but this didn't mean he never drank. Minor indiscretions such as pilfering a drink or two weren't beyond him. This wasn't his defining trait, but a little booze party at his place for his friends wasn't that implausible after all.

*\*\**

His reputation in shreds, Rajesh Talwar was released from Dasna jail on 11 July 2008. His release took place two weeks before a very important event for the CBI: a change of guard at the top. It is a transition that never takes place without a power struggle. The CBI is charged primarily with investigating corruption in high office and serious economic offences, so the director's post is a sensitive one. The intrigue surrounding the exit of Ranjit Sinha in late 2014 is the most recent example that shows how political the appointment can be.

Vijay Shanker and Ashwani Kumar were Indian Police Service (IPS) batchmates, but Shanker enjoyed a career of seniority over Kumar because of early service in the armed forces. Ashwani Kumar, however, may have been politically more connected. He had been a senior officer with the Special Protection Group (SPG), which handles the proximate security of the prime minister, former prime ministers and families of present and former prime ministers. Ashwani Kumar's job at the SPG had been at 10 Janpath, the residence of Congress president Sonia Gandhi.

Vijay Shanker's vote for the next CBI director had been for a CBI veteran investigator, M.L. Sharma. At a party on the eve of his departure on 31 July came informal confirmation that Sharma would be taking over. Arun Kumar held Sharma in very high esteem. In fact, through the course of the Aarushi–Hemraj investigation, he had spoken about the case more with Sharma than with Shanker. He was happy with the turn events were taking. But the day after the party, things changed. Sharma, it turned out, wasn't going to be the next director. The position would be Ashwani Kumar's.

Shanker told me he had no discussions at all about the Aarushi case as he handed over charge to his successor, Ashwani Kumar. 'Directors don't investigate cases, so they are never really talked about as you hand over charge,' he said.

This may seem odd, given that there was almost non-stop coverage of the double murders at the time, but there was another reason why the case wasn't part of any discussions between the outgoing director and the incumbent: there was no meeting between them.

'I retired at the end of July and my successor joined about three days later,' said Shanker.

Within a week of his taking over, Ashwani Kumar held a meeting about the Noida double murder investigation. The media pressure was unrelenting, and the new director needed to get a grip on the case. At the meeting Ashwani Kumar said that he had watched Arun Kumar's press conference of the previous month with rapt attention as an ordinary viewer, and felt it didn't show the agency in a good light. This was because there had been several minutes of silence at the beginning of the press conference, during which Arun Kumar and others sat facing the cameras saying nothing. It made the CBI look tentative. This, the new director felt, was embarrassing.

This silence had indeed filled out several minutes. It also had a simple explanation: some channels had set up their cameras and gone live, broadcasting pictures. Others were still sorting out their equipment and connections. Arun Kumar had no response to his director's charge. But the first meeting on the Aarushi case hadn't gone well.

Through the month of August, Kumar and his team had worked on Vijay Mandal to turn approver, and testify against Krishna and Rajkumar. That deal was as good as struck; all that was required was the director's approval. Ashwani Kumar was away in Kolkata when his approval was sought. He turned it down. Why?

Arun Kumar's track record had become the subject of rumour within the CBI. He had earlier investigated two high-profile cases: the Nithari murders and the killing of Rizwanur Rahman, a computer engineer who was allegedly murdered in Kolkata in 2007 after marrying Priyanka Todi, the industrialist Ashok Todi's daughter. Though public perception was that the Todis had killed Rizwan and made it appear a suicide, the CBI finally found it to be a case of suicide. Similarly, in the Nithari murder case in Noida, in which remains of women and children were found in a drain behind Moninder Singh Pandher's house, Kumar's initial investigation found that only his servant Surinder Koli was the culprit.

An impression may have been created about the cases Arun Kumar handled: the wealthy and powerful who were initially suspects in sensational cases managed to get off as innocent.

Arun Kumar told me he was aware of these rumours. Ashwani Kumar would have been as well. From thinking he had the case wrapped up, the investigator found he was back where he had started. In early September, the three new suspects were released on bail, for lack of evidence against them.

Kumar felt direct DNA or blood evidence was his best chance now. CFSL test results hadn't yielded anything on any of the suspects. Dozens of samples had gone to the Centre for DNA Fingerprinting and Diagnostics (CDFD), Hyderabad. Kumar decided to lie low and await the reports from there.

The most voluminous of these arrived in early November. And no sooner had they entered the CGO Complex than the scandalous part of the report was immediately leaked to the press. Aarushi's vaginal swabs had been sent to the government lab in Noida after the post-mortem. Dr Sunil Dohare had not even marked them as Aarushi's—he had just wrapped the slides in paper and handed them to a runner who took them to the pathologist Richa Saxena at the Government District Hospital, Sector 30, Noida. Why hadn't Dohare at least marked the slides? In his fourth interview with the CBI, on 30 September 2009, Dohare calmly said, 'There is no procedure of collection of swab in our district and in entire UP state.'

Within hours of the post-mortem, Saxena received the samples. She tested them for semen and biological fluids, found none present, and sent her report on 16 May itself. Then she put the slides away in a steel almirah in her office along with all other slides.

A couple of weeks later, when she was in Patna, she received a call about the slides from the CBI. She directed them to the almirah. Of the samples that went to the CFSL, a forensic scientist found traces of Aarushi's DNA, but also DNA from another female source—given their handling, this would come as no surprise.

This anomaly forced the CFSL to send the samples to Hyderabad's CDFD for DNA testing in July 2008. The report from Hyderabad was even more troubling than the one from CFSL. It concluded that the DNA extracted was 'not from the biological daughter of . . . Dr Rajesh Talwar . . . and Dr Nupur Talwar'.

The traces of Aarushi's DNA seem to have just disappeared at the Hyderabad lab. Now there was speculation that the slides had been swapped. Half-hearted inquiries about how this might have happened followed. But there was no real explanation by the CBI for the discrepancy. Some unnamed sources in the agency said that there had been a genuine mistake, that this wasn't a cover-up. Others put out the story that the Talwars had used their 'influence' and were responsible for the 'swap'.

A layer of plausibility was added to this theory. The Talwars knew the pathologist Richa Saxena. Their children went to the same school, and Saxena had once interacted with them on a dental matter. That interaction could hardly have been termed 'friendly', according to the Talwars. In fact, it was a dispute over a bill. But things were even more complicated than that. Richa Saxena also happened to be married to Dr Naresh Raj. A paediatrician by training, Dr Raj had conducted the post-mortem on Hemraj's body, and appeared happy to fall in line with whatever investigators were saying. His wife, however, wasn't going to be pressured.

Saxena had a track record of standing up to this kind of thing. A few years ago, a powerful cartel of doctors who ran an illegal blood bank in Muzaffarnagar had tried to threaten her not to test blood samples that would incriminate them. They failed, and were eventually convicted.

The CBI tried to discredit Saxena, saying she had discipline issues, and was in a running battle with her superiors at the government hospital.

According to Saxena, her records were snatched from her in early April 2008—a month or so before the murders. She told CBI investigators that there were orders to bar her entry into the hospital so that she could be marked absent. In addition, the hospital administration had withheld her salary. She said she turned up for duty every day despite all this, and had taken her grievances to the Allahabad High Court.

Saxena confirmed to the CBI that the samples the hospital received were stored unsealed—and that contamination could not be ruled out as a result. When investigators summoned her again a year later, in November 2009, she told them firmly that there was no foul play and that she was willing to go through a lie detector or any other test if required. But the thing to note here is that the CBI's own lab, CFSL, had found Aarushi's DNA on the slides. They had had custody of the material till that time. They had sent the slides to the Hyderabad lab; the Talwars had not.

A whole new angle to the case seemed to be opening up, in which lay infinite avenues of speculation. New stories now began circulating: the Talwars had used their influence to swap samples to prevent the discovery of a sex act having been committed; Aarushi was adopted, which explained why her parents didn't love her and eventually killed her. Arun Kumar had not succeeded in building a case against the servants. And now, in November 2008, there seemed to be evidence implicating the man whose release he had sought in July.

Both the agency and the media turned their focus on the 'biological daughter' issue. Neither Arun Kumar nor anyone in his team noticed anything interesting in a dense little bit which appeared a few lines above it.

If anyone had bothered to look at item number two, on the preceding page, they would have found the hard evidence required to charge Krishna:

. . . Exhibit R (two razors, articles said to be of Mr Hemraj), Z20 (one pillow cover, purple coloured cloth) and exhibit Z30 (one bedcover, multicoloured) with suspected spots of blood are from the same male individual . . .

Stripped of the numbers and the jargon, this is what it meant. The razor and the multicoloured bedcover belonged to Hemraj, and his DNA was detected on these. Hemraj's DNA was found in the traces of blood on an item that did not belong to him: the purple pillow cover belonged to Krishna.

This was a potential case-cracker: it suggested that Krishna was at the scene of the crime. It could have been the proof Arun Kumar and his team were looking for against Krishna. But for that it would first have to be noticed.

Arun Kumar and his team were instead preoccupied with trying to limit the damage to their reputations. They now came under pressure to subject the Talwars to narco and brain-mapping tests. In January, the Talwars travelled to Gandhinagar and were from then on in the hands of Dr S.L. Vaya, who put them through a polygraph test as well as a brain-mapping test. The results cleared them of any suspicion. Dr Vaya looked at the test reports of the three servants, one of whom, Rajkumar, she had personally administered the test to, and the contrast between the two sets of tests was definitive: she told me that the Talwars clearly appeared innocent and the servants guilty.

As far as Dr Vaya was concerned she felt no need to put the Talwars through the invasive narco analysis test, particularly because Rajesh Talwar was on anti-depressants and Nupur Talwar was on medication to help conceive another child; the chemistry of the narco test would interfere with the chemistry of these separate medications. Arun Kumar accepted Dr Vaya's recommendation.

*** 

The curious case of the vaginal swabs and other errors of omission probably cost the first CBI team its assignment. In mid-2008, Arun Kumar had jumped the gun and as good as held the servants guilty in a press conference, even though all he had to go on were brain-mapping and narco tests. His team could not file a charge sheet, or take the investigation forward. The confusion over the swabs threw the investigation off by a number of months and was the final straw. The boss wasn't happy.

Unnamed CBI sources spoke on Ashwani Kumar's behalf to share the director's views. As the team was reconstituted in September 2009, the *Indian Express* wrote: 'The CBI director was unhappy with Arun Kumar's "line of investigation" ever since he joined last year. "The case was transferred to Dehradun since no development has emerged in the investigation even after all these months," the source said. "The forensic reports have also gone against CBI's line of probe."' Ironically the very evidence that would have helped the CBI had been sitting on the investigators' desk for more than two months.

How common is it for the CBI to reconstitute a whole team? 'My successors are the ones who need to answer this,' Vijay Shanker told me later. 'Either you have sacked a person for not having done his job properly, and you reconstitute. Or you give good reasons why you are reconstituting. These are matters of life and death! And you are laying down the foundation of justice.'

The reason here ostensibly was that it was sixteen months after the murders and the case was going nowhere. So the CBI brass advised a change in the line of investigation. In effect it was really saying: 'It's got to be the parents, get them, close this damn thing.' Why did the CBI go after the Talwars? This is a complex question, the answer to which comes in distinct parts—parts that may have nothing to do with each other.

For me it started with an unforgivable act of incompetence on the CBI's part in missing a crucial finding of the CDFD report—that Hemraj's DNA was found on Krishna's pillow cover. The second reason was a consequence of that error: the direction of the investigation was changed, and a licence given to follow the new line without any ethical restraints. The third element is the most difficult to understand when the context is law or policing. This was that the investigator simply did not 'like' the Talwars, especially Nupur Talwar. From Nupur's account of their interactions, it becomes clear that she wasn't intimidated by the new CBI investigator, Additional Superintendent of Police A.G.L. Kaul. This is something the Indian constabulary isn't used to—in their experience, it is only the influential guilty who are not intimidated by the threat of prosecution.

Kaul came into the case in September 2009, a little more than a year after the CBI took over. His boss, Neelabh Kishore, who was officially in charge of the case, was based in Dehradun. Kishore in turn reported to Javed Ahmed in Lucknow. But for all practical purposes, Kaul led the investigation. Kaul was in his early fifties, a balding man of average height with a rather large belly, which became even more substantial through the investigation. (The Ghaziabad regulars would greet him saying *Healthy lag rahe ho, Kaul sahab.*')

The superintendent had the air of a man who knew everything about everything, and then some. Part of this may have been because of the way some journalists pandered to him, nodding vigorously as he gave his short, low-decibel, briefings. Kaul was selective about who he briefed, but he seldom said much. He did, however, unfailingly give the impression that he knew a lot more—a tiny twisted smile would appear on his face at times, as if to say 'We have this thing tied up, the sensational stuff you're looking for will be revealed shortly.' Sometimes, after having been briefed this way, reporter colleagues would tell me, 'Just sit down one day with Kaul sahab, he will tell you everything.'

CBI officers could be assigned one of three branches in the organization: anti-corruption (against public servants, such as the investigation into the fodder or coal scams), economic offences (that result in losses to the national exchequer, such as major tax evasion/fraud, for example, the fake stamp paper racket run by Abdul Karim Telgi) or special crimes. Major crimes such as the Rajiv Gandhi assassination or various terror attacks come under the last category. So do dowry deaths involving the families of politicians, murders that may have a political angle to them—and therefore the possibility of abuse of influence—and murders of ordinary citizens that make too many headlines.

But special crimes investigations do not always have a high profile; in fact, most cases never make it to the papers in any significant way.

Most CBI officers will tell you that anti-corruption and economic offences are the preferred postings: the sensitivity and scale of the investigations undertaken make for much more interesting work. The darker side to this is that it offers CBI officers inclined that way much greater opportunities for making money or influence-peddling.

A special crimes position isn't, therefore, exactly prized. A direct recruit into the force, Kaul was in the economic offences wing in his early years. There, a departmental inquiry was held against him on a corruption charge, of which he was later cleared.

Arun Kumar was too senior to be Kaul's immediate boss, but he had upbraided Kaul both privately and publicly when Kaul was under his charge: Kumar had information that Kaul had been trying to extort money from people implicated in a dowry death case.

As his superior, Kumar was also privy to a list that the CBI guards with zeal. This is the ODI list: Officers of Doubtful Integrity. He told me Kaul was consistently on it. It's fair to ask why Kumar didn't just sack Kaul. But that's not how governments work: the government servant is too well protected for that—not just by the law, but by other colleagues who watch each other's back. The worst that happens is a transfer or a denial of promotion. Kaul was due to make the rank of superintendent earlier than he did, but was superseded.

Working within the system, the easy way out for Kumar was to avoid assigning Kaul to sensitive cases or ones in which he would need to interact with Kaul regularly. For instance, in the Nithari investigation, of which he was in charge, Kumar gave Kaul only a bit part. In the Aarushi–Hemraj investigation, no part at all. I learned from various people in the CBI that Kaul's reputation within the CBI had another facet: not everyone approved of his methods, but he was also seen as someone who got the job done—at a cost.

Kaul had for example in the past used the sex angle in a case effectively. The infusion of sex into a story worked very well in the media; it focused public opinion not on the facts of the case, but on the character of the suspects. In the notorious killing of the human rights activist Shehla Masood in Bhopal, which he had investigated, the media was supplied lurid excerpts from a somewhat dubious diary that Zahida Parvez, the alleged mastermind, maintained.

Parvez's motive in arranging the hit on the activist was jealousy. She purportedly suspected Masood of having an affair with a politician she herself was involved with. Within two days of Kaul taking over as investigating officer, the contents of the diary were all over the press.

Kaul was also known to have settled on a quarry and then coerced the suspect's friends/close associates to testify against them. The 2003 murder of Ram Avtar Jaggi, a Nationalist Congress Party (NCP) politician in Chhattisgarh, was one such. Kaul's theory at the time was that a political rival had bumped off Jaggi. He decided the culprit was Amit Jogi, son of the Congressman and former Chhattisgarh chief minister Ajit Jogi.

The conspiracy to murder Jaggi was hatched in a hotel room in Raipur, with Amit Jogi as its mastermind, said the investigator. Kaul then got a man who had known Jogi for decades to say under oath that the chief minister's son was the chief conspirator and director of operations. The scene described by the witness defied credulity. He claimed there were more than a dozen people present in the hotel room at one point or another; some were called, some came, some went, and some stayed, as Jogi hatched his plan. Along with Amit Jogi, dozens were arrested on the basis of this and other similar statements.

Jogi was acquitted in 2007 after spending nearly a year in jail because Kaul had been careless. It turned out that on the night in question one of Jogi's close friends whom his star witness had named hadn't been in the Raipur hotel at all. He was in the United Kingdom. It wasn't just him. Two other people whom the CBI claimed were in the hotel were also in the UK. A fourth was in Patna. Those who were out of the country produced their passports and immigration records. Kaul promptly had these seized for 'verification'. The CBI kept the passports for over a year, Amit Jogi told me, leaving the affected people running around trying to put together UK immigration records, passenger manifests of the flights they took, hotel reservations and records of credit card transactions.

The CBI's image is built upon the notion that it is more competent and more neutral than the police (it reports to the central vigilance commission and the department of personnel, Government of India; the police report to their respective state governments). That the CBI's recruits are largely from the same pool as the police is somehow forgotten.

The announcement that the CBI has taken over an investigation is routinely treated as good news. It comes with the suggestion that there is intent to get to the bottom of whatever the matter is. With this comes expectation. In the Aarushi case, for instance, the magistrate who sent the case for trial reflected the general belief that the CBI had disappointed not just her, but the country, by saying that it didn't have enough evidence to convict anyone when it submitted its closure report.

This faith that the CBI has the ability to crack every case, nail every culprit, isn't rooted in reality. It recalls, without irony, those 1970s' films starring the legendary Raaj Kumar as the CBI officer zipping down to a crime scene in an Ambassador Mark 2, with his assistant—a terrified German shepherd struggling to maintain balance on its roof—and solving mysteries by simply looking at the suspects as he smoked a cigarette. The reality is different. What does the CBI do in cases where winning a conviction seems difficult? The Jogi case reported in the press is instructive.

Firoz Siddiqui is at once a journalist, a detective and a murder conspirator out on bail. He has also wet his beak in Raipur's political soup, and is seen as an Amit Jogi follower.

In line with his strategy, Kaul summoned Siddiqui and asked him to record a statement under Section 164 saying that he knew of Amit Jogi's plan to get rid of his rival Ram Avtar Jaggi, and that it was hatched at a particular location.

'I told him I knew nothing about this. How could I just make it up?' Siddiqui told me. Kaul first tried to coax Siddiqui, and when this failed, told him that he was asking for trouble if he didn't comply. 'He said he would arrest me, but I refused to give a 164,' said Siddiqui.

Then, late one night, Kaul summoned Siddiqui to a guest house in Raipur saying he needed assistance with the identification of some people in photographs related to the case. When Siddiqui reached there, he was told that his visit had nothing to do with any photographs. He was there only to record his 164, failing which he would be arrested.

Over the next several hours, Siddiqui kept insisting he could not make up a story. At 4 a.m., Kaul woke up Siddiqui's brother Raees and summoned him to the guest house. 'He told Raees, "Try and drill some sense into your brother—does your family need all this hassle?"'

In the end, Siddiqui was arrested. In CBI custody for the next fortnight, he says he thought up a plan. He began to pretend that he was ready to spit out his 164. The arrest, the effect it was having on his family and his financial situation were all too much for him to take.

Kaul was pleased, and told Siddiqui he would grant him a second chance. Just before the statement was recorded, Siddiqui requested Kaul to talk to his brother Raees and explain things, reassure him that no harm would come to the family. Kaul agreed. What he did not know was that Raees was recording the conversation and several more that were to follow. In them, Kaul is heard saying that he cooked up the charge sheet; that the court was under his control, at least in the matter of granting reprieves; that the Siddiqui family would be taken care of financially.

He promised Raees a fleet of Innova cars to start a taxi service, and said he had already sent some money to the Siddiquis. (Siddiqui told me that his family received Rs 25,000, and that they accepted it since it was part of the sting operation to nab a crooked cop.) The tapes went straight to the media of course, causing a storm in Raipur. They were also submitted in court. But Kaul simply denied that it was his voice. The court asked if the officer would be willing to offer a voice sample for matching. Kaul refused. (By law, you need not give evidence against yourself.)

Jogi spent ten months in jail, before eventually being acquitted. Four years after his 2007 acquittal, the CBI challenged it and the matter is now in the Supreme Court. As for Siddiqui, the lower court convicted him, along with dozens of others, but in the light of the quality of evidence, he was granted bail by the high court.

***

In the Aarushi–Hemraj case, Kaul's groundwork had been done by the UP policeman Gurdarshan Singh. The media had already been given a sniff of sex; it was more a question of serving a spiced-up version of what Singh had said at the time.

Within two weeks of Javed Ahmed, Neelabh Kishore and A.G.L. Kaul taking over, the first steps for coming up with a 'new' theory were taken. The process was formally started on 25 September 2009, with an email from Ahmed to the director of the Forensic Science Laboratory, Gandhinagar. The email made a specific request that Dr M.S. Dahiya, then a deputy director at the lab, be asked to conduct a 'crime scene reconstruction'.

Why Dahiya? On the professional front, there was his work on the 2002 Godhra train burning incident to be considered. Dahiya's services (or, more accurately, the services of forensic scientists) were requested two months after the incident, in which 59 Hindu activists were burnt alive in a compartment of the Sabarmati Express. By the time Dahiya and Co. reached the scene, almost all physical evidence had been seriously compromised. So Dahiya conducted a crime scene reconstruction, simulating the throwing of fuel from outside the train carriage using water. He argued that this wasn't how the train was set alight.

What he suggested instead became controversial: that the fire was started inside the compartment, by miscreants who had boarded the train. Some people interpreted Dahiya's report to mean the culprits were already on board. Although there have been convictions in the Godhra case—and in the cases of the riots that followed the incident—the issue has never quite been settled. A crime scene reconstruction is, after all, just a theory.

The Aarushi case required a theory, and Kaul turned to Dahiya. Within days of the first contact with Dahiya, things began moving at a frenetic pace. Within a fortnight, the whole complexion of the investigation would change, even though the available material remained exactly the same. Not much could be done about the material. But what about people? People, as it turned out, could change.

I put myself in Kaul's shoes and considered the challenge before him as he took over the investigation. At times it appeared that his brief was to look at new angles and wrap up the case. But here was a set of documents—the servants' scientific test results—that suggested the earlier investigation may have been in the right direction. If they stood the test of further investigation, they could also point to the direction the investigation could take.

Within two days of his taking over as investigating officer, the CBI claimed it had recovered Aarushi's cellphone with the help of the Delhi police. It was also around this time that Hemraj's cellphone was found to be 'active' in Punjab. Arun Kumar's team had gone on the basis of the narco and other tests on the servants who admitted to knowing how the phones were disposed of, but they had failed to recover anything. Kaul had made one recovery, and didn't pursue the 'active in Punjab' lead at all. But with the recovery of

Aarushi's phone the servants' narco revelations—which said they had destroyed the phones—stood discredited. It could now be argued that the tests weren't dependable. They were simply kept on file, and away from the courts and the media.

The servants' narco reports out of the way, Kaul turned to what he could try and cull out from the scientific tests done on the Talwars during Arun Kumar's time. Rajesh and Nupur had undergone multiple polygraph tests and the reports indicated their innocence. There was also the January 2009 brain-mapping and polygraph reports from FSL Gandhinagar.

These reports too were very clear. In her comprehensive forensic analysis report, Dr Vaya wrote that there was 'no indication suggesting that they either directly or indirectly participated in the murder of Aarushi or Hemraj'. The lab's findings only indicated 'that both of them are victims of the circumstances of the ghastly murders of Aarushi and Hemraj'.

This was not how Kaul saw it at all. He enlisted Dr Dahiya's help in reinterpreting the reports. Between them, they prepared an unofficial two-page summary with their own version, picking out indicators of the Talwars having hidden Aarushi's cellphone and of Rajesh striking Hemraj on the head.

The previous year, Dr Vaya and her team of scientists had been so convinced by the tests they had conducted on Rajesh and Nupur that they found narco analysis unnecessary. Kaul and Dahiya now went to her with their own interpretation—and argued the case for subjecting the Talwars to narco tests.

Dr Vaya was incensed. She pointed out to them that specific findings in these kinds of tests couldn't be cherry-picked to suit a hypothesis. That conclusions could only be drawn from comprehensive analysis that supports a logical sequence of events. She also told them that the tests on the servants both in her lab and in others consistently pointed to their involvement. If the Nupur and Rajesh reports suggested they had hidden Aarushi's phone, the same indications were there in the tests conducted on the servants. Surely, argued Dr Vaya, all of them could not have hidden Aarushi's phone. Finally, she let Kaul and Dahiya know that neither of them were behavioural scientists. This was her area of expertise, not theirs.

Kaul and Dahiya did not want to stand down. They insisted on narco analysis being done on the Talwars. Dr Vaya told them that she had no problems conducting the tests as long as there was consent, and a court order. Kaul set about getting both, but that would take some months.

To establish that there was a new, viable line of investigation two things needed attention: the weapon(s) and the motive. The khukri was now out, but a scalpel seemed suspicious enough when wielded by a surgeon—even a dentist. For the motive, Kaul and Dahiya could fall back on Gurdarshan Singh's earlier statements. But this would require leavening and kneading the dough again. The central theme in the new theory relied heavily on the personal details of the Talwars: their profession, lifestyle, their relationship with their daughter—and, crucially, her relationships with boys.

To accomplish this, Kaul turned his attention to, and there isn't a more delicate way to put this, Aarushi's vagina. He returned to the post-mortem report, and to Dr Sunil Dohare, the man who had conducted it. In his post-mortem report, Dr Dohare had detected nothing abnormal with regard to Aarushi's genitals. He had mentioned a whitish discharge from both the uterus and the vagina, but this wasn't unusual in girls Aarushi's age.

Dohare had sat on an eight-man AIIMS expert committee which submitted its report in September 2008. Dr Naresh Raj, the doctor who conducted Hemraj's post-mortem, was also on the committee. The AIIMS committee deliberated over the facts for a good two months and submitted what it described as its 'considered opinion', an opinion endorsed on every page by Dr Dohare and Dr Raj. There was 'nothing abnormal detected' with regard to Aarushi's sexual organs.

But a month later, in October 2008, the CBI recorded a second statement from Dr Dohare. (His first, after the post-mortem, was recorded a few months earlier.) On the bottom of the first page was the line: 'During post-mortem examination I observed that the vaginal cavity of the deceased was dilated.' This was not a finding but an observation. Perhaps Dohare was explaining why he obtained vaginal swabs. Had it been anything more, the doctor was surely bound to record it in his report. He hadn't, but Kaul seized upon the line.

On 30 September 2009, five days after Dahiya was requested to come on board, Dohare was summoned to the CBI's camp office in Ghaziabad. Dohare's statement—his third—that day was nothing short of startling. He picked up from where he had left off a year earlier, and told Kaul: 'On external examination, the vaginal opening was found prominently wide open. Vaginal cavity and cervix was clearly visible . . . Hymen was ruptured and healed (old).'

Surely this was significant enough to mention in the post-mortem report? Or at least to bring up in the deliberations of the expert committee? Kaul pre-empted these questions by asking them himself.

> Kaul: During your examination you have found certain peculiar facts about the private parts of the body but the same have not been mentioned in the PM report. Why?
> Dohare: Comments about the private parts of the body were not mentioned in the PM report as the findings were non-specific and were very strange.

It is worth mentioning that Dr Dohare had never conducted an autopsy on a female before Aarushi's body came to his table.

That was the explanation he later gave for not recording a word about the 'very strange' things he had seen in his post-mortem report. And with each statement he gave, the orifice seemed to expand. It had started by being 'dilated', now it was 'wide open', so wide that the cervix was visible. In a fourth statement that Kaul recorded in May 2010, Dohare would become even more explicit about what he had seen two years earlier.

But his September 2009 statement was significant for one other reason. It was the first time that he mentioned Aarushi's ruptured (and healed) hymen. Aarushi's Facebook and Orkut accounts, and her cellphone records, showed she was in touch with a number of boys. Dohare's belated revelation about her ruptured hymen put a different spin on it altogether. It didn't matter to the vast majority of those who were told this story that hymens can rupture for reasons other than the loss of virginity. The leavening that was required for Gurdarshan Singh's claims that the girl was 'characterless' was now complete. Aarushi was sexually active—so wasn't it possible that she was sleeping with the servant? There was no difference between what Gurdarshan Singh said and what Kaul alleged—they were both insinuations. All Kaul did was use a doctor's opinion to support the insinuation. He thus completed the circle—and made a thirteen-year-old girl the villain of the case.

The status of Aarushi's hymen, as described by Dohare in September 2009, was quite specific and not very strange. So why didn't he include it in the post-mortem report? One reasonable explanation can be found if we ask ourselves the corollary: Why did Dohare choose to speak now?

The CBI had been in a panic over the alleged swapping of Aarushi's vaginal slides. The previous team had taken a lot of criticism for it, and the new one desperately sought explanations. In this regard, Dohare had come dangerously close to incriminating himself. He had admitted that he hadn't even bothered to mark the slides.

Right after Kaul was finished with Dohare, the investigating officer sent one of his underlings to record more statements— of the two sweepers who were in the room when Dohare was conducting his autopsy.

They had been interviewed a year earlier and had talked about the slides and the assistance they provided during post-mortems. Now, hours after Kaul had spoken to Dohare, they added a new paragraph to what they had said earlier. The operative part of it was: Aarushi's vagina was very wide open, and neither of them had seen such a thing before. Sweepers have no medical qualification to give an opinion in this instance. Yet the CBI obtained their statements.

\*\*\*

On 9 October, Dahiya travelled to Delhi to inspect the crime scene. According to him, there wasn't much to inspect: the house had been painted (with the CBI's permission) and put up for rent. Upon inspecting the roof, Dahiya gave Kaul his only concrete suggestion.

This was to do a simulation experiment involving a body being dragged by two people. Under Kaul's instructions, this 'scientific experiment' was eventually conducted, but the low level of any actual science was evident from the props used, such as diluted Shalimar paint (red), which had none of the physical or chemical properties of blood except perhaps its colour. But this would only be conducted in December 2010, when the CBI's closure report was being filed. For now, the 'evidence gaps' in Kaul's and Dahiya's theory had to be filled.

Aarushi's post-mortem doctor had given an opinion, however belated, that Aarushi may have been engaged in sex with Hemraj. Dr Talwar appeared to have a motive. He was a father who felt enraged and was compelled to take his daughter's life in the defence of family honour.

The CBI had begun to close in on a motive but what about the execution of the crime? For this, Kaul and Dahiya reminded themselves that Rajesh Talwar wasn't just a father. He was also a doctor. Somebody, one would assume, who would be precise in the use of a surgical instrument.

Kaul then turned his attention to the paediatrician Dr Naresh Raj, the man who had conducted Hemraj's autopsy. Both Dohare and Raj had earlier suggested that the khukri (recovered from Krishna's house and sent to them for examination) may have caused the fatal blunt injuries, but the weapon's cutting edge wasn't sharp enough, so the possibility of it causing the slits to the throat was remote.

Kaul summoned Dr Raj to his office in Delhi and recorded a brief, telling, statement. On 12 October 2009, Dr Raj told Kaul that the injury to Hemraj's neck was caused by a 'very sharp edged light instrument'. Kaul wanted something more specific, so he asked Raj what inference he could draw from the fact that the cuts to the neck of both victims were identical. Raj said: 'The identical position of the injury and the skill with which the cut was made clearly point towards a surgically trained person.'

At the time, the CBI had just one suspect. Dr Rajesh Talwar. And although he was a dentist, he did have some surgical training, didn't he? It was a neat fit. The pieces of the new theory were falling in place, and there were 'experts' willing to testify on different aspects of it.

But one question remained. Dr Raj, like Dr Dohare, had mentioned none of this to earlier investigators. He was also on the AIIMS panel which was specifically asked to answer the same questions. He had said nothing. So why now?

There is one more thing worth mentioning here. Kaul never seized any of Dr Talwar's surgical instruments. Throughout the investigation and the trial the prosecution insisted that a scalpel was used, but Kaul had never actually ever seen the kind of scalpels dentists use. He admitted that he hadn't even bothered to buy one for the sake of curiosity. The question of having any expert examine even a likeness of the weapon never arose. As far as Kaul was concerned, the suggestion of surgical skill was enough.

In November, a month after Dr Raj's new testimony, Kaul summoned Richa Saxena. That is when she firmly told Kaul that there had been no foul play with the slides of the vaginal swabs, and that she was willing to go through a lie detector or any other test if required.

\*\*\*

While the issue of the cuts to the neck had now been 'settled' by Kaul and Dahiya, there was a small problem. According to the examiners, the victims' necks had been slit either after they were dead or while they were dying. The blunt injuries that smashed their skulls had caused death. So even if a sharp, light weapon was used in the course of the murders, it wasn't the murder weapon.

The post-mortem doctors and the AIIMS committee had so far said that the culprit had wielded a khukri, whose blunt side could have been used. But with the servants out of the frame of suspicion, so was the khukri. Rajesh Talwar's feelings as a father and training as a doctor had fit into Kaul and Dahiya's thesis. What else was Rajesh Talwar? He was a golfer, of course.

The Talwars' practice was flourishing, and one of the markers of a successful professional in middle-class India is membership of a golf club. Dr Talwar was a novice, but he did own a set of golf clubs—or, as the CBI preferred to call them, golf sticks. The head of a golf club is, of course, heavy and blunt.

In July 2008, the Talwars' driver Umesh Sharma had given investigators a detailed statement about what he recalled in the days leading up to the murder and its immediate aftermath. Umesh had said that two golf clubs were always in Dr Talwar's Hyundai Santro, and that four or five months before the incident, when he took the car for servicing, he had removed the clubs and several other items from the boot. All these things, he said, he had kept in Hemraj's room.

In the first pictures that the police took of Hemraj's room, however, only one golf club could be seen. That the room was in a mess at the time, with the police force turning everything over, and that the other club may simply have been out of the frame, was not something Kaul wanted to consider. He and Dahiya had found their heavy, blunt object.

On 13 October, Dahiya was formally asked to write his crime scene reconstruction report. He sent it in on 26 October. It is marked 'Document 79' and is the defining document of the case. Three days after Dahiya's report, the CBI demanded that the Talwars hand over Rajesh's golf kit. They did so readily, on 30 October 2009.

Going through the record, a pattern seemed to emerge of the roles of Kaul and Dahiya.

25 Sept 2009: The CBI requests the CFSL for the services not of 'a scientist', but of Dahiya.

30 Sept: Dohare modifies his statement to say the vagina was wide open and the cervix was clearly visible, implying that there had been sexual intercourse which someone had tried to erase evidence of. The statements of two sweepers are taken, who also attest to vaginal dilation.

9 Oct: Dahiya is taken to the crime scene, where he does his mental reconstruction. Afterwards, he has detailed discussions with Kaul in his office.

12 Oct: Naresh Raj submits a report in which he says the slit across the throat was caused by a surgical instrument.

13 Oct: CBI sends a formal questionnaire to Dahiya.
26 Oct: Dahiya files his report.

***

The prosecution relied heavily on Document 79. This could be summed up in four words: father, doctor, golfer, murderer. This was the prosecution's case in the trial court in June 2012.

Dahiya's document is a masterpiece in several ways. It reveals things about Dahiya the man. Two of his traits he shared with Kaul. The first was the belief that before you even start investigations, you must get a story in place; the facts could be made to follow. The second was the ability to be the authority on subjects that were clearly beyond his area of expertise. A third, more complex, facet of Dahiya's personality also came through. His belief systems—rooted in the culture of North India's Jats.

The Jats governed by their khap panchayats are widely regarded as a conservative community engaging in honour killing. Does everyone in the community believe in these practices? Certainly not. But is it easier for them to believe that others might kill for honour? Most likely, yes.

In Document 79, it is possible that Dahiya was projecting a belief system, a moral code, on to the Talwar family. A colleague of Dahiya's at FSL Gandhinagar told me that he was 'unable to shake that aspect off and think beyond. This is who he is.' Here is Dahiya on 'honour' and 'psychology':

All these circumstances indicate the possibility of someone interested in the honour of the deceased girl and/or her family being active on this count. As far as human psychology is concerned, finding one's adolescent daughter in the company of a domestic servant at the dead of night in her bedroom is a grave provocation that can lead to an emotional upsurge

beyond human control and beyond rationality . . .
Though no conclusive evidence to that effect can be
obtained from photographs and other limited facts,
an intensive probe in that direction is certainly
warranted.

And:

The common/similar nature and dimensions of the
injuries inflicted on both the deceased establish the
common origin of their assassin(s). This similarity
also goes to *prove* [emphasis added] that they were
the victims of similar anger or grievance against them.

And:

. . . Those keenly interested in the virtuosity and
honour of Ms Aarushi and the Talwar family could
be behind this incident that appears to have its roots
somewhere in an improper/immoral conduct of either
or both the deceased.

Dahiya made other striking claims. He had been provided
photographs of Aarushi's room, on the basis of which he
notes with supreme confidence that 'two distinct impact
splatters on the wall behind the headrest of Ms Aarushi also
goes to *prove* [emphasis added] the contention of Mr Hemraj
having been caused head injuries in the room of Aarushi
itself'. ('Impact splatter' is a term of bloodstain pattern
analysis. Here Dahiya is saying he saw two distinct patterns
of blood splatter on the wall and his conclusion is that the
splatters arise from two different people.)

A serious contradiction naturally followed. Dahiya was
at pains to explain how the culprits had wiped all bloodstains
and chance fingerprints, utilizing the 'well-lit' conditions

inside the house. Somehow, though, they had forgotten the blood splattered on the bedroom wall. And somehow, no trace of Hemraj's blood was found when forensic labs tested samples of it.

Hemraj and Aarushi were murdered in the same room, on the same bed, according to Dahiya, but the murderers were able to wipe all traces of the servant's blood from the room while leaving untouched all of Aarushi's. Science will have some trouble explaining this feat, and Dahiya offers no help.

The fact is that Hemraj's blood/DNA/semen or traces of any other biological fluid were never found in Aarushi's room—and dozens of forensic samples were collected. Those who offered the simple explanation that no such evidence was found perhaps because it wasn't there, possibly because Hemraj wasn't killed in Aarushi's room, were dismissed as being biased or irrational. It was far more plausible that the murderers distinguished between blood groups and wiped one set clean—after all they were doctors.

\*\*\*

As any student of science knows, a really small change in initial conditions can lead to colossal divergences in results. In this case, the premise Dr Dahiya relied on was false. His starting point was the 'fact' that Hemraj's blood was found in Aarushi's room.

From there, sitting in his office in Gujarat, he dreamt up the scenario that read like a judgement rather than a 'crime scene analysis', Document 79's actual title.

The 'fact' that Hemraj's blood was found in Aarushi's room can be traced to an error in a 2008 letter written by a CBI SP called Dhankar, which listed the seizures of items from Aarushi's and Hemraj's rooms. Dhankar included a bloodstained pillow cover and pillow belonging to Hemraj as recovered from the teenager's room whereas these items were actually recovered from Hemraj's room, not Aarushi's.

A year after Dahiya's analysis, this error was corrected thrice: the CBI's closure report said no blood of Hemraj was found in Aarushi's room; in a submission to the Supreme Court, the agency specifically mentioned that the two items were seized from Hemraj's room; and in court, the original tag attached to the pillow cover was displayed.

In his analysis, Dahiya takes off from the point where Hemraj is in Aarushi's room at a clearly inappropriate time: around midnight. 'It has been attempted to be projected that Mr Hemraj was assaulted and killed on the rooftop,' he writes. '. . . The presence of the blood of Mr Hemraj on the pillow in the bedroom of Ms Aarushi, however, negates that plea conclusively.'

I spoke to Dahiya about his 'premise' in July 2012. He told me that he had only gone by what was 'provided' to him, in between lots of 'I cannot remember's. He was listed as a witness and I asked him whether he would clarify in court that he had been given faulty information. He then ended the conversation with that most reliable excuse: the matter was sub judice.

*\*\**

Document 79 was also conclusive about the weapons used. The throats of the victims were alleged to have been cut by a sharp surgical instrument of the kind Rajesh Talwar may have possessed.

With the motive and one weapon sorted by the Dahiya–Dohare–Raj triad, what remained was settling on the blunt murder weapon that actually delivered the death blows. Apart from the Talwars' driver Umesh Sharma's early statement that he had kept two clubs in Hemraj's room several months before the murders, there was no mention of the golf clubs by any investigator before Dahiya arrived on the scene.

On 13 October, the CBI sent a questionnaire to Dahiya in which he was specifically asked whether the triangular-shaped injuries on the heads of the victims could have been caused by a golf club. The golf clubs had not yet been seized, so the question of sending them for forensic testing did not arise. And even thereafter, neither post-mortem doctor was ever shown the clubs to ascertain whether the dimensions of the wounds on the victims matched those of the alleged weapon.

Dahiya, sitting in Gandhinagar, didn't get to see them either. Nor had he ever investigated a case where a golf club was a murder weapon. He would later say that he based his thesis on information supplied to him by Kaul—that the injuries were 'triangular shaped'—and not on the opinion of an expert who had actually inspected the clubs. Nevertheless, the golf club as a murder weapon was born.

Dahiya duly wrote out Kaul's question, sans a question mark, as a finding: 'The triangular-shaped head injury suggests that the weapon of assault must have been a golf club.' Between sending Dahiya his simple question and the Gandhinagar man's reply, Kaul attempted some investigation on the golf clubs. On 16 October, he summoned the Talwars' driver Umesh to his office. Umesh came back weeping, and with a burst eardrum, babbling that Kaul kept asking him where he had hidden the murder weapon, how much money he had been paid, and so on. Kaul recorded a statement in English that day (Umesh spoke no English) and confirmed with Umesh that he had kept two golf clubs in Hemraj's room. Asked if he could identify them, Umesh said he was not sure, but that he may be able to if he was shown the clubs.

Rajesh told me: 'When he beat him up, I called up Neelabh Kishore. He started saying very sorry sir, really sorry.' Nupur imagined that Kaul and Kishore were playing the old good cop–bad cop with them. 'He was always like that. "We have to change this IO," he says. And you know what he asked me? "It was in the CBI this happened? Are you sure? Lodhi Road?" I said yes very much Lodhi Road CBI office. "Ohh," he says, "we have to change this IO."'

Rajesh Talwar sought an appointment with the CBI director to complain, but could reach only the special director. He says he was assured that such a thing wouldn't happen again, but rues the fact that he didn't file a formal police complaint.

Kaul needed stronger evidence regarding the clubs. He didn't get it, but he could rely on Dahiya to introduce it as the 'new' murder weapon. After suggesting that a golf club could have been the weapon of assault, Dahiya expanded on his theme:

> There is also some possibility of a hockey stick to have been used, if there are some strong reasons to rule out the use of a golf club. A golf club is heavy enough to fracture the skull; it has a long handle that allows the assailant to maintain distance from the victim; it can be struck with great speed and force; it can leave a triangular cavity at the point of impact on the skull and it can cause an injury that matches with the dimensions of injuries recorded in the present case.

\*\*\*

Document 79, with its errors, speculation and astounding claims, would guide not just the investigation, but also the trial. Dahiya's report introduced several new things, but one of the most important was the phrase 'dressing up' of the crime scene, a charge the Talwars would have to live with from October 2009 onward. This, despite the fact that the flat was filled with blood and fingerprints, and a bloodstained bottle of whisky sat on the dining table asking to be noticed.

If the Talwars were so careful, why leave such obvious clues? One explanation was that it is precisely why they would do it: they didn't want to make the clean-up look too perfect. Or that they wanted to divert suspicion towards Hemraj, who it was initially believed had gone missing after killing Aarushi and helping himself to a drink. Dahiya also suggested that Hemraj was wrapped in a sheet after being fatally wounded in Aarushi's room and carried to the terrace where he was dragged to a spot which concealed the body.

All these themes would play out during the trial, but before that Kaul had to try and establish that a golf club was the murder weapon. He sent the golf kit to the biology division of the CFSL shortly after it was seized. Those tests yielded nothing by way of blood or DNA. On 10 November 2009, the clubs were sent to the physics division, where they lay till they were finally unsealed on 15 April 2010. It is only then, six months after the golf club theory was floated, that their dimensions were actually measured. A report would follow three months later.

***

September 2009 was the first time Nupur and Rajesh Talwar met Kaul and Neelabh Kishore. The officers of the new team wanted to take a look at the crime scene. The Talwars had moved out of their Noida flat by then, but were there to show the CBI men around. 'We wanted to cooperate to the fullest extent,' Rajesh told me later. But the couple had the niggling feeling that something was wrong even before any pleasantries were exchanged. Kishore was polite in his greetings, Rajesh recalled. 'The minute you see somebody, you can make out—there's something wrong there. At the stairs I shook hands with Neelabh Kishore. But Kaul intentionally did not shake my hand.'

Rajesh had been a suspect early in the investigation and spent nearly two months in jail before being released. Now, he suddenly felt like a suspect all over again. He would later tell Nupur that he had a bad feeling about Kaul. She told me, 'I also felt it, in fact we talked about it. I said why is he giving us these dirty looks? He asked, what kind of bed sheet did Aarushi use? I said blue bed sheet with a Disney print on it . . . He gave me a look as if I was lying. I said ya, that is what she was using. I knew there was something wrong, immediately.' That first meeting would define not just the relationship that Kaul and his team would have with the Talwars, but also the line of investigation. Kaul, like so many other people, may have got the impression that Nupur Talwar was cold and manipulative—and a little too assertive for his liking.

Kaul and his subordinates were interviewing other family members as well. One such interaction, with Nupur's parents, Bhalachandra and Lata Chitnis, was going well till Kaul asked their opinion on Nupur and Rajesh's relationship. Lata Chitnis told him that the marriage was very happy, the family tight-knit. Kaul waved this away in a manner that seemed inappropriate to the retired air force officer. He told the CBI man that it was his daughter he was talking about, and that he expected more decency. Kaul flared up, telling the old couple that he would drag them to the CBI office in Delhi day after day if they didn't answer questions properly. A heated argument ensued, during which Chitnis reminded Kaul that he wasn't impressed by the threat. He was a senior citizen: it was his right to be interviewed at home. Kaul backed down.

One of the last meetings the Talwars had with Kaul was at the Talwars' Hauz Khas apartment, and it was similar to the first, but by now, late 2010, everyone's tone had changed to open hostility. Especially between Kaul and Nupur Talwar.

Nupur clearly remembers that meeting. 'He was sitting in the lobby . . . He said I'll get twenty witnesses to say that she was covered with a white sheet,' she said. Kaul was referring to the flannel blanket that Aarushi was found covered with, which one of the UP policemen had described as a white blanket. This semantic difference apparently made it seem to Kaul that they were talking about two different articles, when they were talking about the same thing; and to his mind, it could have meant something as sinister as destruction of evidence.

'I said no, she was not covered with a white sheet,' Nupur Talwar said. 'I then said either your witnesses are lying or you are lying, because she was covered with that flannel sheet with circle patterns, which you keep seeing on TV shows everywhere. Then he started staring at me in a dirty kind of way. So then I told him you talk properly, behave properly. I told him I don't want you talking this way to me. I said I'm not lying to you, I've never lied to you.'

***

It seemed Nupur Talwar had annoyed Kaul because she wasn't intimidated by him in person. So he came up with his own little psy-ops project. He created a special email address in order to communicate with Rajesh and Nupur Talwar: 'hemraj.jalvayuvihar@gmail.com', under the username 'Hemraj Singh'. All emails to and from 'hemraj.jalvayuvihar@gmail.com' were official. Rajesh Talwar would receive email summons from this address. When he was asked for his consent to undergo narco analysis, for instance, 'Hemraj Singh' wrote him a mail on the CBI's behalf.

As official conduct, the creation of this creepy alias was indefensible. As a pressure tactic against suspects who were expected to respond to mails purportedly coming from the 'person' they were supposed to have killed, it was crude.

The issue of the 'Hemraj' emails first appeared in the *Indian Express* (1 May 2011). This was when the magistrate's decision to send the case to trial was being challenged by the Talwars. The report stated that, according to the agency, the mails were a prank. The CBI spokesperson, Dharini Mishra, went on record to say: 'Our investigation officer has told us that no such mail has been sent by the CBI.' This officer, presumably, would be Kaul. Ironically, the spokesperson was also asked whether the CBI would investigate who was posing as Kaul. To which she replied that the agency didn't take such things up 'suo motu'. This is where the matter rested.

The *Express* report had a CBI denial built into it because of an error. The email address it cited was 'hemraj. jalvayuvihar.com@gmail.com. The mails in question were sent from 'hemraj.jalvayuvihar@gmail.com'. The extra .com left room for a tenuous denial.

But what is tenuous breaks soon enough. In documents it submitted to the Supreme Court in April 2012, the CBI included a printout of a December 2009 email sent to Rajesh Talwar regarding the Talwars' consent for narco tests. Clearly printed, at the top of the page, was the source: 'hemraj singh <hemraj.jalvayuvihar@gmail.com>'.

Rajesh Talwar's reply was addressed to 'Mr Kaul'.

This isn't the only place where 'hemraj.jalvayuvihar@ gmail.com' makes an appearance. Court documents showed the address was created specifically for the Talwars and those perceived to be on their side. Ajay Chaddha, a family friend, also received at least one email from Hemraj/Kaul.

No email communication with the Talwars that the CBI placed on record comes from anyone except this 'Hemraj Singh'. In the case of the Talwars' consent for narco analysis, for instance, the Hemraj/Kaul mail is used to make the CBI case in the Supreme Court. The Talwars had said they willingly agreed to the tests while pleading that the case be reviewed. The CBI countered by saying that the accused agreed only 'conditionally'. It referred to the email by Rajesh Talwar addressed to Hemraj/Kaul in which he said he was giving his consent to the tests in the 'interest of justice' provided there was an assurance that the procedure was not hazardous to his health.

It may not appear that way, but CBI officers do have official email addresses. 'Hemraj' did not write to managers at Airtel or Vodafone requesting cellphone details relevant to the Aarushi investigation. According to records, such emails were sent using addresses ending with @cbi.gov.in.

The chief information officer, CBI, Dharini Mishra, exchanged telephone calls, SMSs and emails with me several times in August 2012. At first she denied anybody in the CBI could ever have sent the 'hemraj' emails. In the space of approximately an hour, however, she had changed her statement several times, arriving at a final version in an email.

The transcripts of the conversations, SMSs and email are illuminating.

*Call at 1.50 p.m. 9 August 2012, on Ms Mishra's landline, (011) 24361156.*

Avirook Sen: What is the standard procedure while sending summons via email?

Dharini Mishra: They are sent from the official IDs that end with @cbi.gov.in. In case there are network problems, officers might sometimes use their personal emails, but these normally bear the name of the officer. In no event will they use an obscure email address.

Sen: The Talwars received summons and other queries from an email ID that read 'hemraj.jalvayuvihar@gmail.com'. You denied this in an *Express* story from May 2011.

Mishra: You are writing about the Aarushi case? These mails were not sent by the CBI. This is not possible.

Sen: Do you stand by that denial?

Mishra: Yes, yes.

Sen: There are documents in court that the CBI has submitted that contain the address . . .

Mishra: What?? Okay give me 10 minutes, I will call you back. If I don't call back, then you can say I stand by my earlier denial.

Mishra called back at 2.13 p.m.

Mishra: Okay, I have spoken to the officers. They say they have used this email ID for some time due to some very special reason.

Sen: You said you had spoken to the officers when you last issued a denial. Does that mean that denial was incorrect?

Mishra: You are trying to make a story out of nothing . . .

Sen: Can you tell me what 'special reasons' there might have been?

Mishra: That we cannot disclose.

Sen: I will quote this conversation in its entirety . . .

Mishra: You cannot do that! You are just making a big story out of nothing. Please listen to me. You did not tell me you were going to quote me. You started by asking a general question, but then you started asking specifics . . . I knew there was something fishy.

Sen: I have told you what story I am working on and what documents I am relying on. These are CBI documents. I did not invent them.

Mishra: You can only quote me on what I say exactly. I am going to write to the *Mirror* [the publication I wrote for]. I will send you an SMS and then an email. That is all you can quote me on. Do not try to make a big story out of this.

Mishra did message back shortly thereafter: 'Regarding your query in the Aarushi case—the matter is sub judice therefore CBI will not comment on court proceedings, evidence in court etc.'

Sen: Is this your final statement? Tks.

Mishra: Regarding your query about issuance of summons by e-mail—the same is normally done by official e-mail. In rare occasions, personal or other e-mail ID can be used.

Mishra: I've sent two sms es and being followed up by e-mail also. Rgds Dharini Mishra, CIO, CBI.

After our conversation, Mishra called up a news agency and issued a short statement saying that the ID had indeed been created by the CBI for use during investigations. A two-paragraph report, no questions asked, went on the wires sometime the same evening. It baffled everyone who was following the story: I wondered why the CBI suddenly decided to put out such a story. In the jargon of our trade, this was a 'spoiler'. Information put out so that the sting is taken out of an exposé.

Ashwani Kumar, director of the CBI from August 2008 to November 2010, was part of the email exchanges. He was copied on several emails, including one from Nupur Talwar in April 2010 complaining that his officers were leaking damaging stories. Kumar thought nothing of the bizarrely named 'colleague' who popped up in his inbox from time to time.

Kaul's boss Neelabh Kishore sent and received mails from the ID several times. For instance, when Nupur

Talwar wrote asking for permission to rent out the Jalvayu Vihar flat, and when Kishore summoned them to his office in May 2010. Kaul's subordinates used it too. The Hemraj mail-trail thus ran right across the ranks of the CBI: from inspector to director.

The emails were not limited to the period of investigation either, as Dharini Mishra claimed in her belated clarification. The investigation was over in December 2010, but CBI officers kept writing to the Talwars till May 2012—when the matter had moved to the courts and trial proceedings had begun. Judge Shyam Lal mentions the emails in his judgement as if there was nothing at all amiss. He merely lists what he thinks is an unremarkable fact, saying Kaul had created the email ID to stay in touch with the accused during investigation.

Gautam Patel, who later became a judge at the Mumbai High Court, had this to say about the Hemraj emails in a column for the *Mumbai Mirror*:

> To describe this conduct as disturbing is to put it mildly. It is downright dangerous, certainly dubious and calls into question the CBI's motives and intentions, especially given that the CBI, like every arm of the government, has official email addresses. The implications of permitting this conduct are serious. A non-official email ID has been created and used to introduce material into the record of a court trying a criminal case. Does this contaminate the entire evidence pool? Does it jeopardize the integrity of the judicial record?
>
> Why should any government agency be allowed to communicate with anyone using a non-official address? Imagine what might happen if, say, the Enforcement Directorate or Income Tax starting sending us emails from unverifiable gmail or hotmail

addresses. How would we even know if these emails were authentic, spam or some new form of digital trickery? Have agencies like the revenue services ever communicated with anyone in this manner? Has the CBI itself ever created or used non-official addresses in any investigation previously? If it has not, then why is it doing so now? And what is to be made of its many denials?

These are the kinds of questions that the CBI has been asked repeatedly, but perhaps not enough times. These are the kinds of questions it should answer in court. But for that, the court needs to know. I was a little taken aback by Judge Shyam Lal's simple, unquestioning acceptance of the email address. The Hemraj emails had earlier been submitted to the Supreme Court too. It had said nothing about them. Judge Shyam Lal also blandly recorded the fact that the address had been created.

\*\*\*

In early March 2010, Kaul's team received a minor setback.

Kaul finally got the consent and the court order for the narco tests for the Talwars. Kaul had accused the Talwars of avoiding the narco tests the previous January. Nupur tried to explain that it was Dr Vaya's opinion that there was no need for one at the time. If the investigation required it, they had no objections.

In February 2010, the Talwars travelled to Gandhinagar to undergo their tests. The scientist there found them cooperative but Dr Vaya told them clearly that this round of testing was different: they had come to the lab as prime suspects. The Talwars each told their stories in a trance as videotapes rolled. The scientists had been given the new hypothesis, and at one point Nupur was asked about her friends. She mentioned a Dr Dogra, and there was alarm.

Was he the same man who spoke with the post-mortem doctor? 'Tell us more about him,' the scientists asked Nupur. She told them she was talking about a lady doctor. Someone who she had met at a function after Aarushi's death. This Dr Dogra had just lost a son in a road accident. They became friends because of their shared grief. The conclusions drawn from the narco were clear, and in line with Dr Vaya's assessment a year earlier: no information regarding the Talwars' participation in the crimes was revealed.

Kaul received the report in early March 2010. But it didn't have what he and Dahiya were looking for. Instead, it said that, for the Talwars, Aarushi was a 'long awaited, precious child'. And that the parents' 'behaviour throughout indicated that they have nothing more to lose compared to what they have lost'. The Talwars' narco also as good as negated the honour killing motive—their value systems wouldn't allow it. The results said: 'Considering the parents' intellectual capacity, outlook and open-minded attitude, it will be easy for them to accept even the most unacceptable behaviour of their daughter compared to losing her permanently.'

The scientists who conducted the narco tests also suggested the CBI should investigate whether the Talwars had been drugged on the night of the murders—Nupur had revealed that she felt extremely drowsy that night, and although Rajesh was a late sleeper he fell fast asleep after a telephone call around 11.30 p.m.

But with this report, Kaul would have to find other material to build his case. It would be useful if a witness turned—if a witness who had helped the Talwars' cause gradually turned against them. Such a witness came to Kaul, in the form of K.K. Gautam.

\*\*\*

Gautam's statement to the first team of the CBI led by Arun Kumar has him learning about the murders on 17 May. He doesn't know the dentist couple, but his eye doctor—a friend of Rajesh's brother Dinesh—insists that he visit the Talwars and he goes to the flat. There, he notices, with his policeman's eye, that there are depressions on Hemraj's bed that suggest three people have sat on it. That there are three glasses on the floor, and the servant's bathroom is dirty, as if several people have used it and not flushed.

Gautam had lied in his first statement in 2008. He may not have wanted to go into his role on that first day—helping speed up Aarushi's post-mortem. In April 2010, about two years later, Gautam was summoned by the CBI once again. This time, A.G.L. Kaul recorded a further statement.

Gautam now said that he had read his previous statement and would like to 'clarify' certain things. First, that he found out that Aarushi had been killed a day before: his eye doctor, Sushil Choudhry, had called him and asked if he could help get the post-mortem report released quickly. So far, so good. But this was followed by the claim that Dr Choudhry had also asked him whether he could use his influence as a former policeman to get the word 'rape' left out of the post-mortem report. Gautam told Kaul that he refused to help in this regard.

This claim that Sushil Choudhry, a friend of a friend, called to try and use Gautam's influence to omit the word 'rape' was the central part of Gautam's testimony. In the trial court in 2012, Gautam went beyond just clarifications. His early statements had him saying he had conducted an 'inspection' of the premises and observed things like the depressions on Hemraj's bed which suggested the presence of others in the flat. He told the trial court that he had said no such thing to his interviewers in 2008. He had no idea how this and other details suggesting the presence of outsiders had found their way into his statement.

At the time that he gave his clarifications to Kaul in 2010, he had not mentioned that there were embellishments by the CBI officer recording his first statement. In fact he had said he read his earlier statement over as he gave his second, and just wished to clarify 'some points'.

Gautam's turnaround was swifter than the change he underwent from mid-ranking policeman to post-retirement education entrepreneur as patron of Invertis University, formerly Invertis Institute of Management Studies. There seem to be several reasons linked to Gautam's turnaround.

In mid-March 2010, Kaul was picking up pieces of the puzzle that would compose his theory. During this time he spoke to Ajay Chaddha, the Talwars' friend. Chaddha had been at the crime scene on both 16 and 17 May 2008, and Kaul asked him if he thought there was anything unusual that he noticed.

Chaddha recounted an odd incident that took place on 17 May. The Talwars had left for Haridwar to immerse Aarushi's ashes, and he had stayed behind in the flat. In the afternoon, K.K. Gautam arrived with a man, who was introduced as someone from a detective agency, and two women. Gautam asked Chaddha if they could see Aarushi's room. Since the Talwars weren't present, Chaddha politely refused. But the four people hung around, and one of the women asked to use the washroom.

Chaddha couldn't turn that request down, so he showed her to the guest toilet that could be accessed through the living area. Chaddha felt she was spending unusually long in the washroom, when the second woman also asked to use the toilet. With the guest toilet occupied, Chaddha was left with no choice but to ask her to use Aarushi's. He showed her the way through Aarushi's bedroom. The two toilets had a connecting door on the inside, which meant that you could access Aarushi's bedroom from the guest toilet via her toilet.

Chaddha recalled that the women may have spent between ten and fifteen minutes in the toilets. Though he had met Gautam that morning, the man from the 'detective agency' and the women were strangers. He wondered why they had come to the flat and what they were doing in the toilets for that long. Kaul asked him if he could recall the names of any of the three strangers; Chaddha couldn't.

But on the evening of 20 March 2010, while watching a television programme on News24, Chaddha recognized a panellist, Usha Thakur, as one of the women who had come to the Talwars' with Gautam. On 22 March Chaddha emailed Kaul telling him that, though he had seen her just once, he was almost certain that it was Usha Thakur who had accompanied Gautam to the flat on 17 May 2008.

As it happened Usha Thakur, a local social activist, had just been questioned by the CBI a few days before, on 18 March. Shortly after the murders, she had claimed that Hemraj had approached her for help five days before he was killed. He had apparently heard of her work for the victims of the Nithari killings. According to interviews Thakur gave at the time, Hemraj was very distressed about a possible threat to his life and wanted to speak to her in private. This conversation didn't take place because she didn't have the time that day.

Thakur was an ardent supporter of Gurdarshan Singh's theory about the murders, and remains one to this day. Within ten days of the killings, she told reporters that the Talwars were responsible. The CBI took note of this and wanted to know why Hemraj had gone to her, and what role she played. Her replies, as reported in the press, were exactly what she had told journalists in May 2008, just after the murders. There was no mention of her visiting the flat with K.K. Gautam. Four days later, Ajay Chaddha's mail popped into Kaul's inbox.

K.K. Gautam had never said anything about returning to the flat. He said he had left once the police took over (post his heroics in the morning: finding Hemraj's body, inspecting the crime scene, etc.). He didn't mention anything about a detective agency or two women. That was perhaps because there wasn't really any detective agency, just that Gautam's friend Usha Thakur wanted a first-hand look at the scene of the crime.

Kaul told Chaddha that he would summon Gautam to his office so Chaddha could confront him. On the afternoon of 1 April 2010, Chaddha arrived at Kaul's second-floor office in block 4 of the CGO Complex. Gautam had also been called, but he was waiting in another room.

Chaddha told me, 'When Kaul called Gautam in, and I recounted his visit to the apartment, he just denied it flatly. He said he had never seen me before. I found this very strange. I told Kaul that I had no incentive to lie about such a thing. I had been asked if I thought something unusual had happened, and I thought this was unusual.'

What made Chaddha more credible was that he had been consistent about this—investigators had recorded him telling them about the visit in 2008. Gautam now had a lot of explaining to do. What was he trying to do back in the flat? Who was the supposed detective? Why had he taken the two women there?

In the weeks preceding the meeting between Chaddha and Gautam, the CBI had also looked into his links with Invertis University and seized his medical records from his eye doctor, Sushil Choudhry. Gautam may have retired on a government salary, but he would boast to Choudhry about the large house one of his sons had in South Africa and the sterling achievements of the other. Invertis University is a sprawling 70-odd-acre campus with an 'avant garde' (their description) building on the outskirts of Bareilly that attracts semi-rural 'degree' aspirants. Gautam's son Umesh is the chancellor of the university, another son is the pro vice chancellor, and their wives are involved in various important capacities. The cellphone that Gautam was using was registered under the name of this institution.

Kaul had caught Gautam lying about his sly little afternoon visit to the crime scene on 17 May, but he also seemed to have much more on the retired policeman. Arun Kumar had been out of the investigation for several months by now, but he received a surprise telephone call from Gautam. Kumar knew Gautam well and not just by reputation. Early in his career, the IPS officer had served in Bareilly and Gautam had been a subordinate.

The most casual observers of the goings-on in the state of Uttar Pradesh would probably know that the universe that that state's bureaucracy occupies has rules and mores that are different from what we may otherwise encounter. One of the traditions in the UP bureaucracy was the often reported annual 'most corrupt officer' contest. The public was excluded from the extensive search this required given the highly competitive field, but the award's merit rested, in a way, in this exclusion. It was a brutal peer review exercise. The kind that one might perhaps have to go through to get published by, say, *Nature*. (Or, for that matter, by Penguin.)

The Neera Yadav case spoke to the ways of that universe. She was accused of corruption, and convicted in November 2012. Which is when the *Times of India* said:

> Yadav, a 1971 batch IAS, became the first woman chief secretary of UP in 2005 when Mulayam [Singh Yadav] was CM. This flew in the face of IAS service rules as the CBI had filed the charge-sheet in the Noida scam. Her stint lasted barely six months, and she [was] removed on October 6, 2005, by an apex court directive. Earlier, in 1997, she was adjudged one of three most corrupt officers in UP by the UP IAS Association.

The top echelons of the UP bureaucracy had their own traditions; those lower down had theirs, even if these were less known. There are two informal indexes that aid decisions regarding transfers and postings in the UP police. These help superior officers place the right people in the right areas. One is the 'HLI' or 'high loot index', which rates a locality. For instance, a part of town that is full of markets and businesses would be a 'high loot index' area. In other words, a lucrative place for a policeman to be.

The other index is the RHI, or the 'Robin Hood index', and this rates personnel. A cop who has a high 'RHI' mark isn't someone who, as the name might suggest, robs from the rich and gives to the poor. He simply robs. That is, extorts. When decisions regarding assignments are taken, superior officers try to keep in mind HLI and RHI and find a balance. If, for instance, a high RHI station house officer is posted to a station that's in a low HLI area, chaos could ensue. Low HLI means fewer extortion opportunities, and a high RHI cop's appetite would not be satisfied. So the few businesses in the area would be put under an unfair amount of pressure. Police officers from Uttar Pradesh talk about these indexes without irony.

Gautam had immense respect for his senior. Now he sought Kumar's advice on how to escape the situation he found himself in. He told Kumar that he was being trapped into changing his testimony.

Kumar asked him the details. Gautam was initially reticent, but grew increasingly desperate in subsequent calls till he finally told Kumar what the problem was. What was at stake wasn't just a lie or two about his visit to the crime scene. Kaul had confronted him with information of a deeply personal nature. He had also communicated he was eager to use it unless Gautam agreed to change his statement. Arun Kumar heard him out, and then told him there was nothing he could do to help. I checked with

Gautam who confirmed the calls but was non-committal about what had happened.

Two weeks after the encounter with Chaddha, Gautam made his fresh statement to Kaul incriminating the Talwars. There was no further probe by the CBI on his alleged visit and Kaul had got another piece of the puzzle whose complete picture would be the indictment of the Talwars.

Gautam's companions' visit to the two washrooms was a reminder of something else that was seldom recalled during the investigation and the trial. This was that the door to Aarushi's bedroom was not the only way to enter her room. The guest washroom allowed access to her toilet, and thereafter into her bedroom. To this day, very few people are aware of this fact. But does it not open up the possibility of an assailant entering Aarushi's room through her toilet without having a key—or being 'allowed in'?

\*\*\*

In the third week of May 2010, the scene shifted to Dehradun, where Neelabh Kishore had summoned the Talwars. In the course of this conversation, Nupur Talwar told Kishore that in 2009, before the golf kit was seized, she and a family friend, Ajay Chaddha, had gone to the Jalvayu Vihar flat to supervise pest control and do some cleaning. The Talwars had moved to Azad Apartments near IIT Delhi, and their old home had been lying vacant and neglected for many months. As they emptied a loft, said Nupur, they found a golf club, some of Aarushi's toys and some junk. The club was carried back and placed along with the others in Rajesh's kit. At the time, it had been over a year since Rajesh had last played golf.

Three things happened in quick succession. The first was a report in the *Pioneer* dated 24 May quoting 'top-ranking' and other nameless CBI sources, who were all convinced that the Talwars had committed the crime. In journalistic parlance we call such a story a trial balloon, and this was the first one that mapped out the CBI's new case. This story, with its various inaccuracies, read less like a news report and more like a charge sheet and did the job of reviving interest in the case, putting the CBI in a positive light and cementing public perception of the Talwars as the killers.

The story contained the same wrong information about Hemraj's blood being found in Aarushi's room—on her pillow. It had other shades of Dahiya: 'Somebody was desperate to ensure that the crime did not look like a case of honour killing,' a CBI official told the paper.

It also said that the victims were hit by 'a golf club, or similar object'. Another detail was added when the *Pioneer* reported that a golf club was 'missing': 'Sources said that the CBI was looking for a missing golf club which could be Talwar's. "So far he has denied that any club from his golf set is missing, but we are not convinced," said a CBI official.'

It is difficult to say whether this was a mistake the paper made or whether the CBI official, who was the source of so much information, wasn't aware that Rajesh Talwar's golf kit—with all its 12 clubs in it—had been seized by the agency in October the previous year.

In the public mind, however, an impression had been created that Rajesh Talwar was behaving suspiciously about his golf clubs—he was hiding one of them.

This worked very well for Kaul as he segued into his next step. This was yet another interview with Dr Sunil Dohare. His fifth statement to the CBI was recorded four days after the *Pioneer* story appeared and was still fresh in everyone's mind.

Kaul asked Dohare whether a golf club could have killed Aarushi. Dohare answered: 'The injury on the forehead of Aarushi was V-shaped and had been made with a heavy blunt instrument. It is possible that the injury could have been caused by the golf club.'

There was just a little more work for the CBI to do, now that suspicion had been raised about a golf club and two experts, Dahiya and Dohare, had agreed that it could be the murder weapon. This task centred on the golf club found in the loft, which Nupur Talwar had mentioned in Dehradun.

Kaul (or 'Hemraj') wrote to Ajay Chaddha on the matter, and received a detailed reply on 1 June 2010. Chaddha corroborated what Nupur had said. That they sorted the stuff, discarded some things, placed some back and kept the golf club, an iron, aside.

He also wrote:

> I clearly remember, looking at the head of the golf stick to see whether any blood or such stuff was there but it did not appear as there was anything. Later on Rajesh visited the house and we mentioned to him about the stick, to which he remarked that the whole golf kit had been lying in the loft and one of the sticks may have got left behind. He too had a look at the sticks and had the same view as us.

To summarize, Rajesh Talwar had a golf set of 12 clubs which he kept in a loft near the drawing room of his apartment. At some point, when the golf kit was being taken out, one club was left behind, but it wasn't an absence sorely felt by Rajesh Talwar since he was not an advanced player of the game. A few months before the murder, he used two clubs and then had them sent back with his driver Umesh for Hemraj to keep with the rest of the kit. Some months after the murder, while cleaning out the flat, Nupur found the 12th club and had it put back with the kit. Thus, when the CBI seized the golf kit, it had the entire set.

Kaul saw the whole story differently: Chaddha was an old friend of the Talwars, and meant well, but this email was spun as proof that the Talwars had hidden an incriminating piece of evidence. On the record, there is nothing to show that the Talwars were asked about the golf clubs before 29 October 2009, when the CBI told them the kit had to be handed over. But the impression created in the media, and carried through to the trial, was that the failure to report the 'recovery' of the club when the flat was being cleaned in early 2009 was an act of concealment.

It is reasonable to assume that even if the fatal blows were struck with a golf club, it would have to be a particular golf club. There are four types of clubs: the driver, the wood, the iron and the putter. Each has a distinct shape, with the driver and wood having large heads, and the putter having a flat head. Each bears a number; in fact there are eight irons in a set, each with the head at a lower angle. So was the club found in the loft the murder weapon? What marking did it bear?

The CFSL said the examination of the 12 golf clubs, under a microscope, 'reveal[s] that negligible amount of soil was found sticking in the cavity of the numbers engraved at the bottom portion of the head of the golf clubs marked exhibits 3 and 5' in comparison to the soil found on all the other clubs. One of the two 'cleaner' clubs was a wood, the other was an iron.

That this report came eight months after the seizure and all manner of handling, by various people at the CBI and the CFSL, didn't matter. The iron that had less dirt had to be the murder weapon: it had been cleaned. This is the story that the CBI put out, and stuck to.

But which golf club was it? According to Kaul's authoritative December 2010 closure report, it was the club bearing the engraving number '5'.

There was one problem with this that Kaul had failed to notice: the club bearing the engraving '5' wasn't the iron that appeared to have been cleaned. The two 'cleaner' clubs were a 3 wood (which wasn't a suspect) and a 4 iron.

When the discrepancy was pointed out in the course of the trial, the 4 iron became the weapon of offence. No explanation was offered. This was the fourth time the weapon responsible for the blunt injuries had changed. The police initially suspected a hammer; the AIIMS medical committee said it was a khukri; Kaul said 5 iron; the trial court was told it was a 4 iron.

***

Ajay Chaddha was central to the story of the golf club. Chaddha was born in Amritsar, where Rajesh's mother was from, and the families knew each other well. Chaddha had started a medical supplies business and Rajesh allowed him the use of a cabin in his Hauz Khas clinic for this.

Although his email was crucial and he was listed as a witness, Chaddha was never asked to testify for the prosecution. Tall, light-eyed and blessed with North Indian good looks, Chaddha would, however, turn up in court on many dates. He was one of the first friends of the family to reach the Talwars' flat on the day of the murders, and spent the night there, helping with the post-mortem and the cremation. The next day, he was returning home in the morning when he heard about the discovery of Hemraj's body. He took a U-turn at the DND flyover and came back to the flat. Chaddha was a source of support to the Talwars through the investigation as well. In May 2010, for instance, he had accompanied them to Dehradun, where the issue of the golf club came up.

Chaddha had had a couple of interesting interactions with Kaul before the exchange of the golf club emails. In January 2010, the investigating officer summoned him to his office to record a statement. Chaddha says Kaul began by showing him photographs of the crime scene and reminding him of the brutality with which the murders were committed, but soon enough he was on to another theme.

'He told me, "You know they have done it, why defend them and make more trouble for yourself? Testify for us." I told him that I was convinced of their innocence and had already told investigators what I knew of the events of that day,' Chaddha told me.

Nevertheless, he said, he was willing to answer any questions Kaul may have had. Kaul appeared to have the impression that Rajesh Talwar and Chaddha were related. Chaddha clarified that they were not. Towards the end of a meandering interview, during which Kaul repeatedly reminded Chaddha that he was only inviting trouble if he stood by the Talwars, Kaul pulled out what to me was his cheapest trick.

During her narco tests, under the influence of a cocktail of drugs, Nupur Talwar had said many things of a personal nature, including her love for Rajesh. In one line, she had also said that she had, on one occasion, had physical relations with Chaddha. This was when Rajesh was in jail, and Chaddha was the only one among their friends who had stood by their side.

The scientists who conducted the test didn't judge the statement on whether it was true or not. Unlike brain-mapping, in which an experience a subject has participated in and one the subject has only heard about produce two different brain-states which can be directly measured, the effect of narco analysis is a lack of inhibition in expressing both thoughts and experiences. Narco analysis cannot determine if what Nupur said was true or false; only that she was being honest about her feelings for Chaddha. Scientists call this transparency; it is common in narco narration.

In the servants' narco analysis, to put this in perspective, the scientists found no transparency at all, and repeated attempts at deception. The servants' narco analysis in fact confirmed the brain-mapping, in which they placed themselves at the scene of the crime.

Kaul, of course, had read the report and latched on to this juicy bit. 'He told me he would tell my family that I was having an affair with Nupur, that he had proof,' said Chaddha. 'I told him, go ahead, do your worst.' In the statement recorded that day, Kaul asked Chaddha whether he was having an extramarital affair with Nupur. Chaddha's reply was, 'That is a stupid question.' He wasn't having an affair.

Nuggets like these were great fodder for the media. The more important aspect of the scientific tests on Nupur (and Rajesh) was that there was no deception in their answers. But with a swirl of rumours about the allegedly promiscuous lifestyle of the Talwars already in circulation, the suggestion of an extramarital affair was seen as too juicy to ignore—even if it were circulated as an additional rumour. The last question to Chaddha, according to his January 2010 statement to Kaul, was whether he knew anything about a golf club that had gone missing. Chaddha purportedly replied that he had faint memories of some inquiries in this regard in the early part of the investigation.

I asked Chaddha why he didn't tell Kaul that, in early 2009, he and Nupur had found a club in the loft. 'I was never asked this question at all,' he said. I pointed out that the January statement bore an 'ROAC' (read over and corrected by the witness). Didn't he do this? 'Absolutely not. I am not just certain, I am two hundred per cent certain,' Chaddha said.

This was like another statement that Chaddha gave on 29 July 2010 which too wasn't read over and corrected by him. In it, Kaul confronted him with the same question I asked: Why hadn't he mentioned the 'recovery' of the golf club in January?

But in this interview with Kaul well after his email of 1 June 2010, the investigating officer records Chaddha as saying he didn't tell the CBI about the club in the loft when asked earlier because he didn't remember the incident clearly at the time (in January 2010). This statement is filled with evasive answers about the missing club. Chaddha insisted the question was inserted. He hadn't signed the document, and was never shown a copy of the transcript, he told me. Kaul, however, signed off on it, claiming that it had been read over and corrected. But something about the statement Kaul recorded in January 2010 was odd, the question on the missing golf club ended the transcript, but the one preceding it was significant:

> Kaul: Is it correct that you are very close to Nupur Talwar including having extramarital relations with her?
> Chaddha: This is a stupid question. Yes I am quite close to her as I feel that she is a victim of tragedy. No I do not have extramarital relations with her.

Kaul had told Chaddha that he had proof of the affair, but the narco report was submitted on 9 March 2010. It was striking that Kaul was able to confront Chaddha about his affair with Nupur Talwar in January, more than two months before Nupur's report arrived.

*** 

The CBI's claim that the Talwars had not given 'satisfactory' answers about the 'missing golf club' are based entirely on what Chaddha purportedly told Kaul. Nothing on the record shows the CBI asking the Talwars any questions about the golf club at any time before the full set was seized in October 2009. But Kaul found a way around this. He cast Chaddha as someone answering on behalf of the Talwars. And providing unsatisfactory answers. In court, this story was given a wicked twist. The Talwars claimed that they had never asked Chaddha to speak on their behalf while contesting the admission of the email as evidence. Kaul would tell the court that he was speaking on their behalf because he was a 'relative'.

One of the first things Chaddha had done when he met Kaul was tell him clearly that he wasn't a relative. Rajesh's mother and his mother were just neighbours in Amritsar. Chaddha never testified, and the court held that since Kaul's claim wasn't refuted, Chaddha was indeed a relative, and was therefore speaking on the Talwars' behalf.

Though he remains a loyal friend to the Talwars, Chaddha's 1 June email, detailing the circumstances about the recovery of one golf club during the cleaning of the Noida flat, caused serious damage to the defence. One day during the trial, while having the usual late lunch at a restaurant just outside the court, the Talwars' trial lawyer Tanveer Ahmed Mir told Rajesh in mock despair: 'Doctor sahab, if you really had to murder somebody, you should have murdered Ajay Chaddha.'

\*\*\*

In November 2010, Ashwani Kumar was moving out of the CBI and into an obscure academic job for a period of 'cooling off' before he would head to the Raj Bhawan in Manipur. The Talwar case had progressed (if that is the right word) during his tenure with big leaps and no real proof; it wasn't sound enough for court.

It fell to Kumar's successor, Amar Pratap Singh, to make the announcement that the CBI would not press charges against anyone, and declare the investigation closed. It wasn't a happy task, but Singh wanted it out of the way at the very start of his term. He called a meeting of the officers involved within a week or so of taking charge.

Arun Kumar was invited to join the meeting even though he was no longer part of the organization. The new director felt Kumar's input was important since he had conducted the early investigation.

The others who attended included the IPS officer Javed Ahmed, who was in overall charge, and his subordinate Neelabh Kishore, who was based in Dehradun. A.G.L. Kaul was present of course. So was the CBI counsel R.K. Saini.

It was Kaul who spoke the most at this meeting, laying out why he felt that there was a case to be framed against the Talwars. The golf club, the scalpel, the unusual Internet activity—the router was apparently switched on and off through the night, suggesting someone was awake—the post-mortem doctors' revised reports, all of this went into his narrative.

His seniors listened, but were not convinced that there was enough to go to court with. The CBI's director of prosecution, who was also there, pointed out that the whole case was circumstantial. For that to result in a conviction, the chain of circumstances could have no gaps at all. There were glaring holes that Kaul could not explain.

Saini spoke up for Kaul. He pointed out that the Talwars could not escape the burden of proof: they were in the house and it was up to them to explain how the murders took place. But the director of prosecution shot this down pointing out that the burden of proof (under Section 106 of the Indian Evidence Act) was applicable in cases like dowry deaths, and couldn't be stretched to frame charges in this one.

Arun Kumar heard all of this without comment. The director then asked him his opinion. He told the meeting that he agreed with the view that no case could be made out against the Talwars, and since there was nothing further on the servants' front, the best course was not to charge anyone.

It was decided that the CBI would file a closure report, which is a final report marking the end of investigation and

listing the conclusions. Amar Pratap Singh told Kaul, as the
investigating officer, to write the report. As far as everyone
in the room was concerned, the case was closed.

***

Perhaps it is incorrect to say 'everyone'. A.G.L. Kaul seemed
to have continued with his investigation. In mid-December
Kaul, with some help from Dahiya, conducted a 'crime scene
reconstruction' experiment on the terrace of the Talwars' flat.
The purpose of this was to show that it was possible for
two people to wrap a body in a sheet, carry it up one floor
and drag it across the terrace. There were no other suspects
at the time, so the 'two people' could only be Rajesh and
Nupur Talwar.

In mid-December, Kaul recorded statements incriminating
the Talwars from Rajesh's friends Dr Rohit Kochar and
Dr Rajeev Varshney before a magistrate, under Section 164
of the CrPC. This gave a serious and unusual twist to the case.

Kaul had wanted to record Ajay Chaddha's statement,
about the discovery of the missing golf club, under Section
164. It would have been a valuable piece of evidence for Kaul,
but Chaddha had not obliged. So Kaul turned to Kochar and
Varshney, who had turned up at the flat on the morning of
16 May 2008 on hearing that Aarushi had been murdered.

The middle-class professional in urban India wants very
little to do with the state beyond things like passports, pan
cards and railway tickets. As for the police (which includes
the CBI), we would like to avoid any interaction at all. Being
associated, in any way, with a murder case of this notoriety
would count as serious misfortune. The best course was to
put distance between the event and your own, decent, if
unremarkable, life.

There were people who reflected this attitude fairly
clearly in this case. One of the Talwars' neighbours shifted

out altogether. Another, Puneesh Rai Tandon, who lived in the flat below, and whose terrace abuts the Talwars', told investigators that his family was 'not having social relations [with the Talwars] as they belonged to upper strata of society and we are middle-class persons. Apart from this, they are doctors maintaining high and different social circle and we belong to defence background.'

Puneesh Tandon, a software consultant, was indeed from a defence background—his father, Avnish Rai Tandon, was a vice admiral in the Indian Navy. But so was Nupur, despite what he told investigators, as her father, Bhalachandra Chitnis, had retired as group captain in the air force. The Tandons had a posh home in the hill resort of Naukuchiatal, which the Talwars had visited. Rajesh Talwar remembers too the parties on his terrace which Tandon had attended.

For Tandon, it was pragmatic not to mention these social interactions. After all, apart from the unfortunate, and unavoidable, circumstance that two murders had been committed in the flat above, he and his family had nothing to do with the event. And wanted nothing to do with it.

Kochar and Varshney were well acquainted with the Talwars. Rajesh would routinely make dinner plans on Thursdays with the Kochars, and Varshney had known Rajesh for twenty-five years. They were at the scene early like Chaddha. But unlike Chaddha, Kochar and Varshney were eager to put distance between themselves and the Talwars. And unlike Chaddha, Kochar and Varshney agreed to record statements under Section 164. Their statements corroborated each other's.

Kochar and Varshney were initially persuaded by Kaul to give statements under Section 161, and they did so in June 2010, two years after the incident. Kaul then ensured they would not retract and had them make the statement under Section 164 in December 2010—just two weeks before the CBI filed its closure report.

Both men said they had noticed traces of blood on the stairs to the terrace and alerted Rajesh on the day of the murder. They both said that Rajesh started up the stairs when informed of the fact, then suddenly turned back and didn't pay any attention when he was asked for the keys to the terrace. This behaviour was seen as compelling evidence of guilt.

Kochar's and Varshney's Section 164 statements were powerful evidence. But not because they could not be refuted with logic or fact. Their strength lay in the emotions they evoked, even in a judge. Kochar and Varshney were testifying against their *friend*, Rajesh Talwar.

Varshney's statement to Kaul begins with a sentence that is simple, and in some ways almost touching. It reads: 'Dr Rajesh Talwar is my friend.' In the absence of other reasons, the only thing that would compel a friend to give evidence against another was an obligation to tell the truth. Were there any other reasons in this case?

When Kaul had met the two men earlier in June 2010, his line of questioning made his line of investigation obvious. Kaul records Kochar as saying that he and Rajesh regularly met for 'drinks' and dinner on Thursdays. That 'non-veg' food was served even though it was Thursday. That Nupur Talwar was 'very particular' about her appearance. And that, even on what should have been the saddest day of her life—the morning after the murders—he found her 'looking in the mirror' in Aarushi's room.

Although anyone living in Delhi will know that eating 'non-veg' on a Thursday isn't such a big deal, it does suggest that the consumers are liberal. And therefore different. The Indian middle class is largely Hindu conservative.

Each statement that alluded to any perceived non-conformity in their lifestyle chipped away at the character of the Talwars and put their conduct at the time of the murders and thereafter in precisely the context that the CBI wanted. A question such as 'What kind of person would look in the mirror to check her appearance when her daughter is lying murdered next to her?' was loaded with the presumption of guilt.

The power of suggestion of what seems like such a trivial fact should not be underestimated. It has led to murder convictions—in the recent past, and from the Ghaziabad courts. In the Nithari murder case, in which Moninder Singh Pandher and his servant Surinder Koli were accused of raping, killing, dismembering and disposing of 17 children, including ten girls, although Koli had confessed (and later retracted), Pandher was found guilty of having a hand in the murder of 14-year-old Rimpa Haldar and was sentenced to death, though he was not found guilty in the cases of each of the other victims. This verdict was arrived at because Surinder said his evil instincts were aroused when he saw his master drink and romp with prostitutes. Pandher was seen as a debauch. For the court, the leap to murderer was a small one. Pandher was acquitted by the high court because he was able to prove that he was in Australia at the time of that particular murder.

Everything about Kaul recording Varshney's and Kochar's statements under Section 164 was unusual. First, the need to do it: statements under Section 164 are normally recorded when investigators want a confession that stands up in court, or when a witness has turned approver, and the police want to ensure he doesn't do a U-turn during his testimony. In practice, the police use Section 164 sparingly: it is binding, and ties not just the witness down, but the investigator too. It doesn't leave room for manoeuvre, which is often necessary while pressing for convictions.

Varshney and Kochar were neither confessing nor had they turned approvers. That they were asked to give statements before a magistrate suggested design. The design becomes clear from where the statements were recorded, who they were sent to, and when.

Kaul didn't present his two witnesses before a magistrate in Ghaziabad, even though the case was under the jurisdiction of that court. He took them to Delhi's Karkardooma courts. This wasn't due process, but this did not trouble him. When I spoke to Kochar after the trial, he said that neither he nor Varshney thought at any time that what they said would be used against the Talwars. 'I wanted to help my friend,' Kochar said.

Kaul had met them several times before this, and it was Kaul's subordinate Arvind Jaitley who organized their trip to Karkardooma. They were told that statements they had made in previous interviews with the CBI contained some inconsistencies in language. The statement before the magistrate would put all of this to rest. 'We had no idea that a closure report was to be filed and that no charges were being framed against the Talwars,' Kochar said.

Kaul arranged for the statements to be sent directly to Preeti Singh, the Ghaziabad magistrate to whom the closure report would be submitted. This was done fifteen days before the closure report was actually filed in Preeti Singh's court. This is unheard of. Statements are submitted as part of a report, not to give advance notice to the magistrate about what to expect.

***

The Talwars were horrified to read A.G.L. Kaul's closure report. Dated 29 December 2010, it could be summarized thus: The CBI knew that the parents had committed the murders; unfortunately, they could not prove it. The report read like a charge sheet, without the final charge. In the report's own words:

The findings of the investigation reveal a number of circumstances that indicate the involvement of the parents in the crime and the cover up. However there are a number of critical and serious gaps in the circumstances which make it difficult to string together the sequence of events and motive behind the gruesome murder . . .

In view of the aforesaid shortcomings in the evidence, it is felt that sufficient evidence is not available to prove the offence U/s 302/201 IPC against accused Dr. Rajesh Talwar beyond reasonable doubt. It is, therefore, prayed that the case may be allowed to be closed due to insufficient evidence.

Detailed reasons for ruling out the servants and outsiders were provided. Such as the servants would not dare consume liquor in the house knowing that the master and mistress were in. And that there was no sign of forced entry.

The reasons for not pursuing the case were far clearer. Hemraj's blood wasn't found in Aarushi's room or on the clothes of the Talwars. The unusual Internet activity continued inexplicably through the next day, when no one was on the Internet and the flat was full of policemen. There were no incriminating fingerprints or any other forensic evidence connecting the Talwars to the crimes. All the evidence the CBI could point to was clearly circumstantial.

But there was a viciousness about parts of the closure report. The scientific tests done on the Talwars were emphatic about their lack of involvement in (and knowledge of) the crimes, but Kaul chose to describe these reports as 'not conclusive'.

Similarly, the closure report stated: 'The hymen of Aarushi was ruptured and was having old tear and was fibriated', and 'the vaginal orifice of deceased Aarushi was unduly large and the mouth of cervix was visible'. These were never mentioned in the post-mortem report, nor did the closure report state how these findings were opinions drawn up years after the event.

The report also mentioned that 'a whitish discharge was present inside the vaginal cavity and mouth of cervix of deceased Aarushi', which is normal, particularly since the closure report says 'the pathologist reported absence of semen'. Then why bring up the whitish discharge at all?

'There were no signs of urine or any other body fluid on the underwear or pyjama of Aarushi,' the closure report states, which can mean anything but was used by the CBI in their theory that Aarushi's genitalia had been cleaned up of evidence.

The scientific tests of the servants, possibly the most damaging of the tests and the ones that could have yielded a solid case had they been pursued in investigation, are summarily dismissed in a single line: 'During investigation Dr. Rajesh Talwar, Dr. Nupur Talwar, Dr. Dinesh Talwar, Dr. Sushil Choudhary, Dr. Richa Saxena, suspect servants namely, Krishna, Raj Kumar & Vijay Mandal were subjected to various scientific tests including Lie Detection Test, Brain Fingerprinting Test and Narco Analysis Tests. The test results for all the suspects were found to be inconclusive.' Disingenuously, the servants' tests had been lumped not only with the Talwars' but also with those of people obviously innocent.

The Talwars were outraged, and shortly after the closure report was submitted to a magistrate's court, on 25 January 2011, they filed a protest petition claiming their innocence and demanding a proper investigation. As they were on their way to do this, a deranged youth attacked Rajesh with a meat cleaver. This senseless act of violence was committed in full public view, and with police all around. Rajesh Talwar was permanently disfigured.

Magistrate Preeti Singh rejected the Talwars' plea and turned the closure report into a charge sheet, repeatedly referring to the suspicious bottle of 'Valentine's' (meaning

Ballantine's) and censuring the CBI for saying it didn't have enough evidence. She thought there was—and that both parents should be charged with murder and destruction of evidence; in addition Rajesh was culpable for lodging a false FIR blaming Hemraj for the murder of his daughter.

Her order said:

> When this incident occurred at that time four members were present in the house—Dr Rajesh Talwar, Dr Nupur Talwar, Aarushi and servant Hem Raj; Aarushi and Hem Raj, the two of the four were found dead . . . On the basis of evidence of all the above witnesses and circumstantial evidence available in case diary during investigation it was expected from the Investigating Officer to submit chargesheet against Dr Rajesh Talwar and Dr Nupur Talwar.

The court had had two other options: of either accepting the closure report as it stood or ordering a fresh investigation. Yet Preeti Singh chose to send this to trial, and from her order it was apparent that not only did she have reverence for the CBI—'Here it is pertinent to mention that the CBI is the highest investigating agency of the country in which the public of the country has full confidence'—she could not believe that such a high-profile case could have an ignominious end.

Rajesh was recovering from the cleaver attack, and his lawyers filed an application asking that he be exempted from personal appearance before the magistrate. Preeti Singh dismissed this plea summarily.

In a country where politicians and people of influence unashamedly, and with the cooperation of both the medical and legal fraternity, manage to spend time in hospital whenever the spectre of jail or court appears on the horizon, Preeti Singh's order might have seemed harsh.

The attack on Rajesh Talwar was real, and nearly fatal; it seemed unfair to force him to come to court in the state he was in. The Talwars applied for transfer of the case out of Ghaziabad on the grounds of security, inconvenience— and, crucially, bias. One argument forwarded was that Preeti Singh had already concluded that the Talwars were guilty. The Talwars couldn't hope to get justice in such a situation. They moved the Allahabad High Court (since that was the appellate court for all UP lower courts such as Ghaziabad's).

This matter was dismissed in the Allahabad High Court and went all the way to the Supreme Court, which, in 2012, took a grim view of what the Talwars had contended. It said that it could have taken action against the Talwars for implying that the court was biased, but had decided to let them off this one time. 'We consider it just and appropriate to warn the petitioners from any such impertinence in future.'

***

One of the heartening consequences of the legal battle that the Talwars had undertaken was that they now had to be given access to investigation documents. How, and on what basis, had charges been framed against them? The CBI was predictably mean-spirited about this, giving the Talwars copies of only some documents. Among these was one that the CBI believed was inconsequential. This was Document 48. It had detailed forensic reports from CDFD Hyderabad and buried in the code and jargon of its pages was the strongest possible lead to the identity of the actual murderer, namely, the evidence of Hemraj's blood on Krishna's pillowcase.

It would be a gross understatement to say Dinesh Talwar was protective about his younger brother Rajesh. No one has been more passionate about Rajesh's defence. Dinesh was of similar stature to Rajesh, had the same portliness, and was a man with an astonishing capacity for painstaking work. He seemed to live for details and, to the frustration of those around him, he sometimes got lost in them. Given a document, he would not be happy until he had read it forwards, backwards and sideways several times over.

He had reached Allahabad to help challenge the lower court order and was staying at a friend's place. There he settled down one night to pay Document 48 his full attention. He was a religious man and while going through the papers, he accidentally touched his phone and one of his favourite bhajans began playing:

'*Ibadat kar, ibadat kar,*' submit to God, it went.

'I was just taking a break from looking at the documents and this thing just started off . . . So I prayed a little bit, and started looking at the documents again, and suddenly this thing came up . . .'

In professional jargon, the document noted that the profile found on 'Z20 (one pillow cover, purple coloured cloth)' and the profiles extracted from the palm print on the terrace, the whisky bottle, Hemraj's comb and Hemraj's bed sheet, 'was from the same male individual', that is, Hemraj.

The purple-coloured pillow cover was the only item recovered from outside the Talwars' flat. It didn't belong to Hemraj. It belonged to Krishna, who lived in L-14. Dinesh Talwar stared at the document in disbelief.

'It was very clear-cut. So I thought let me see if it's really the same pillow cover. To be hundred per cent sure. So I traced it to the previous document, then to the seizure memo. By chance all the three documents were there. We were given only a few documents then, but these three were there. I checked and rechecked at least thrice.

'I thought this is unbelievable! How could this evidence have been missed, because they already had the narcos which said the servants were involved.'

There had been a raid at Krishna's house after the 12 June 2008 narco analysis which indicated deception, and in which Krishna and Rajkumar each said that they saw the other commit the murders. Krishna had been arrested on 13 June and, after the raid, the CBI on 14 June found and seized the pillowcase.

'By that time it was two o'clock at night. You can't phone someone at two o'clock at night. My problem was, now what do I do? I always think the worst for myself. I thought, if I die, what happens? How do I leave this, who's going to understand what's going on?

'This had to go somewhere—in a manner that it's not missed. Then the only way I could do this is by texting Rebecca John [the Talwars' lawyer].'

The next day, Dinesh spoke to Rebecca. 'She said this is explosive, and we filed an affidavit on this. I had this niggling doubt that they might change documents. So I actually asked Rebecca, she said that won't happen. That the document was already filed with the court.' This piece of naivety, based on the belief that the system is fair, was to cost the Talwars their best chance of a defence.

\*\*\*

The Talwars filed their application in the court, saying there was evidence clearly incriminating someone other than them, but within days of this, on 10 March 2011, two photographs of the exhibits materialized.

Each of the photographs showed a pillow cover. One white, belonging to Hemraj, and one purple, belonging to Krishna. At the bottom of the photographs were scraps of paper that did not remotely resemble any CDFD stationery. These scraps had exhibit numbers written on them. In the report, submitted more than two years earlier, Hemraj's pillow cover was exhibit Z-14 and Krishna's Z-20.

In the photographs of 10 March, however, the 'labels' had them the other way around. Z-20 became Hemraj's pillow cover, Z-14 Krishna's. This revision meant Hemraj's DNA had been found on Hemraj's pillow cover, and nothing was found on Krishna's.

These pillow covers would have been in sealed envelopes, shut with a CDFD seal. Someone needed to have opened the seals, removed the pillow covers from their marked envelopes, and placed handwritten labels, one of which was held down by a pencil that is clearly visible in the photographs. Then photos of the two pillow covers were shot. But not by the CDFD.

The court was shown the photographs of the evidence on 10 March and told that the mix-up was the result of a 'typographical error'. The photographs were only displayed before the judge, not submitted as evidence. Had they been submitted, questions about their authenticity might have arisen at a later stage.

On 17 March, the Allahabad High Court came to the conclusion that it was 'clear' from the photographs that there had been a typographical error, and that the Talwars' prayer must therefore be rejected. Bizarrely, even as it was saying this, the court in its order made another typographical error and got the exhibit numbers mixed up again. Nevertheless, the Talwars would either have to go higher or back to Ghaziabad.

As pieces of forgery, it would be a challenge to find poorer examples. The exhibits under CDFD seals came in November 2008 and these seals could be broken only by the orders of a court, or before it. No court had seen them/passed any such orders at the time, so how could the photographs of the pillow covers have been taken?

Madhusudan Reddy, one of the scientists connected with the case, told me that no photographs of the items were taken at the lab. The question of handwritten scraps of paper on the original samples with the alleged CDFD exhibit captions was therefore irrelevant. It implied that the handwritten scraps were introduced into the parcels, and this implied the seals were broken without the court's witness or knowledge. And the sealed parcels were in the possession of the CBI/CFSL at the time.

A second reason catches the forgery out even more directly. Not only are the 'labels' unsigned and undated, whoever wrote out the swapped exhibit numbers also copied them down wrong from the original stickers. He added a serial number where none existed.

There was a third point that surely merited some consideration. The lab that had prepared the report had not even been contacted when the photographs were shown in court to make the typo claim. After all, the alleged error was at the CDFD end. Should they not, at the very least, confirm that one of their typists had made a mistake?

The Allahabad High Court never asked for the photographs to be placed on record. Nor did it tell the CBI to get a clarification from the lab before it passed any orders. On the basis of two photographs, it rejected the Talwars' prayer.

\*\*\*

There was more to follow. Having secured the high court's order in their favour on 17 March 2011, the CBI wrote to the CDFD. They didn't just write, Kaul flew to Hyderabad and camped there. But here is what the CDFD officially heard:

'It appears that due to a typographical error, the description of the exhibits Z-14 and Z-20 in the report dated 6.11.2008 have been interchanged.'

How does it suddenly 'appear' nearly two and a half years after the original report, and more important after the Talwars have pointed to a clear piece of evidence incriminating Krishna? Kaul, who was not supposed to even have opened the parcels, had not just magically produced photographs of the exhibits under seal, he had also suggested that there was an error at the CDFD's end. An error that concerned one specific, case-turning, sample.

On 24 March, the CBI received a brief clarification from the CDFD saying that Kaul was right, that there had been a typographical error. That is, Z-20 was actually Hemraj's pillow cover, and his blood had been found on it. It took just a sentence to remove the keystone on which the Talwars might have mounted their best defence.

This was the sequence of events: Dinesh Talwar discovers the evidence against Krishna; the Talwars file an affidavit; the CBI produces two dubious photographs and claims a typo, without any confirmation from the supposed source of the error; the judge accepts the argument, rules in favour of the agency; the CBI gets its clarification after Kaul travels to Hyderabad.

With the Allahabad High Court order in hand, it became that much easier for Kaul to get the CDFD to simply agree with the suggestion in his letter. After all, a high court was convinced—why would the CDFD take an opposing position?

But the original report is still there for everyone to see. The improbability of the samples being interchanged is evident. The exhibits are ordered in a way that samples from one person or one area are listed one after the other. Hemraj's belongings, for instance, are all serialized together, his undergarments, slippers, watch, sheet and pillow cover come one after the other. The 'typo' breaks that sequence for no apparent reason—something belonging to Krishna makes its way into what is Hemraj's list. The full description of Krishna's pillow cover—'purple coloured cloth'—appears no less than six times in the report. Six typos?

Surely someone would have to explain. I asked both the CDFD director J. Gowrishankar and Reddy about this: their explanations were vague. When I sent Gowrishankar the photographs he said that the photos were unauthenticated so he could not comment on them; then he gave a long-winded description of general procedures followed while labelling. In the end, he said he could not comment on the specifics.

Dinesh Talwar was distraught at this turn of events. In anger and frustration, he told me, 'What is the credibility of any document when you can change them?' What the Talwars hadn't realized at the time was that a trial was inevitable. Had they kept the secret of Document 48 to themselves, all they would have had to do was ask a CDFD scientist if he stood by the report during the trial. That would authenticate the document. And by then, it would be too late for anyone to turn Z-20 into Z-14.

\*\*\*

With the typographical error now accepted by the high court and acknowledged by the Hyderabad forensic lab, the road ahead was barrier-free. Kaul and his team had returned to the honour killing story first floated by the UP police, but they had fleshed out a set of circumstances that led to it. On the basis of photographs supplied to him, and the crucial nugget of false information that Hemraj's blood was found on Aarushi's bed, the Gandhinagar forensic scientist Dahiya had woven his epic around parents capable of filicide. He had taken cues from the Talwars' lifestyle and their profession to settle on the murder weapons: a golf club and a scalpel.

Two doctors had agreed with Dahiya's 'findings'. Two years after examining her, one suggested that Aarushi was sexually active, and that her private parts had been cleaned to erase any evidence. An important witness had turned—saying that the Talwars had approached him to use his influence to get the word 'rape' omitted from their daughter's post-mortem report.

It now looked as if the CBI had an imagined motive with speculative weapons to go with it. It had no hard evidence. The hard evidence pointed at someone else. But that was due to a typist's mistake. The road to Judge Shyam Lal's court in Ghaziabad was clear.

Postscript: The Case of the Pillow and the Pillow Cover

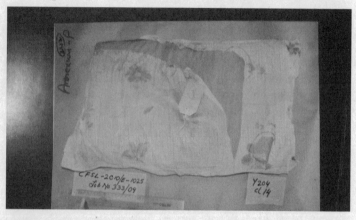

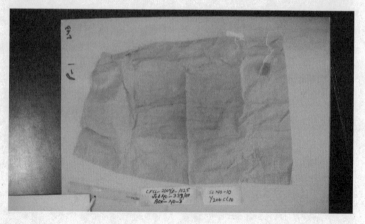

These photographs are of two case-turning pieces of forensic evidence: a pillow and pillow cover seized from Hemraj's room in the Talwars' flat, and a purple pillow cover seized from Krishna's bed at L-14 Jalvayu Vihar, a few houses away.

They were flashed before an Allahabad High Court judge by the CBI in 2011. The agency argued that there was a typographical error in the reports on the two covers. The original report said Hemraj's blood had been found on Krishna's pillow cover, pointing to his involvement in the crimes. When the Talwars pointed this out, the CBI said the findings had been swapped, offering the photographs as proof.

Here are the questions the agency did not answer about the photographs:

1. The pillow covers were under seal. No court authorized the opening of the seals, so on whose authority were the pictures taken?
2. Who took the pictures?
3. When were they taken?

The CBI's A.G.L. Kaul gave no clear responses to any of these questions.

But how were these pictures passed off as 'official' before the Allahabad High Court when there were obvious discrepancies?

The official laboratory label on Hemraj's pillow and pillow cover read: **CFSL-2009/E-1025 Job No. 333/09 RC 1 (S)/08/ SCR-III CBI DL Y204 CL-14**

The official label on Krishna's purple pillow cover read: **CFSL-2009/E-1025 Job No. 333/09 RC-1(S)/08 SCR 3 CBI ND Y204 CL 10**

These descriptions are clearly different from those read from the scraps of paper held down by a pencil in the photographs. Who wrote the descriptions by hand? Who authorized this? How is the integrity of the evidence protected if seals are broken to take pictures? These are the questions that the CBI did not answer.

# Part Two
# The Trial

On 4 June 2012, I was on the road to Ghaziabad, a distance of about 50 kilometres from Gurgaon, where I live. I was going to attend the first hearing in the trial. In the preceding months the Talwars had pleaded desperately to have the case shifted to a court in Delhi. They gave reasons as disparate as distance (they had moved to Delhi) and their fear that they would not get a fair trial in Ghaziabad. Higher courts slapped them around for doing this and the Supreme Court was particularly scathing.

So Ghaziabad, a settlement struggling in that odd pace between village and city, it was going to be. On my way, I passed scores of towers under construction, and hundreds of hoardings trying to sell a thousand square foot piece of heaven. Their names were pregnant with promise: Imperia, Laurel, Riviera and Wave City, whose tagline on billboards read 'The city that thinks for you'. There were also a disproportionately large number of billboards of educational institutions peddling degrees, claiming things like 'recognised under the "B" category by govt.' Ghaziabad was trying to 'get there'.

On the roads, both drivers and pedestrians seemed to take just a few more risks—or were they just liberties? When I entered the court complex, I found a minor traffic jam had resulted in casual calls to vandalize a car (which, incidentally, had a policeman sitting in it). No damage was actually done.

You enter the CBI's special fast-track court through a narrow iron gate situated at one corner of the maze of tin and concrete that is Ghaziabad's 'kacheri'. To the right of the gate is a public toilet with limited facilities—the urinal sees heavy use and no cleaning; the two private stalls are padlocked, one of them with a bold sign on its door saying, for some reason, 'notice board'.

To the left of the gate is a large crate where rubbish is dumped (it was finally removed as the trial came to a close). The waste came mainly from the eateries that lined the lanes of the complex, or anyone else who wished to contribute. Sprinkled among the food stalls are stand-alone Xerox machines, plugged mysteriously into invisible power supply points. Then there are the stalls for typists and passport photo specialists. This could be a court complex in any other provincial town.

Once you get past the excrement on the right and the waste to the left, you enter a walled compound with a courtyard, scarring whose middle is an open, often brimming, three-foot-deep drain, in whose depths lies the backlog of many years of filth. In the early days of the trial, Dinesh Talwar neglected to 'mind the gap' and fell into the drain. He escaped without injury, but one leg of his trousers had muck till the thigh.

The culture (work or otherwise) in Ghaziabad is defined by the most powerful body on the premises: the Ghaziabad Bar Association, whose pink building you pass as you take a side entrance into the court premises. There is a chhole-kulche wala at hand, and a statue of Chaudhary Charan Singh, in which the former prime minister appears positively simian. His arms are folded in front of him at knee level, as if the sculptor, having been on course till then, suddenly discovered he'd run out of stone for the bottom half of his work. Charan Singh's statue, with its orangutan arms and dachshund legs, nevertheless seemed to smile benignly at whatever went on in court.

Towering over the courtyard is a water tank into which a monkey may or may not have fallen to its death some years ago. (The veracity of this story is disputed: some veteran advocates swear it is true and only use a nearby tube well; shopowners who use and peddle the water laugh off the suggestion.) At any rate, the tank overflows with unfailing regularity, the spill gathering exactly at the foot of the steps of court no. 2. Here, a layer of slime forms in the wet season—and it fells prosecutors and defendants without bias. A few weeks after the drain got Dinesh Talwar, Group Captain Chitnis escaped a nasty injury when an agile young policeman grabbed him just as he was about to hit his head on the steps after having slipped on the slime. The octogenarian has trouble with depth perception. At lunchtime, the steps, the slime, the drain would often seem like an obstacle course to him, as he brought back cold drinks or biscuits for his daughter and son-in-law.

There are about two lakh cases pending in Ghaziabad. All 'under one roof', according to the court website. But the CBI special courts are in an annexe. Here, 'high-profile' cases are moved along with urgency. For instance, the accused in the Nithari killings appear in the same courtroom as the Talwars. In the court opposite, a scam involving retired judges is being heard.

Our court system is three-tiered. While a case is usually first heard by a lower court, any orders that are passed during the trial may be challenged, but this must be done one level up, which is the high court of the state (Allahabad in the case of UP, as the crime was committed in Noida). If the high court's decision is to be challenged, this must be done the next level up, which is the Supreme Court of India (and even here, the Supreme Court may, if the case warrants it, review its own decision). There are times when an appeal can be made directly to the Supreme Court, without having to go to the high court, through what is known as a Special Leave Petition (and the Talwars took this route once). The legal battle is fought on many fronts, and the prizes from these must be displayed in the trial court in the most favourable light, and the scars hidden as best as possible. The rigid hierarchy of the judiciary means lower courts take their cue from the ones above.

On my first day at the Ghaziabad complex, I was slightly alarmed by the number of guns and gunmen (apart from the police) that I saw on the premises. They were there in so many of the tiny lawyers' chambers that I lost count. There was also a casual menace about them that I found a little unsettling. I wondered why a court needed so many guns.

A Ghaziabad regular told me the guns were required 'for protection'.

'From whom?'

He laughed, almost spitting out the samosa he was eating. 'From other lawyers.'

Some months later, I would know exactly what he meant when the adjacent main building saw a scene out of a Bollywood gangster movie being played out. A western UP gang war had spilled into the premises. The target was a Meerut goon called Udham Singh who ran from one courtroom to another to escape bullets. He was seriously injured, as were four other people—there were pools of blood in courtrooms and verandas.

Udham Singh was an undertrial charged with several murders. His three assailants were gangsters he was expected to testify against. They arrived in court dressed as lawyers, in black jackets and white trousers—their leader, Yogesh Bhadoria, had made the cinematic additions of a bowler hat and a false moustache to his attire. The gunmen walked right through the long-out-of-order metal detectors of the court with a range of weapons, and opened fire once Udham Singh was brought to the first-floor courtroom in the main building.

Three other litigants were injured as the gunmen chased their mark. A security man opened fire and hit one of the assailants; another was apprehended. But Bhadoria, of the moustache and hat, jumped off the first floor on to a waiting car and made a dramatic escape.

In Ghaziabad, no one was surprised, least of all the lawyers or the gunmen on guard (or having tea). Over the past ten years or so there had been at least five potentially fatal attacks on the premises. Rajesh Talwar was the victim of one in early 2011. That is how it worked in western Uttar Pradesh.

But as lawyers and litigants ran for their lives from the court on the day of the Bhadoria shoot-out, the trial in the annexe's 'Fast Tract [sic] Court No. 2' where the Talwars' case was being held soldiered on—the only court to keep functioning through the day's bizarre events.

The courtroom was about the size of a standard 'drawing-cum-dining' in Delhi's suburbs. The dock was in the corner, its railing was broken, so was a leg, giving the impression that it might lean forward too far some day, keel over at the judge's feet, pleading to be repaired.

The judge was Shyam Lal. He was a small man, his grey, balding head just about visible beyond the tall desk he sat behind, the judge's high chair dwarfing him. He seemed unexceptional. In the Ghaziabad courts, he had acquired the reputation of being honest and firm. There was one other thing about him—he would usually convict. The Ghaziabad regulars had a name for him: 'Saza Lal'. Or sometimes, just 'Saza'.

Judge Shyam Lal was an anomaly in Ghaziabad for yet another reason: his work ethic, which in the Ghaziabad context especially was outstanding. Although the courtroom shoot-out was an extreme circumstance, Judge Shyam Lal's court often worked when others wouldn't. Daily power cuts through the summer, for instance, which left the court's computer dead. When the stenographer didn't turn up, the judge would take down testimonies by hand. He even ignored a strike or two, called by the bar association.

But there was something about the Aarushi–Hemraj trial that made Judge Shyam Lal work just a little harder. The reason was fairly obvious: this was the biggest case he would adjudicate, India's most anticipated murder trial in recent memory. And when it commenced the judge knew he had just under a year and a half to wrap it up. He was due to retire in November 2013.

From the outset Judge Shyam Lal's relationship with the lawyers who appeared for the defence wasn't the best. The Talwars' advocates Satyaketu Singh and Manoj Sisodia were old Ghaziabad hands who knew him well. Often there would be loud slanging matches in court, mostly directed at the CBI counsel R.K. Saini, but partly directed at the judge. Saini, on the other hand, appeared to have good relations with Judge Shyam Lal. While waiting for the transcripts of the proceedings at the end of the day, I often saw Saini spend a good half-hour with the judge in his chamber behind the courtroom.

***

Today, 4 June, was also the first time I saw Nupur Talwar. Rajesh was already out on bail, but Nupur was in custody in Dasna jail. Over the two-and-a-half-year investigation, Nupur was never an accused. That changed after the Ghaziabad magistrate Preeti Singh issued summons to both Rajesh and Nupur to stand trial in early February 2011. Over the year that followed, the couple ran from court to court to challenge the Ghaziabad magistrate's order, without success. In its orders in early 2012, the Supreme Court rejected their pleas to quash Preeti Singh's summons, upheld the non-bailable arrest warrant the magistrate had issued against Nupur and ordered her to appear before the lower court. When she did that, on 30 April 2012, Nupur Talwar was taken into judicial custody and sent to Dasna.

The Talwars' entry into court was dramatic that first day as it would be in these early stages. They appeared separately but suddenly, through the tall shrubs under the water tank, accompanied by policemen. This part of the court was out of bounds for everyone except the police and officials, and the route avoided the cameras situated at the common entrance near the toilet. It was also safer, considering Rajesh Talwar had been attacked in the more crowded part of the court on the other side.

Their 'entry point' was a breach in the wall of the annexe's courtyard. But as a seasoned reporter put it: 'In Ghaziabad, holes in the wall always expand.' Nupur Talwar made her entrance through that hole in the wall on the first day of the trial. There were policemen ahead of her, policewomen by her side, policemen behind, but she gave the impression that she was outpacing all of them. Bar the occasional darting of her eyes, as if a mental camera was taking Polaroids of the scene around her, she showed no anxiety.

She passed her parents during her brisk walk into court. Her father stood there about to speak, but got no more than a sideways glance from her. He held out his hand, but this gesture too went almost unacknowledged: his palm barely brushed her arm. She looked ahead, at the door of the courtroom.

In the year and a half that I followed the trial, I saw many defendants in other cases enter and leave the court premises. In the eyes of most, guilty or not, you could almost read the words 'show mercy'. In their bearing, you saw the less-than-equalness that we associate with the 'accused' in our courts. There was none of that in Nupur Talwar. Despite her washed but not pressed salwar kameez, a clue to where she might be coming from, she seemed to walk in as if the police around her were props, that she was coming to the court on her own terms. If you were searching for emotions on her face, the only one that you might have found was determination. This mismatch had a strange effect on the people watching: they seemed to stiffen up,

even make way for her. Nupur Talwar was not just another
accused; she wasn't like any other accused.

On this day though, Nupur and Rajesh's trial would not
begin. The prosecution was to have called its first witnesses,
but the untimely death of a member of the Ghaziabad
Bar Association meant the court had to stop working. An
advocate tangentially involved in the case told the waiting
cameras: '*Condolence ho gaya.*' This was not to be taken
lightly. Just after his arrest, for instance, Rajesh Talwar had
to make an appearance on a day when members of the Gujjar
community had called a strike. This incensed a mob—work
was being done in court despite their call. A group of men
vented their anger by thrashing Nupur Talwar's brother and
Ajay Chaddha.

The first witness, the photographer and fingerprint
expert Constable Chunnilal Gautam, would have to appear
four days later.

\*\*\*

Constable Chunnilal Gautam, a man with light, smiling
eyes, had the sort of respectable portliness that you might
associate with a regular patron of one of Ghaziabad's decent
Vaishno dhabas. He had joined the UP police in 1987, and
was resigned about his work. 'Who likes taking pictures of
dead bodies every second day?' he asked me. To get away
from this he had decided to become a lifelong student. On his
own initiative he had successfully completed an MA and a
law degree. He was now pursuing a PhD in Hindi literature.

Chunnilal was one of the first policemen on the
crime scene; he had taken the first photographs and lifted
fingerprints. When he arrived at the Talwars' Noida home
on the morning after Aarushi's murder, Chunnilal testified,
this is what he saw: Aarushi's body covered with a white
sheet, which when pulled back revealed her fatal wounds.

Blood spattered on the walls but no traces of red on the toys on her bed. Her pyjamas low around her waist, the cleft of her buttocks showing, untied string dangling on each side.

The details were what made his testimony potent. Blood spattered on the walls, but unsoiled toys (implication: placed later by killers who had feelings for Aarushi). Pyjama strings untied, buttocks showing (implication: someone pulled the pyjamas up after the murder). Only the couple in the dock could have had a hand in this alleged rearrangement of the crime scene. In the absence of any hard evidence, Chunnilal's testimony was seen as the first links in an incriminating chain of circumstantial evidence.

However, his first impression, in a statement recorded by the UP police on 31 May 2008—Aarushi was murdered on 16 May—had none of these details. In a fresh statement of the CBI investigation team under Kaul in 2010, he departed substantially from what he had said in 2008. During the trial, he stuck to this new version.

His memory on everything but this new story failed him completely in court, however. To every uncomfortable question the cross-examiner posed, Chunnilal smiled and said: 'Dhyan nahin hai' (I can't remember). In a page and a quarter of one transcript of his testimony, this phrase appears eighteen times. It became a joke in court. But Chunnilal had a lot to answer for. He admitted he hadn't inspected the toys, so how could he be so sure about the absence of blood? Why weren't the toys seized? Had he noticed that Aarushi's cotton pyjamas had an elastic band, a common feature in these casual garments, which can be worn without tying the strings?

Again: 'Dhyan nahin hai.'

Chunnilal, as it turned out, wasn't much of an expert at anything apart from ducking questions. The fingerprints he lifted from the scene were useless to the labs, and his photos were in a complete mess—several prints submitted with negatives were mismatched. Where were these missing pictures? These would have been vital for the defence, but Chunnilal had lost his memory.

*** 

Of the items on the scene that morning, the most intriguing was the bottle of Ballantine's Scotch whisky. The company's tagline is 'Leave an impression', but in the present case, it turned out that there weren't any particularly useful impressions on it. This was down to Chunnilal, whose familiarity with the process of lifting prints competently appeared limited. He didn't know, for instance, what chemicals had to be used. He said he used a 'black powder'.

The UP police had seized the bottle, supposedly covered with fingerprints and blood, two-thirds of its contents consumed. But this is what the CBI's closure report of December 2010 had to say about the bottle: 'Presence of a scotch bottle without glasses on the dining table of Dr. Rajesh Talwar with blood of both the victims on it indicates the involvement of inmates [read parents] as it was unlikely that an intruder would return to the flat to take liquor after committing two murders.'

As C.N. Bhattacharya, the acting director of the CFSL, told me on a later occasion, the collection, packing, handling and sealing of samples were of paramount importance. The bottle of Ballantine's could have thus yielded important bits of forensic evidence had fingerprints been properly collected. In fact by the time the third investigating team weighed the evidence—or lack of it—it was speculated that there were no fingerprints on the bottle, and a story appeared in the *Hindustan Times*, quoting sources, saying that no fingerprints on the bottle meant that the Talwars must have worn gloves while allegedly committing the crime. This glove theory, however, never made it to the closure report or to the trial.

\*\*\*

Through the sapping summer of 2012, the court would hear the case an average of twice a week. A steady stream of witnesses for the prosecution came and went. It was clear that one of the CBI's strategies in court was to draw a picture of the Talwars as an immoral and emotionless couple, who had suppressed the fact of their daughter's rape and had her genitals cleaned. It was at this time that one of the oddest testimonies of the trial (and there were a few bizarre ones to follow) was recorded.

Sanjay Chauhan was a city magistrate in Noida then, and said he had arrived at the Talwars' flat at 7.30 a.m. on 16 May. He had no real business there, but had noticed that there were several mediapeople and policemen around the Jalvayu Vihar neighbourhood when he was driving home after his 'morning walk'. He was curious, asked around and reached the Talwars' flat. The CBI said he was testifying not as an official, but in his 'personal capacity'.

Chauhan said he found Rajesh and Nupur 'roaming' from room to room, talking to visitors. He also observed that they avoided going near Aarushi's body and showed no signs of grief, which he found 'surprising'. He added that he noticed bloodstains on the steps and railing leading up to the terrace, which was locked. He, however, made no official mention of this to anyone that day.

The city magistrate had mentioned that he lived in Greater Noida, so Dinesh Talwar pulled out his smartphone outside the court and Google-mapped the distance from Chauhan's home to Sector 25, where the Talwars lived. It was 28 kilometres. This meant Chauhan drove 56 kilometres a day just to take a walk. This was incredible, but it wasn't all. He was asked about landmarks around where he walked and couldn't name even one. He told the court that he would travel all this way because the facilities for walking in Greater Noida were inadequate and the area unsafe.

Chauhan looked like he could use some morning walking, but it wasn't as if he was invisible. So how was it that no one remembers seeing him in the flat? And what was the purpose of his testimony? Witnesses who were summoned later would support his claim about the Talwars' conduct. A Jalvayu Vihar security guard also told the court that the Talwars were not weeping when he rushed to their flat on being told about the murder. To investigators who spoke to him right after the incident, however, the guard had said Rajesh and Nupur Talwar were in tears and in shock.

The guard and the morning-walker's depositions threw up the following suggestion: if you have lost a loved one in a violent crime and do not weep at the exact times future witnesses for the prosecution arrive at your home, then you must be guilty. It didn't matter that there was no proof Chauhan was at the scene at all, or that the guard had said the opposite earlier. Or that there were a number of witnesses who saw the Talwars weep.

\*\*\*

In matters of observation of behaviour, people can, and do, express a subjective opinion. But what about in matters concerning science?

Dr Sunil Kumar Dohare, the medical officer who conducted the post-mortem on Aarushi's body, appeared in court that summer to say what he had earlier told Kaul. That Aarushi's vaginal cavity was so dilated he could see her cervix. When he was asked why he hadn't recorded these facts in his autopsy report, Dohare gave a slightly different answer from what he had told Kaul. Then he had said his findings were 'non-specific' and 'very strange'. Now he told the court that they were 'subjective'.

There is no such thing as a 'subjective finding'. A finding is by definition objective and verifiable. An article in the respected *Journal of the American Medical Association* describes 'subjective findings' as 'self-contradictory and time-dishonored' and goes on to say, 'By definition, findings are either objective demonstrations of abnormality, or the objective lack of demonstrable signs of abnormality.'

But Dohare went on to expand on his theme. He told the court that the wide opening of the vaginal cavity indicated that Aarushi's private parts had been 'manipulated' after her death. The presence of a 'whitish discharge' suggested possible cleaning, because the discharge wasn't evenly spread.

Dr Dohare is a man of average build in his early forties. The two most noticeable things about him were his thick glasses, through which his eyes seem to bulge, and a weak chin. He had a tendency to explain rather than answer directly, and was at pains to tell the court about his limited role in the AIIMS post-mortem report on Aarushi—he had 'signed it' but not 'prepared it'.

When the court broke for the day, I asked Dr Dohare about the AIIMS document. Why had he signed it when he took no responsibility for its contents? He began by explaining he was not an expert in the other fields included in the terms of reference, and then was glad to be rescued by a CBI officer standing nearby. The CBI man said, 'He wasn't asked this question,' and chaperoned Dohare away. His job for the day was done.

Dr Dohare was among the most important witnesses in the trial. His testimony was one of the pillars that propped up the case against the Talwars. In it were his 'expert opinion' of the weapons used and the tampering with

Aarushi's body. In it, the CBI argued, were both the motive and the method for the murders.

Although those were early days, the CBI believed that the man who followed Dohare in the witness stand (so to speak—since there is no stand in the fast-track court, the witness simply stands facing the judge) would clinch a conviction.

Dr B.K. Mohapatra was one of the CFSL scientists who had conducted DNA tests on all the evidence collected from the crime scene: scrapings from blood-specked walls, the khukri, various articles of bloodstained bedding, all of it went to Mohapatra. He had joined the investigation right from the time the CBI took over in June 2008, a fortnight after the crimes. The CFSL is an extension of the CBI, and Mohapatra was part of a team of scientists and investigators who had gone to the crime scene hunting for clues.

Dr Mohapatra had several days of appearances ahead of him. His deposition involved as many as 152 exhibits—many of which had to be physically held up in court. He had to testify on eight separate forensic reports. He also had to provide details of every seal, noting and letter that concerned the CFSL.

It was in the course of these days that I sensed a growing confidence in the manner in which everyone on the CBI's side conducted themselves. I had read Mohapatra's reports and wondered what I might have missed that made the prosecution so sure of themselves. I felt the most important aspect of Mohapatra's testimony would be an incriminating presence of DNA. The prosecution could walk away with the case if, for instance, Hemraj's DNA was discovered in Aarushi's room. This would establish his presence there, and therefore Rajesh Talwar's motive.

It was for the lack of hard evidence such as this that the CBI was forced to file a closure report. Had they found fresh evidence since then?

At lunchtime one day I found Mohapatra sitting unaccompanied in the courtroom, minding two large folders on a table in front. He was a short, spectacled man, with a thick Odiya accent that sometimes confused people from the north ('blood', for instance, would become 'blawed'). He looked simple, and so were his concerns. As I sat next to him, he complained about the unpleasant extended summer, and the long waits in court. He then said it must be very hard work for reporters as well. He had seen us standing at the courtroom's door all day because we weren't allowed in. I mumbled something about everyone having to do a job, when he asked me: 'Do you get TA/DA?' I told him we didn't, but he was entitled to allowances, surely. He nodded, and I thought how the government had taken over the scientist in Mohapatra.

I got down to my question. Was there any proof that Hemraj's DNA was found in Aarushi's room?

Mohapatra gave me a canny answer: 'How do you know it wasn't?'

From my understanding of his reports, I said, and from the CBI's admitted position. He said that I should wait and hear his testimony.

In court Mohapatra finally made his revelation: a bloodstained blue-and-white pillow cover on which Hemraj's DNA was detected was recovered from Aarushi's room.

Yet just a few months before Mohapatra's testimony, while referring to the same piece of evidence, the agency had told the Supreme Court: 'One pillow cover was also seized from the room of the deceased Hemraj and the same was also sent for forensic examination . . .'

The CBI counsel R.K. Saini explained that Dr Mohapatra could not be expected to remember the sources of various items seized, even if he was part of the team collecting evidence. He was therefore relying on a letter written three days after the seizures by an SP, CBI. SP Dhankar, however, was not part of the 12-member team that inspected the Talwars' premises on 1 June 2008.

Reporting on the day's developments, websites and newspapers went with 'Partial Male DNA Found on Aarushi's Pillow' or variations of it; no mention was made of the CBI's affidavit to the Supreme Court or to the closure report.

For a month after Mohapatra had made the claim, the CBI stuck stubbornly to the line that traces of Hemraj's blood were found in Aarushi's room. Eventually, by end-August, it became clear that the agency had been misleading the court. Hemraj's pillow cover, which Mohapatra had said was seized from Aarushi's room, was unsealed and displayed. A cloth tag attached to it said: 'Pillow and pillow cover, blood stained (from servant's room)'. This was the primary record of the seizure. The tag bore the signatures of Mohapatra's CFSL colleague Dr Rajinder Singh and CBI inspector Pankaj Bansal.

R.K. Saini, the tonsured CBI counsel, whose right eyebrow twitches uncontrollably during any exciting event, had at first tried to dismiss the exhibit, with a *'Yeh to ho gaya'* (We are done with this). But when Mohapatra, slightly shamefaced, read out the tag, Saini, far from being embarrassed by the failed stunt, said it would make no difference at all. And he was proved right.

\*\*\*

'Preparation of fish curry starts from catching fish!' Only a Bengali would use such a metaphor while trying to explain the processes of forensic science, and of course C.N. Bhattacharya was very much a Bengali.

'Is it not?' he continued, as I nodded in complete agreement. I had gone to meet the acting director of the CFSL in his office in the CGO Complex, where the CBI is also headquartered.

He was a charmingly simple man. Interested in his science, the pursuit of which appeared to give him genuine satisfaction. If he were an exhibit, he would be one that proved an earlier generation of Bengalis was still thriving. He assumed, for instance, that everyone spoke and understood Bengali—this left his Delhi staff bewildered. It was the festive season, and he was missing the atmosphere of Kolkata during Pujas. '*Yaa devi sarvabhute . . .*' he bellowed involuntarily early on in our conversation. '*Pujor aamej, pujor aamej . . .*' (the puja mood/ambience) he kept repeating.

I had sought the interview with Bhattacharya to understand the CFSL's role a little better. From what I had seen in the trial, the integrity of the samples displayed and of the scientists testifying seemed questionable to say the least. Bhattacharya's allusion to fish curry had to do with the collection, packing, handling and sealing of samples, and somewhat naively he said that courts throw out forensic evidence if any of these things aren't done properly. (He had obviously not attended the Talwars' trial.)

Then I brought up the trickier question of the relationship between the CBI and the CFSL. I gave Bhattacharya a quick wrap of his subordinate Mohapatra's performance in court. Why would a CFSL scientist go to these lengths for the CBI? Wasn't the CFSL supposed to be an independent body, even if its primary purpose was to assist the CBI?

Bhattacharya was a ballistics expert, far more comfortable talking about, say, subsonic handgun projectiles. He became cautious, but he also seemed concerned. He wouldn't go into any integrity issues, but he looked out of his ninth-floor window and said there were 'people of all types'.

'You mean those that can be influenced . . . and those that can't?'

'Yes, something like that. See, ours is an extension of the CBI, we operate from the same complex. Some things are there that I personally do not like . . . it is quite common to be called by the CBI to their offices . . . Some people accept this. I find them going and reporting.'

When I asked if the CFSL's independence suffered as a result of this culture, Bhattacharya didn't want to answer the question. He had told me several times during the conversation that he was only filling in as director till someone was appointed permanently. He looked away again, and said, 'You could say there is a parallel administration.'

Our conversation ended with Bhattacharya passing on instructions to one of his staff—a North Indian lady called Babita—in Bengali, about work that had been left pending. He was heading out of office and relished the prospect: 'How many cups of black tea can you have?'

His 'Mrs' hadn't yet arrived in Delhi, and he was living on a camp cot, he told me. But with incredible warmth, he also asked if I would join him for dinner in his quarters—of a simple Bengali meal of mashed boiled eggs and potatoes, with rice—just to do 'adda', whenever I found the time.

Neeraj Kumar, a former CBI officer who headed its Special Task Force probing the 1993 Mumbai blasts and later became the Delhi police commissioner, told me about two cases in which a well-known scientist was suspected of corruption because he gave findings that completely undid what were, by all accounts, open-and-shut cases. In his view, this corruption among some scientists provided the CBI extra leverage over the CFSL when required.

The CBI investigates a case, collects evidence. It then takes this to a lab under its control for analysis by scientists who are aware of their subordinate status, even if this isn't official. There is no separation between investigation and prosecution, so the agency has its own counsel, who then briefs the scientists on what they should say. The testimonies and arguments take place in a designated CBI court, like the one in Ghaziabad.

\*\*\*

At the tea stall, under the sheesham tree or in the squalid lanes that connected everything in the Ghaziabad court, there was one topic of conversation that reared up as a refrain. This was about how the Talwars managed to pay their bills.

The Talwars' financial means found its way into Judge Shyam Lal's court through an application filed by them in early November 2012. The defence counsel pleaded that the accused, Drs Rajesh and Nupur Talwar, needed to earn their living in order to mount their defence. Unpredictable court dates—each date consumed a full day—did not leave room for them to pursue their vocation to earn the money they required for sustenance. For once, the court ordered in favour of the defendants. It would hear the matter twice a week, on Tuesdays and Wednesdays, rather than at random.

Starting at the top, the Supreme Court, where Nupur Talwar was granted bail in September, there was a distinguished law firm—Karanjawala and Co., run by the socially connected Raian Karanjawala—and a set of redoubtable (and very expensive) lawyers who appeared on the Talwars' behalf. Among them were the former solicitor general Harish Salve, future attorney general of India Mukul Rohatgi, former additional solicitor general K.V. Vishwanathan and Rebecca John, a prominent criminal lawyer.

Lawyers' fees in the Supreme Court can be bizarre: Rs 10 lakh to Rs 15 lakh per appearance is the norm at the very top. Subrata Roy, India's chit fund king, for instance, might well have to write off a hotel or two to pay his Supreme Court lawyers as he tries to accumulate the thousands of crores he is required to deposit to get out of the cooler. The thing about the Aarushi case, however, was that some top lawyers chose to do it for free.

Rebecca John told me she was moved and convinced by the Talwars' story. Connections within the family led them to Salve. Salve was unaffordable, but he agreed with a nod (rather than the theatrical bow he reserves for the Supreme Court) and no money. Not everyone was free, however. But not everyone operated by card rates either. I happened to overhear a brief negotiation (the boss lawyer is never involved in these, it's the job of his assistants) where a fee of just under Rs 3.5 lakh was agreed upon for one appearance by a prominent Supreme Court lawyer, substantially less than 'card'.

In the lower courts, the financial arrangements were different. Here, livings had to be earned in the present continuous. In the Allahabad High Court, where the Talwars went first, they spent about Rs 1 lakh in fees each time they litigated.

In Ghaziabad, a set of four lawyers usually appeared on their behalf. All of them honest, committed professionals who knew the system and were also trying to make a living. The two people who featured through the trial were Manoj Sisodia, an amiable man whose tiny office was the hub of everything the defence did—including press briefings—and Satyaketu Singh, whose 10 foot by 10 foot space was down the same lane.

From what I gathered, the Ghaziabad lawyers were paid on a retainer basis and, with additional costs, the Talwars were spending anywhere between Rs 50,000 and a lakh a month. This, of course, didn't include the fees of their criminal lawyer Tanveer Ahmed Mir who would come to the case a few months after the trial had begun.

Where did they get the money from? Rajesh Talwar said he and Nupur—just out on bail—were grateful for patients who were still loyal to them. Their consultation fee was Rs 500, but, as anyone who's been to a dentist knows, the costs of dental work can add up. The earnings from his clinic covered living expenses, Rajesh told me. I visited the Hauz Khas clinic a few times, and found the place slightly derelict and in disrepair. A neglected aquarium held a few fish struggling to survive—but what else would you expect given their situation?

The Jalvayu Vihar flat, where they lost what was most precious to them, continued to give them a rental return in the region of Rs 20,000 a month. They later also rented out the Hauz Khas clinic, and these rents covered the salaries of employees like their driver Umesh and Rajesh Talwar's man Friday, Vikas Sethi.

That still left a substantial shortfall. Rajesh said that he was grateful to 'friends and family' for financial support. One friend based abroad sent him a large sum of money at the beginning of the trial, and had promised to wire more. The Talwars had also sold their clinic in Noida to a member of the family for around Rs 70 lakh, and this helped them stay afloat. Additionally, the savings of Dinesh and Vandana Talwar were also almost depleted by the Talwars' legal costs.

Tanveer Ahmed Mir had advised his clients to go even further: sell their properties. He believed that it was the only chance they had. This wasn't greedy lawyerspeak. Mir believed that lawyers worked best if you paid them.

Pro bono work, noble as it is, has direct disadvantages for the client—especially in a case like the Talwars'. Lawyers who offer their time and energy for this kind of work usually do it for issues of wide public interest, say, high-level corruption or big environment cases. The defence of the Talwars in the mysterious murders of their daughter and servant didn't fit the standard definition of 'public interest'. It appeared more to be a case of something the *public was interested in*.

When the public interest aspect is overshadowed by 'personal tragedy', pro bono work is of a different nature—it becomes, without being overly cynical, about favours to individuals in need. The contract that binds the paid-for lawyer to his client isn't there, and even if the lawyer's conscience urges him to help, he might find that his time has already been paid for by others who require his services.

The question of availability of someone like Harish Salve came up several times in Supreme Court matters. The Talwars either waited for a window or paid for a replacement. Although the latter meant spending money, the former—working dates in sync with their ace's schedule—may well have been more costly. The CBI inevitably brought the charge that the Talwars were deliberately delaying things, to the point that it was about the only thing the Supreme Court heard.

***

Events over the months of July, August and September illustrated how multilayered a murder trial can be. The Talwars were fighting their case at three different courts—the trial court, the Allahabad High Court and the Supreme Court. The most pressing case in the Supreme Court was getting bail for Nupur. The CBI, however, wanted Rajesh back in jail and had moved the Allahabad High Court. The two pleas mirrored each other. Nupur pleaded that she should be granted bail because she had been charged with the same offences as Rajesh, and he was free. The CBI argued that Nupur had been sent to custody, so why shouldn't Rajesh be treated the same way?

The CBI told the Supreme Court that Nupur Talwar was likely to influence witnesses if she was let out of jail. The court asked for a list of those the agency felt were vulnerable, and 13 names were provided. It then directed that the testimonies of these 13 be recorded expeditiously over the following month.

This was a stiff target given Mohapatra's lengthy and complicated testimony. The defence needed a lot more time to deal with Mohapatra and the 13 additional witnesses. Completing this before the Supreme Court's 17 September deadline seemed near impossible.

There were other things to contend with, like strikes, or forced holidays on occasions like Valmiki Jayanti. Caste is a big factor in the Ghaziabad bar elections, and the lower castes are a sizeable constituency. Gender is a big factor too; the bar shut the court down for Karva Chauth so that its female members were not inconvenienced. Also, there seemed to be an unfortunate pattern: on an average two lawyers seemed to depart the Ghaziabad bar forever each month and the court could not be allowed to function during 'condolence'.

The defence had other troubles as well. It needed the expertise of its counsel G.P. Thareja, a lawyer who understood forensics, for Mohapatra's cross-examination. Thareja, a former judge, was a grandfatherly figure who would arrive in court drenched in sweat from his assignments in Delhi, slip on a pair of sandals and begin work. (The judge couldn't see his footwear under his robe.) Thareja worked closely with Dinesh Talwar, and seemed to have a genuine affection for Nupur, whom he addressed as 'beti', as he drew her aside to speak to her in what privacy the court allowed. He was doing the case pro bono, but was available only on two days of the week.

This created a peculiar situation in court. As the trial judge urged its lawyers to begin cross-examination, the defence filed an application saying they were not competent to conduct it without Thareja. Mohapatra, in a sharp blue shirt, his bag of papers on the table in front of him, kept waiting.

Keeping the Supreme Court deadline in mind, the defence moved another application pleading the forensics man's cross-examination—a crucial piece in the case, but bound to be lengthy—be taken up after the trial court was done with the 13 witnesses named by the CBI. Judge Shyam Lal rejected this application.

The defence put up the application once again, this time in greater detail. It said Mohapatra's cross-examination would take at least six or seven court dates and that the Talwars had just one lawyer competent to conduct it. Also, the volume of material to be gone through was massive. Thareja had to be given a fair amount of time to prepare.

The CBI replied that repeated applications were being filed 'just to delay the trial'. Commenting on the fact that the defence had kept a witness waiting for a whole day, the trial judge issued a terse directive. He said 'in the interest of justice' he was giving the Talwars one 'last opportunity' to cross-examine the witness on 21 August.

There seemed to be a distinct bias against the defence team. They would, for example, never be given any indication as to which prosecution witness would appear at the next hearing and then be expected to cross-examine them the day they appeared. Frustrated by the daily surprises being sprung on them, the Talwars pleaded with the court several times to direct the prosecution to let them know which witness was being called on the next date. Giving the other side this information isn't just a matter of form, they argued, it impacted preparation for cross-examination. The prosecution never did this—even via a telephone call.

In late July, the court directed the CBI to give the defence adequate notice. This was to no avail: the defence was never given the names of the witnesses, and almost every hearing would begin with the same recriminations.

The witnesses could not just come on their own, so how were they appearing? The answer to this was in a set of certified copies of summons issued by the court to these witnesses. The forms contained the name of the witness and the date on which he/she needed to appear. Sometimes the forms were ready days in advance. This meant the prosecution knew who would appear. The judge signed the summons, so the court knew as well. The only party left in the dark was the defence. That's how it worked.

Meanwhile, the Supreme Court reviewed the progress made in the examination of the 13 CBI witnesses. On 17 September it heard that some witnesses had been dropped, others were yet to be found, and so on. Additional Solicitor General Sidharth Luthra argued for more time, and said the trial would be over by the year end. Not much time to go, so why not keep Nupur in jail?

To which Harish Salve, appearing for the defence, said wryly: 'Let's keep the trial in Ghaziabad.'

By then, the court's mind appeared to have been made up. Bail would be granted. So Luthra begged for more time for the examination of his witnesses. The CBI got eight more days. Nupur Talwar would be out on bail on 25 September.

Salve viewed this seeking of an extra week of detention as mean-spirited. Outside, he told Luthra, 'Cry baby CBI asks for just a few more days. Cry baby CBI.' Luthra didn't know how to react, and mumbled something about winning some and losing some.

It seemed to me an interesting exchange. Salve was one of India's leading lawyers; Luthra wasn't in the same bracket as him. That Salve would react in this manner told me how polarizing this case was. A month earlier, there had been much fist-pumping in the Supreme Court on the other side, when Nupur Talwar's stay in jail was extended till the examination of the 13 witnesses was done. But the reactions in the Supreme Court were barely remarkable in comparison with the bitterness that by now was on view daily in Ghaziabad.

\*\*\*

K.K. Gautam, the retired policeman, arrived without warning just after B.K. Mohapatra's lengthy cross-examination had been completed.

Gautam did exactly what the prosecution hoped for. He testified that Dinesh Talwar's friend Dr Sushil Choudhry had called him to ask whether he could use his influence to prevent the word 'rape' being mentioned in the post-mortem report. He also told the court that he hadn't conducted any 'formal inspection' of the crime scene, and that he had no idea why the CBI investigators from the earlier team had included so many things in his statement to them that he had not, in fact, said.

And what about the fact that he had lied to investigators in the first place? That his involvement began on the morning after the murders, and not a day later [with the discovery of Hemraj's body]? Gautam coolly replied that his statements were the 'same', but with 'some differences'. The court was satisfied. R.K. Saini was beaming.

\*\*\*

On 3 September 2012, Bharti Mandal turned up in court, as usual without warning to the defence. Her testimony was vital to the CBI and her importance was explained to me by the CBI inspector Arvind Jaitley. Jaitley was a tall man in his late thirties with an air of casual calm about him. He stood out among the prosecution's team because of his sense of propriety. He was convinced about the Talwars' guilt, but he didn't see this as a reason to get nasty. At the tea stall outside the court, a lawyer was asking Jaitley about his belief in the parents' guilt. Jaitley told us he didn't want to get into the merits of the case. But the CBI, he felt, had just one task to accomplish to win it: *It had to convince the court that the Talwars' flat was locked from the inside when Bharti Mandal rang the bell at 6 a.m.*

Once the court was made to understand this, the prosecution was home. This was perfectly reasonable. If the door was found locked from the inside in the morning, it would stand to reason the murderer was still in the flat. The burden of explaining the murders would now shift to the Talwars. It would be up to them to tell the court the story behind every bloodstain, fingerprint, bottle of liquor, missing key, lost phone. The CBI didn't have to prove anything, not even a motive or what the murder weapons were. Four in the house. Two are killed. Either or both the survivors were therefore responsible for the murders. It was like one of Agatha Christie's closed-door mysteries.

This is why Bharti Mandal's testimony had so much riding on it. It was she who had rung the doorbell that morning. It was she who was the first witness at the crime scene. It was she who could tell the court whether the Talwars' door was locked from within.

***

Bharti hadn't been issued summons. She said that CBI personnel had simply picked her up and brought her to court. This was done in secrecy, through an access from the rear to avoid any chance encounters with the media. Dressed in a bright yellow sari, Bharti looked tentative. This was an 'event' in her life, but she wasn't sure whether it was a good one or a bad one. She began her deposition. She had been on leave the previous day, but arrived at the flat at 6 a.m. on 16 May and rang the bell, she told the court. And then:

> I touched the iron [outermost grill] door but it did not
> open . . . Then I pressed the bell again, whereupon
> aunty [Nupur Talwar] opened the wooden door and

stood behind the [second] mesh door and started talking to me.

She asked me where Hemraj had gone and I replied that I didn't know . . . Thereafter, aunty told me that Hemraj must have gone to fetch milk from Mother Dairy . . . She also told me that Hemraj must have *locked the wooden door* [mesh door; emphasis added] and gone to fetch milk . . .

Aunty told me that you sit down, when Hemraj comes back he will open the door for you . . . I then told aunty you give me the keys I will open the door and come in . . . Aunty said all right you go down I will throw you the keys.

I went downstairs and from the balcony aunty told me that the door isn't locked, it's only bolted . . . But I told aunty that she better give me the keys, because if it is locked then I will have to come down again . . . Then aunty threw the long key [to the middle mesh door] from the balcony.

Thereafter, when I came up and put my hand on the outer [grill] door, it opened . . . Then I unbolted the mesh door.

Nupur Talwar had left the innermost wooden door open, and Bharti entered the flat. 'I felt some thief had entered the house and that is why Uncle and Aunty are crying,' she testified. 'Aunty threw her arms around me and started crying, when I asked her why are you crying so much, she said go inside and see what has happened . . .'

The CBI scenario emerged. The reason the outermost grill door wouldn't open was that it was locked from the inside. 'I touched the door but it would not open,' Bharti had said. Nupur Talwar threw the keys down to her maid and, in the couple of minutes Bharti took to come back up, she used the door in Hemraj's room, entered the passage, unlatched the outer door, and bolted the mesh door to make it appear someone had locked them in their house from the outside. She then walked back exactly the way she came.

When Bharti Mandal reached the flat again, she said, 'I returned to the door and put my hand on it and it opened.'

Case solved. Or was it?

***

There were some obvious circumstances that everyone seemed to have overlooked. The first was that even if the Talwars were guilty, it really wasn't necessary for Nupur to play out the elaborate door-latching/key-throwing scene with Bharti Mandal. If her aim was to give the impression that someone had bolted the middle mesh door from the outside, locking them in the house, this could have been achieved far more simply, at leisure and without risk.

Why wait for the maid to turn up? Wouldn't it have been much easier to bolt the middle door well before she arrived? What if the maid had turned back up the stairs for some reason and found Nupur locking and unlocking doors? Would she not be running the risk of confirming guilt right there? The Talwars were cast as sharp, calculating killers. If that were the case, surely they would have realized the worthlessness of the deception. There was easy access to the outer grill door and the middle mesh door through Hemraj's room. Wouldn't it be naive of them to think that nobody would notice this? And did that not make the bolt on the middle door irrelevant?

It did, but the CBI's case was that the outer grill door had been locked *from the inside*, presumably by the killers who could only be the parents. 'I touched the iron door and it did not open,' Bharti had said, as had been suggested to her. There was one more thing to consider about that morning's exchange between Bharti and Nupur. It was

Bharti who suggested that Nupur throw down the keys from the balcony. She knew the house, *but she did not suggest Nupur use the access through Hemraj's room to let her in.* The simple explanation is that it didn't occur to her—or to Nupur—because that access was never used.

One of the many things that troubled me during the course of the trial was that every key witness for the prosecution had told one story at the time of the investigation and a substantially different one in court. Bharti Mandal had been questioned by three different investigators within a month of the crime. Yet she had never mentioned to any of them that she had 'touched' the iron door on the outside and it would not open. Neither had she told any of them how the door behaved when she returned: 'I returned to the door and put my hand on it and it opened.'

The door in question was a tricky one: Shashi Devi, the laundrywoman who visited the flat regularly, had said so to investigators. Shashi Devi was dropped as a prosecution witness, but the CBI's Hari Singh testified that he had recorded her as saying: 'The outermost door of the flat used to remain open all the time. If nobody came out after pressing the bell, I used to *push* the door open which *used to remain jammed in the frame* [emphasis added] and I used to keep the clothes there.'

Could anyone who merely 'touched' it, as Bharti said she had, figure out whether it was locked from inside?

The answer to that question was probably the difference between a conviction and acquittal, but it wasn't what troubled me. In June 2008, Bharti Mandal's memory still fresh, the CBI's Vijay Kumar recorded a statement by her— her third—in which she said clearly that it was only the middle mesh door that was latched. At the trial she said: 'I had *not stated* [emphasis added] to the investigating officer that "I first pushed the outer iron door and saw that the inner [middle] mesh door is closed and latched."'

Bharti's testimony opened up the possibility that the outer door to the Talwars' flat was indeed locked from within. The CBI was confident that this would be enough.

Except that there were a few problems. The biggest of these appeared at the very beginning of the court record from Bharti Mandal's cross-examination: *'Jo mujhe samjhaya gaya hai, wahi bayan main yahan de rahi hoon'* (Whatever was taught/explained to me, I'm saying here).

Bharti said this in the first minutes of her cross-examination, almost at the stroke of the lunch break. The rest of the examination would continue half an hour later. The stern-looking policewoman who chaperoned her to and from court whisked her away. Saini and company, beaming the day before, followed agitated.

When the hearing resumed, the defence objected to the witness leaving the court without permission before the cross-examination was completed. This was against court procedure. (All other witnesses in the case had remained in court during breaks. Mohapatra, the forensic scientist, for instance, had a fixed seat where he sat patiently through breaks.) In an application made right after the break, the defence alleged that the witness was taken away so that she could be schooled.

Judge Shyam Lal, usually so concerned about decorum and procedure—giggling policewomen, ringing cellphones and the like—ignored the application. And when Bharti returned to court, the proceedings took a surreal turn. Her statements to investigators were read out to her line by line. These were recorded in 2008, and were documents that the CBI had told the court it relied upon. Almost without exception, Bharti said she hadn't told the CBI any of the facts attributed to her by the investigators of the time.

From her cross-examination, it appeared the CBI may never have interviewed her at all. That she was saying whatever she had to say for the first time, and only to the court. Including: *'Jo mujhe samjhaya gaya hai, wahi bayan main yahan de rahi hoon.'*

***

Bharti Mandal lived in Noida's Sector 8; her 10 foot by 8 foot room was in the Baans Balli slum. Her friend Kalpana Mandal—the person she replaced in the Talwar household—lived there too, in another room. The settlement is behind a dedicated bamboo market, hence the name. Its presence and sly expansion over the years speaks of the stunning bifurcation of life in Delhi's suburbs.

Across the streets from it are large corporate towers with their signature tinted-glass fronts. Several monuments to the suburban middle-class idyll, such as Jalvayu Vihar, with gates and guards and parks and pools, are within walking distance—for the slum dwellers, that is. Others would take cars or rickshaws to avoid the longish trek.

The slum is enclosed within a ring of busy markets that hawk the leftovers from others nearby that have wealthier patrons. Here, the meat and fish stalls sell innards and claws and heads and offal. The provision store offers the option of buying ingredients measured exactly for a family's next meal: oil carefully poured from the bottle into small pouches tied with string, spoonfuls of spices. The vegetable vendor has the tomatoes from the bottom of the pile—for buyers at the bottom of theirs.

You enter the slum through what appear to be merely gaps between the shops that form its facade. The lanes are no more than three feet wide, including the drains that run along or cut across. There are temples in the slum but not enough toilets for its 1,50,000-odd inhabitants, so these passages are lined with the droppings of children.

Most disconcerting, however, was that Bharti Mandal's home was deep inside a wickedly intricate maze. After just a few yards, all lanes would split into two or three, inviting wrong turns every few seconds, each one costlier than the last.

A year after her deposition, I had tried to reach Bharti Mandal and Kalpana Mandal. Bharti lived a few yards away from a temple, and Sanjay, Kalpana's husband, had escorted me there. Bharti wasn't home, and we decided to return after killing some time in the market outside. There, I lost Sanjay, and thinking that he might have returned to his room, I attempted to reach it on my own. This was pure misadventure. Within minutes, I was lost inside the slum and trying to get out. But each turn I took sucked me deeper into it. Half an hour passed before Sanjay finally found me, slightly dizzy from the experience.

In their home, Kalpana made tea, and began talking about the Talwars.

\*\*\*

Kalpana Mandal came to testify right after Bharti, except that she didn't testify. She had continued working at Nupur's parents' place after the murders, and the CBI had listed her as one of the witnesses Nupur Talwar could influence while arguing against her bail.

In court, the prosecution moved an application saying that it had 'reliably learnt' that the witness had been 'won over' by the defence, which is why she wasn't required to testify. R.K. Saini wasn't in court that day, so his underling B.K. Singh moved the application. I asked Singh what had made the CBI change its mind after bringing the witness to court and guarding her the way they had guarded Bharti. And who exactly had won Kalpana over? Nupur Talwar was in jail.

'*Woh to maine achar dala, thoda . . .*' I did that to add a bit of spice, he said smiling.

Sipping tea in her home, I asked Kalpana about her day in court.

'They [the CBI] came in a Gypsy. They came in the morning about 9.30. They dropped me back also. In the afternoon.

'On the way they asked me . . . "What were they like? Were they good people or bad? Were they fighting?"

'I said they never fought in front of me. It was a good family. To me, they were very good. They have never slapped me, or even scolded me. Never did anything to me . . .

'They then asked about my routine, when I went, what I did.

'In some other homes, they scold you, they keep complaining—this isn't done, or that isn't done. This house they would never say anything. And their parents' house is the same. I've worked there for fourteen years.

'How could I say that they were a bad family? Bad parents? The father would go to drop Aarushi to school every morning at 7.30. So how can I say he was bad? Some days he would go to drop her at private tuitions at 4.30 in the evening. She was never alone. If they were not at home, her grandmother was there. She was really taken care of.

'I saw her grow up . . . She was like my daughter [points to her daughter] and I saw her grow up in front of my eyes. Their children grow up so well, so fast . . . I don't know what they feed them!

'They would always be together, eating together, going out together. They would take Aarushi everywhere. So why wouldn't I make out that they were a happy family?

'I would say in court as well that they were good people. I'd say it in front of everyone. I am not afraid to say it, because that is what I know. And sahab was an "India pass doctor", India pass, he was doing so well, opening clinics everywhere.

'They didn't ask me anything in the court. Whatever little they asked they asked in the car. I just told them they were a good family, what else will I say?

'They [the CBI] never gave me anything to eat in court [laughs]. I came back home and ate.'

Kalpana didn't really know what to make of her day in court, so I asked her about Aarushi.

'She was a very good girl, she would call me Kalpana didi. She would stay at her grandmother's place in the afternoon. When she came back from school she would go there. That is what I saw for three years.'

Did she believe any of what the CBI was saying about her having sex with Hemraj?

'Even we were wondering how they were saying all this. She was a good girl, everyone in the cluster would say that as well . . . When we heard the news we were shocked.

'I've cleaned their house even after Aarushi was killed. But it feels empty . . . I used to get a bad feeling. There was no one around.'

As I was leaving I asked Kalpana and Sanjay about their life in Delhi. Did they like where they lived? There was no living to be made where they came from, said Sanjay. Kalpana offered a more evocative answer: *'Eikhane standard jaiga achhe . . . Deshe dhulo mati . . . kada. Eikhane standard jaiga,'* she said. In the village there was dust and muck, here there was a 'standard' (of living).

This is why the squalid maze of Baans Balli was expanding, and would continue to grow. It was less about what the migrants found here, more about what they had left behind. Sanjay and Kalpana Mandal were happy they were where they were.

Ironically, there was also some comfort in where they were not on 15/16 May 2008. Kalpana Mandal and her husband had gone on leave—to the dust and muck of their rural home—at the time of the murders. They received calls from the CBI when they were there, but one thing was clear, they were far away when the murders happened. There could only be so much pressure the police could put them under.

They were not in the position that Bharti found herself in. Kalpana had known Bharti from their growing-up years in Gourangatala, a little north Bengal village, but they were not friends any more. 'Bharti avoids us,' Kalpana told me.

The murders had cost the Talwars many of their friends; their servants had lost some too.

***

Tanveer Ahmed Mir came into the trial in mid-October 2012. Several significant witnesses, including Bharti Mandal, K.K. Gautam, Dr Sunil Dohare and Dr B.K. Mohapatra, had already testified by then.

Karanjawala and Co., the firm involved in the Talwars' Supreme Court matters, believed that the Talwars required a specialist criminal lawyer in Ghaziabad. Satyaketu Singh, who had held things together competently enough till then, was a civil lawyer by profession.

On the advice of the Delhi firm, the Talwars engaged Tanveer Ahmed Mir. Mir wasn't a stranger to the lower courts—these were the first courts where he had defended many of his clients—but his manner was noticeably different from that of the Ghaziabad regulars'.

Mir was a hard-core criminal lawyer; he believed that those who earned their living the way he did must master the 'art of concealment'. Yet there was a disarming openness about him: outside court, he would talk freely about murderers he helped acquit—and equally about the cases he'd lost, often lacing his stories with colourful profanities. He seemed to live his life as if he was in a game, and like a seasoned player, he accepted that he'd win some and lose some.

Inside the court, he was a different man. Despite the commute from Delhi and very often several hours at a stretch in court, he always appeared fresh and distinguished. Ghaziabad's dust never seemed to settle on him. Also, in contrast to his opposite number, the prosecution counsel R.K. Saini, his manner—towards everyone in court—was extremely respectful. He had a quaint way, part feudal, part Indian army, of addressing people—especially those of lower station—as 'sahab'. He was tough in his cross-examination, but also brought up to be mindful of what the Indian Supreme Court had once called the 'majesty of the court'. Saini, on the other hand, often flew completely off the handle.

There was something else about Mir that reporters especially liked. After the 2011 attack on Rajesh Talwar, the press wasn't allowed to enter the court—apparently because of a security threat. So we would huddle at the open door straining our ears to hear what was going on, always careful to remain out of the somewhat temperamental judge's line of sight. Some of the lawyers, and many of the witnesses, were frequently inaudible. This was in part because proceedings were often like a private three- or four-way conversation between the judge and the opposing sides before him, their backs towards us. Add to this the constant din outside the court, where we stood—policewomen complaining bitterly about extra PT; litigants arguing with lawyers; court officials shooting the breeze (loudly); and so on. Their combined efforts would submerge the words being spoken inside.

But when Mir was on, his stentorian voice carried to us clearly; he was also in the habit of summing up what the witness had said. When Mir first came on the scene, he was seen as another in the long line of 'Delhi' (the Ghaziabad synonym for 'high-flying') lawyers the Talwars had employed. This cemented the widely held belief that they were both wealthy and guilty. How else could they afford these people? And who but the guilty would spend all that money?

As I got to know Mir better, I would sometimes offer him a ride back to Delhi so I'd get his perspective on the day's proceedings. We had each, for our respective purposes, got to know the case—and the Talwars—a little better. A bit frustrated with circumstances, he said that he sometimes contemplated exiting.

I asked him what made him continue.

'This is a beautiful case to argue,' he said. It had acquittal written all over it, and should he be able to take the case, it would be a substantial achievement—it was being watched closely by the legal fraternity.

Mir had a thriving practice, and a great reputation, but hadn't yet made it to the major league. With his characteristic candour, he would say that, in Supreme Court matters, he would be called upon as a 'junior counsel'. (It happened to him in this case too when a matter was before the highest court.) He didn't mind assisting—or perhaps he did, just a bit—but there was no question that he loved to argue.

This case went to the heart of why he wanted to become a lawyer. He had taken on the case because he had worked hard to get such an opportunity. He came to Delhi from Kashmir in the early 1990s. His family were erstwhile feudal lords, and his father was a politician; they probably had more than their fair share of power and privilege in the valley they loved. But Tanveer Ahmed Mir belonged to that generation of Kashmiri youths who were born at the wrong time. When he came of age, the Kashmir agitation was at its height. The winds of those times blew away a lot of ambitions, and as many futures.

He said he got a B.Sc. from the university there, but 'learned nothing'. He came to Delhi to 'achieve something'. For this, he braved its mainland bigotry: no landlord would rent him a house, and he managed the initial years thanks to the kindness of a (Hindu) professor who took him in. At Delhi University, he was a serious student, but sociable enough—an attribute that one day, quite suddenly, would make him part of the story in another sensational Delhi murder, that of Priyadarshini Mattoo, a student who was raped and murdered in her Vasant Kunj flat in the mid-1990s.

'I didn't know Priya that well . . . Just hi, hello terms . . . But one day she walked up to me and requested me to accompany her around campus. There was a bunch of boys bothering her. There was this Bihari gang (the DU campus is notorious for such divides) . . . She felt she would be safer if she had a guy around her. I agreed.'

Young Tanveer woke up the next morning to find the story in the papers. 'Fuck, I said, this can't be true, I was with her the whole day yesterday!'

He hotfooted it to the crime scene and told investigators this. The CBI came calling at his hostel door. They asked him whether there was a thwarted suitor in the picture and when he confirmed this the investigators wanted him to testify.

The news spread and he would find notes threatening his life slipped under his door. 'I was in two minds about whether it was worth it to put myself in the box. I felt troubled, afraid even. I called my dad.'

Tanveer's father heard him out. 'He paused for a while, and then started laughing. After that he said something that I'll never forget. It's why I do what I do. He told me, "You want to become a criminal lawyer . . . and you don't have the courage to be a witness?"'

He appeared in court, of course, as prosecution witness 9. He told the court what he knew without fear, and his testimony helped convict Priyadarshini Mattoo's killer. But it was that day in the witness box, the cross-examination that he had to go through, that gave him a taste of real criminal law. He was addicted. He'd got into that court for the right reasons, but once in it, he loved the game. He began to play.

And here he was, a decade and a half later, defending the Talwars. Had he done it for the right reasons? Did he believe they were innocent? Mir's conviction about the innocence of his clients became deeper as he dug further and further. The Talwars would spend eight to ten hours in his Defence Colony office on many days as the trial commenced—basically being grilled. It became clear to me that Mir felt that after a year of dealing with him, the Talwars had left any 'concealing' to Mir. And that whatever it was they had to conceal, if anything, he could deal with comfortably.

This attitude was different from what I had seen on those early drives back from court, when he and I separately wondered if the Talwars had something to conceal. 'So, Tanveer,' I asked one day, 'what was your gut reaction to the Talwars when you first met them?'

'Honestly?'

'Ya, honestly . . .'

'Rajesh Talwar . . . too soft, too emotional. Not capable of murder . . . would not be able to live with himself . . .'

'And . . . ?'

'Nupur Talwar . . . Yes.'

Having gone through the trial so far, Tanveer Ahmed Mir told me that he would have loved the opportunity to grill K.K. Gautam. He knew something that very few people were aware of about Gautam's involvement. The former policeman was extremely fond of appearing on television, and the vernacular channels loved him for his 'face value'. He had given them several gloating interviews on the morning of the 17th, focusing on his role in the discovery of Hemraj's body, and theorizing, with his experienced policeman's mind, how the murders took place.

Mir had seen raw footage of one of these interviews. In it, when asked where Hemraj was killed, a supremely confident Gautam is seen saying it had to be on the terrace.

Had the body been dragged up to the roof, 'rivers of blood' would have flowed down the stairs, he said. Gautam had told the court that all he saw were some stains leading to the roof.

'I don't know whether the judge would admit this evidence, but I'd certainly have taken the chance,' said Mir. All he would do, he said, was ask Gautam, 'Are you the man in this video?', and then play it in court. 'It would have exposed all his lies and debunked this whole dragging theory.'

There was no guarantee, of course, that Gautam would identify himself in the clip. Given the conduct of witnesses in the case, he may well have said his eyes were failing him and pointed to his treatment under Dr Choudhry. One policeman who was shown a photograph from the roof and asked whether he could see the clearly visible handles on the desert-cooler panel covering Hemraj simply said he could not. Everybody else could. Another policeman claimed he couldn't smell Hemraj's putrefying body. Everybody else could. And later, when A.G.L. Kaul would be shown a copy of a petition he had filed in the Supreme Court, he would tell the Ghaziabad court he had no idea about the document and would simply refuse to recognize it.

Still, Mir felt, it would have been worth a try.

***

As winter came that year, the trial slipped into a more regular pace. The almost childish fights of the early days slipped into more sedate sparring. It was as if both sides were taking a breather after the furious early rounds. But it isn't as if this phase didn't throw up something bizarre or inexplicable on a daily basis.

What had happened to the mobile phones that belonged to Aarushi and Hemraj, for instance? Prosecution witnesses marched in to provide answers, but their testimonies ended up posing questions for the CBI.

The phones used by Aarushi and Hemraj were missing when their bodies were discovered on 16 and 17 May 2008. They were important pieces of evidence because the people who got rid of them were most likely the killers.

While making their case against Aarushi's parents, the CBI suggested that the Talwars were in possession of the phones. In Hemraj's case, a call was completed several hours after his death—at about six on the morning of the 16th, when Nupur Talwar tried to contact him. Records from the service provider showed that this person was in the Jalvayu Vihar area.

The prosecution's case was that the Talwars both made and received this particular call and then got rid of the phone to create the impression that it was with someone else. Hemraj's phone had not been recovered. But the CBI claimed that it was active in Punjab well after the murders. Aarushi's phone was recovered after a year and a half of police work.

Sometime in the summer of 2008, weeks after Aarushi's death, a domestic servant working in the Jalvayu Vihar area found the teenager's mobile phone. It lay in a park. She picked up the instrument and took it home. Four and a half years after the incident, Kusum, the lady who found the phone, was in the witness box.

Kusum took the phone home and a few days later her brother arrived from Bulandshahr and took it away for his use, little realizing what he was getting into. A year and a half later, while the phone was still active, the police traced it and came knocking at the brother's door and picked him up. Kusum and her husband were taken into custody shortly thereafter. They told their simple story.

But it was a story with many gaps—gaps that only a proper investigation could have filled. Kusum told the court that investigators never took her to the spot where she found the phone. And the man who actually used it, her brother Rambhool, was not even on the list of witnesses.

The CBI nevertheless took the line that someone placed (rather than dropped or disposed of) Aarushi's phone in the park in a manner that would tempt a passer-by to pick it up.

They also argued that since all the data on Aarushi's phone had been wiped clean, it could have been the Talwars. There was no logical explanation as to why only the Talwars could have erased the data, and in any event the phone wasn't produced in court—the Talwars were never given the opportunity to have an expert inspect the evidence. The CBI simply stood by its claim.

Without the item itself and with the bland testimony of the bewildered domestic help who said little except that she found the phone in a park, there wasn't much scope for factual contradiction, and even less for any logical conclusions.

But Hemraj's phone was different—and more important in order to solve the mystery. Someone had received a call on the phone after he was dead—in the Jalvayu Vihar area, where all the initial suspects lived. Where was that handset?

In the 2010 closure report, A.G.L. Kaul had made a startling revelation that begged many questions: he claimed that the mobile phone Hemraj had been given by the Talwars was active in Punjab well after the murders. How did the phone get there? Who was using it? Kaul did not provide any answers, neither did he investigate.

During the trial, the CBI was asked how Kaul and his team knew the phone was indeed in Punjab. The witness for the prosecution who came after Kusum had the answer: the agency had no way of knowing.

M.N. Vijayan, nodal officer for Tata Teleservices, was the man who had provided the call details for the phone that Hemraj used. On being questioned, Vijayan told the trial court that he had provided the CBI details only for the one critical call made to the Tata number on the morning of the murders, 16 May 2008. He also said that the phone was never placed under surveillance.

But where was the phone? In fact, it was never found: the closure report merely says it was active somewhere in Punjab. There could have been only one way of getting this information, and that is by finding out from the service provider. The records provided by Tata Teleservices show no activity on the phone beyond that early morning call on 16 May. So how did Kaul know the phone was in Punjab at a later date? Vijayan's testimony made it clear that there was no way he could have known.

***

The case moved at its elephantine pace and the press lost its keen interest in it by November 2012. The CBI was still calling in its witnesses. On the list was Dr Naresh Raj, who had conducted Hemraj's autopsy and whose changed testimony was central to the closure report. Judge Shyam Lal asked when Dr Raj would testify but the CBI had a problem: the agency could not find Dr Raj, even though his whereabouts were a matter of record and he lived in government accommodation.

The following week, as the CBI prepared to bring in a batch of expert witnesses—and the hunt for Dr Raj continued—Saini told the court (with some indignation) that the accused had filed an application under the Right to Information (RTI) Act with the CFSL. The suggestion was, once again: 'Look at the extent they are going to!' The application itself was fairly innocuous. The Talwars sought details of the quality and standards guidelines followed by the lab.

Forensic laboratories around the world make this information public on their websites, but not the CFSL. During the trial, witnesses representing the CFSL had been either non-committal or sketchy in their testimonies with regard to guidelines. The RTI application was filed so that the defence could question CFSL witnesses on whether they had followed procedure in their testing.

The Talwars filed the RTI application one afternoon in November. Its concerns were limited to the CFSL and its guidelines, and had nothing to do with the CBI. Yet the next morning, Saini told the court that such an application had been filed. For an agency that had been working for several weeks on trying to find one of its own witnesses—a doctor in government service—this is pretty fast work.

How did Saini know? Information of this kind is generally passed on, after due process (as I was reminded), through the information department of the CFSL. The officer who headed the department, J.G. Moses, told me he was aware that the RTI was filed, but he had not passed on this information to the CBI: 'I did not tell them,' he said. The thing is, only the Talwars and the CFSL knew the application had been filed. And the Talwars certainly didn't tell Saini.

\*\*\*

In the absence of Dr Raj, other scientists were brought to testify for the prosecution. One of them was Rajinder Singh Dangi, a senior scientist at the CFSL, who came to testify for the prosecution. Dangi had conducted a 'scientific experiment' and submitted a report recreating the crime scene on the roof of the Talwars' flat, specifically about the alleged shifting of Hemraj's body after his murder.

The experiment in question was carried out using every scientific tool required. These were listed methodically as part of the 'forensic opinion': two 10-ml bottles of red paint (Shalimar Superlac); a 10-litre bucket; 4 litres of water; one bed sheet. In addition, there was an unsuspecting volunteer from the lower constabulary—who was made to lie on the sheet, get carried, and then get dragged.

Shalimar Superlac (red) came into the picture because 'recreation of the crime scene' required a 'blood trail'. On the terrace, a sheet was duly soaked in paint, a constable lay on it and was then dragged. It was noticed that the drag marks made by the heels were 'parallel'.

One of the other conclusions drawn from the experiment was that it was indeed possible for two people to drag a body in a sheet up a flight of stairs.

During his cross-examination, Singh was asked why he chose Shalimar paint. Did it have the exact consistency of blood? He didn't have any idea about the densities of blood or paint, said Singh, but he said: '*Woh khoon jaisa tha . . .*' (It was like blood).

The judge didn't take too kindly to this. He chided Singh saying it wasn't the kind of answer that the court expected from an expert. But it didn't stop there. Counsel for the defence asked the witness whether such a demo test referenced any scientific papers. The CFSL scientist responded that it did not and added that there was no 'tradition' which required it to.

Did the Shalimar paint solution clot the way blood does? Singh avoided the court's ridicule on this one and admitted that it did not. Was he briefed that Hemraj was allegedly carried to the terrace by a man and a woman? And was a woman involved in carrying the constable wrapped in a sheet? Singh gave the correct scientific answer to this question: he was not briefed, and no woman was involved.

Why did a senior scientist from one of India's top forensic labs carry out this 'dummy test'? Well, he was asked to. The test was A.G.L. Kaul's brainchild; it was conducted within months of his taking over and about a year and a half after the murders. And what did it actually prove? Singh eventually admitted his findings were 'inconclusive'.

\*\*\*

With most experts having come and gone, it was the turn of the Noida policemen to testify. Part of the Uttar Pradesh police force, they were the first responders and the case's investigators for a fortnight, before the investigation was handed over to the CBI.

Constable Pawan Kumar, a fresh but overweight recruit posted at Noida's Sector 20 police station, had completed his night rounds in his area and just deposited his rifle when a gateman from the Jalvayu Vihar housing complex arrived to say there had been a murder. This was early on the morning of 16 May 2008.

Kumar got to the crime scene by 6.30 a.m. and stayed less than half an hour. He told the trial court that Dr Talwar let him in and then showed him to Aarushi's room. She lay there covered in a white sheet, he said, but her head was exposed. Her throat had been slit.

Kumar got on the phone to his superior when he saw the body, and other policemen arrived soon after. Kumar observed two other things during his brief stay in the Talwars' flat: that an 'aged couple' arrived when he was there. (Aarushi's maternal grandparents, the Chitnises.) He also said that the people in the house were 'normal but tense'.

The recording of that phrase, 'normal but tense', appeared to be the only reason Kumar was called in as a witness. In the CBI's criminal psychology book, at least as far as this trial was concerned, if you were 'normal' after your daughter had been murdered, you were clearly not grieving; however, you would be 'tense' if you were guilty. Hence the compact 'normal but tense'.

The phrase wasn't something that Kumar communicated in any manner to anyone at the time of the murder. During his cross-examination Kumar admitted he hadn't mentioned it to his superior when he called him from the scene; neither did he record this observation in the general diary. The phrase first came up when the CBI's investigators summoned the constable to their office more than a year after the double murders.

The statement was never shown to him, said Kumar. In any case, it was in English, a language he said he studied till 'class six or class eight'. Throughout the trial, whenever a witness had nothing substantial to offer by way of hard evidence, the prosecution's fallback was on the conduct of the Talwars. Through the testimonies of policemen or morning-walkers or friends or crematorium priests, the prosecution wasted no opportunity to suggest that the Talwars were not grieving.

This strategy played very well with the media, which seldom bothered to take into account the subjectivity of the observer or the simple fact that one cannot weep for twelve hours at a stretch.

In Pawan Kumar's case, he repeated the catchphrase dutifully when led on by Saini (the defence objected, and was overruled) and had little else to say. Like other witnesses from the lower constabulary, he recalled very little apart from this—he didn't, for example, know who he was out on his rounds with on the night of the murder, or even the name of his SP. In fact, he remembered so little that the judge gave him some food for thought: 'Eat less,' said Judge Shyam Lal, 'you might remember more.'

***

Each time a policeman came to testify in the Aarushi–Hemraj murder trial, his common sense seemed to have exited.

Subinspector Bachu Singh, in uniform, and wearing thick prescription glasses, made his appearance as a prosecution witness. During the course of his cross-examination, he made an incredible admission: he had no sense of smell, he told the court.

Bachu Singh had volunteered that when he saw the victim Hemraj's body on the terrace, about 36 hours after the manservant had been killed, he found it in mint condition. There was no decomposition, no putrid smell. This tested Judge Shyam Lal's patience. The trial judge let the policeman know that common sense hadn't taken an adjournment: 'What are you talking about? No stink after a body lies outside almost two days in the middle of May?'

This is when Bachu Singh pulled out a classic 'Sir, hamein na badboo ata hai, na khushboo' (I can sense neither stink, nor aroma).

The entertainment continued. R.K. Saini stepped in for his witness, trying to explain that a body may not decompose. In Punjab, where he was from, summer actually sets in around July–August nowadays, he told the court with a twitchy smile. May, when the murders took place, is relatively cool. (For the record, the temperature in the Delhi region on the relevant day in May 2008 was 47 degrees in the shade.)

Having heard Saini out, Judge Shyam Lal asked the witness with undisguised irony whether he too was from Punjab. 'No sir,' said Bachu Singh, 'I am from Mathura.' This is about the only undiluted truth the policeman said in court that day.

The policeman's description of the corpse in court was meant to suggest it was easily identifiable, and this had to be understood in the context of his claim that the Talwar family refused to identify Hemraj positively. Ergo, they were buying time: only the guilty would do that.

Bachu Singh was a seasoned policeman; it was he who wrote out the panchnamas for both murders. But as his day in court wore on, the suspicion that he may have doctored them became increasingly reasonable. In Aarushi's panchnama, for instance, a line appears to have been added (in visibly smaller letters) that her pyjama strings were untied. This fit the theory—formulated two years later—that her genitals were cleaned.

Singh denied he had made this amateurish alteration to the document. He told the court, 'It might appear so . . . But I just did it to fill out the line.'

The judge smiled; the scribe took it down. The fact is that this kind of 'line-filling' was all over the police documents in the Aarushi case. Bachu Singh offered a stunningly simple explanation for this in court: *'Hum aise hi karte hain'* (That's how we do it).

When he appeared in court, with his thick glasses and his amiable, if mischievous, manner, Bachu Singh was hiding a secret that had nothing to do with the case, but had a lot to say about policemen in Uttar Pradesh. He had successfully plotted a murder in his native Mathura at around the same time that he was taking his oath in this murder trial. The policeman was convicted about a year later—for bumping off a woman who was causing trouble for his family. He was sent to the same Dasna, where the Talwars would eventually go.

\*\*\*

Subinspector Dataram Nanoria, the first investigating officer in the case, actually had a conviction against him for the custodial death of a prisoner. He had done time, and was out pending appeal when he came in to testify. Nanoria was among the policemen who had broken the lock to the terrace and discovered Hemraj's body covered by a cooler panel on the morning of 17 May 2008. But he didn't seize the item as evidence—although it may have yielded DNA or fingerprints—because 'it was too large and heavy', he told the court.

So here is where common sense needed to be recalled to court: How could the Talwars, a couple of average build, manage to lift, shift and place an item so heavy exactly where they wanted it, when a posse of policemen (there were at least half a dozen present) could not manage the same feat of strength?

The cooler panel actually had handles, as these things usually do, to make moving them around convenient. Nanoria was shown pictures of the panels with the handles clearly visible. But he steadfastly maintained that he could not see them. The same photographs also showed bed sheets hanging a few feet from where Hemraj's body lay—a crude device used by the killer(s) to prevent clear sight of the body from the adjacent terrace. He could see the sheet, but couldn't explain why he didn't seize it.

***

As part of the parade of policemen who were called to witness was a senior officer who could damage the defence's case most. This was Mahesh Kumar Mishra, the Noida SP, the seniormost officer on the scene. Tanveer Ahmed Mir was genuinely apprehensive about his testimony and cross-examination.

In indignation, rage and, in retrospect, poor legal advice, Rajesh and Nupur Talwar had filed a protest petition against the closure report filed by the CBI. In it they made an admission that had huge potential for damage. They said that they had locked Aarushi's room from the outside at about 11.30 on the night of the murders and kept the key in their bedroom. The Talwars went on to say that they had told Mahesh Mishra about this.

Mishra testified that Dr Talwar also told him that it was possible an intruder took the key from his room and let himself into Aarushi's room. This scenario was outlandish: someone is let into the flat by the Talwars' servant Hemraj; the murderer then slips into the Talwars' bedroom, where the couple are asleep, slips out with the key with which he enters Aarushi's room, murders her, kills Hemraj, drags his body up to the terrace and comes back for a couple of swigs of Ballantine's whisky.

The defence argued that Mishra invented the story. At the heated hearing, defence counsel Mir asked Mishra whether he had put this important fact down on paper anywhere in the first days of the investigation. Mishra's best answer was that he had told his 'superiors' about it.

The first time it was put on record is in Mishra's statement to the CBI nearly two months after the murders. But if Mishra 'invented' the scenario of Dr Talwar locking his daughter in from outside (incidentally, this was the type of locks in hotel rooms, so while Aarushi could open the door from the inside, no one could enter without a key), why did the Talwars claim they had done so in their petition against the closure report?

The Talwars never had a clear explanation for the key. But it wasn't the only way to enter Aarushi's room. As the Usha Thakur adventure revealed, the toilet attached to Aarushi's room was accessible to guests without them having to go through her room. So entry was clearly possible without a key if the toilet wasn't locked from the inside. But facts such as a possible second entry point didn't dispel the niggling doubts about the Talwars' guilt.

The policemen, servants, forensic scientists and the likes were done testifying. As the first quarter of 2013 came to a close, it didn't look like the prosecution had much more to say—only 35 of the 141 listed witnesses had appeared. But that still left three who were essential to the CBI's case.

Prosecution witness number 36 was—finally—Dr Naresh Raj. Dr Raj introduced the potent idea of surgical incisions—the use of a scalpel in the act of the murders. At the trial he would go much further. There was an unmistakable world-weariness about the post-mortem doctor.

He seldom looked up or spoke up in court. In the course of his deposition, a suggestion was made that he was involved in a major medical equipment scam also being investigated by the CBI. This involved scores of doctors and technicians in the Uttar Pradesh health system. On the days the 'NRHM (National Rural Health Mission) scam' hearings took place an alarmingly large number of men of different shapes and sizes would be stuffed into the (well under capacity) courtroom dock, barely able to move. The net had been cast very wide and every government doctor in Noida was afraid he would be implicated. Dr Raj denied any involvement.

He began his deposition: 'I conducted the post-mortem of deceased Hemraj at 9.00 p.m. on the night of 17.05.2008 under artificial light . . .'

The first part of his testimony was going along predicted lines. The prosecutor asked Dr Raj if the cuts to the throats of the victims could have been caused by a scalpel. 'Yes, it can be caused by a surgical scalpel,' he said.

This was expected, and in line with what Dr Raj had told Kaul in his statement in October 2009—that the wounds were caused by a sharp-edged surgical instrument and inflicted by a surgically trained person.

But the testimony soon moved into unexplored territory. Asked to describe the state of Hemraj's body (he saw it 44 hours after the murder), Dr Raj said, 'The penis of the deceased was swollen.' He proceeded to give reasons: 'The swelling in the penis of the deceased was because he was either in the midst of having sexual intercourse or he was about to have sexual intercourse and immediately he died [sic].'

This alarming claim put the focus back on the alleged illicit, socially unacceptable, sex that titillated the Indian middle class.

In response, Tanveer Ahmed Mir referred to a widely accepted forensic science text, Modi's *Textbook of Medical Jurisprudence and Toxicology*, and read out the relevant section on the signs of a body's putrefaction after death. 'From 18 to 36 hours or 48 hours after death, eyes are forced out of their sockets, a frothy reddish fluid or mucus is forced out of the mouth and nostrils, abdomen becomes greatly distended, the penis and scrotum become enormously swollen.'

On what basis had Dr Raj reasoned that Hemraj was having sex or was about to?

'My statement that the reason for swelling found in the penis of the deceased Hemraj was that he was murdered either while he was in the midst of sexual intercourse or just before commencing intercourse is based on my marriage and experience of my marriage . . . I cannot produce any authority in support of my statement.'

That was not all. When Mir suggested to him that the experiences of his marriage surely could have nothing to do with this case, the doctor replied robotically: 'It is incorrect to suggest that my marriage and experiences of my marriage has no connection with the swelling that I found in Hemraj's penis.'

It was unusual testimony.

Dr Raj had been interviewed by investigators on two occasions within months of the post-mortem. Why had he not mentioned his reasons for the swelling in the post-mortem report or to any investigator recording a statement? Why hadn't he put the observation on record in the AIIMS committee report on which he was a key panellist?

'When I conducted the post-mortem of the deceased Hemraj, I did not form the opinion on the reasoning I gave for the swelling in his penis, as such, I did not write this in the post-mortem report. I thought, when somebody asks me the reason, I will tell them.'

Although his reasons appear for the first time in his testimony to the trial court, Dr Raj insisted that it was 'incorrect to say' he didn't reveal them to investigators earlier. As for the AIIMS committee, questions regarding the swelling of the penis never came up.

The cross-examination of Dr Naresh Raj ended in the customary way. Mir told him he was lying in court under pressure from the CBI. Dr Raj said: 'It is incorrect to suggest that my theory about the swelling of Hemraj's penis has been stated by me in the court at the instance of the CBI.'

The subject of the swollen penis was thus laid to rest.

Apart from a confirmation of his opinion that a scalpel was the second murder weapon, the CBI wanted to seed two other ideas through Dr Raj's expert testimony: that Hemraj's body wasn't in a state of decomposition and was therefore easy to recognize (implying that Rajesh Talwar's confusion when confronted by the body was a sign of evasion); and that Aarushi and Hemraj were having sex. Dr Raj was the first prosecution witness to actually say this in court.

\*\*\*

Imagine for a moment that the case for a murder conviction is like a book with 20 chapters. If all 20 are written and published, you have a 'book'. But what if chapters 16 through 19 are missing—just blank pages? It isn't a book any more, is it? At best, it is an incomplete book.

There is no such thing as an incomplete conviction in a murder trial. It is a binary game: guilty or not guilty. In the kind of case that was at hand, one where circumstantial evidence was heavily relied upon, the 'book' didn't just have to have all its chapters, it was necessary for each one to lead to the next. That was the law: every link in the chain of circumstantial evidence has to be fixed, and unbreakable, for a guilty verdict. If the defence was able to manipulate the prosecution in a way that gaps remained, then a wise judge would see them and acquit.

There was another view. If you coaxed the prosecution's witnesses into filling in the blanks by telling a story that was illogical and unfounded on the facts on record, a wise judge would see that too, and he would acquit.

In the Aarushi–Hemraj murders, the issue was whether it was more expeditious for the Talwars to have the CBI leave blank pages or to have them narrate absurd, invented scenarios. The missing 'chapters' had to do with the six hours between midnight of 15 May and 6 a.m. the following day. What took place in the flat during those hours?

Although there had been insinuations to the effect that Aarushi and Hemraj were having sex, the most recent being Dr Raj's theory on Hemraj's post-mortem erection, no witness had directly said so. This was one of the 'blank pages'. No witness had described how the actual assaults took place either, and this was another chunk that was missing.

Within the team of defence lawyers, there was a clear difference of opinion on how to tackle the cross-examination of the two final witnesses in the trial, Dr M.S. Dahiya and A.G.L. Kaul.

Tanveer Ahmed Mir led the defence; Satyaketu Singh, who practised out of Ghaziabad, supported him. It was part of Mir's routine to prepare a questionnaire for all his cross-examinations and run it by his clients, chopping and changing after arriving at a consensus. But Mir had no control over what Singh might ask. This frustrated Mir, but from the Talwars' perspective, it was important to respect the local knowledge and experience that Singh brought to the table. Without the support of the Ghaziabad regulars, the Talwars would be lost in the premises of the 'kacheri'.

Satyaketu Singh had played a significant, perhaps underrated, role in the Talwars' defence. His small chamber was often the alternative venue for the Talwars' less than private conferences with their lawyers. He was basically a civil lawyer—one reason the Talwars felt they had to bring the criminal law specialist Mir in—but he was also someone who had an excellent feel for how the Ghaziabad court worked. He commanded a fair amount of respect in the premises: in part because he had been around for a few decades and knew the system, but mostly because people thought of him as upright. He had a straightforward, even stern, demeanour, and this didn't change when he appeared before Judge Shyam Lal.

For one thing, Singh wasn't afraid to stand up to Judge Shyam Lal. On at least one occasion he had told the judge before a packed court that he was biased against the Talwars. Judge Shyam Lal knew Singh's standing in Ghaziabad—censuring a man like him would prove to be a misadventure. He kept quiet.

In court, Singh's manner was assured, and his delivery was clear. He never sought out the press, nor did he ever make mischievous interventions like challenging the judge's fitness to deliver a verdict because he had technically passed retirement age as other Ghaziabad regulars might have. However, he had often advised the Talwars, through the duration of the trial, to seek a transfer from Judge Shyam Lal's court. He felt they were doomed if they were there. He pointed out that the judge seemed to ignore the compelling arguments that the defence made.

The insistence on this point was another example of the differences in work culture among the Talwars' lawyers. The Ghaziabad lot understood that getting any purchase where they practised meant working the system. Mir's vantage was one from which he had seen the system work—at least in relative terms. The things that went on in Ghaziabad wouldn't get past a judge in the Delhi courts, where Mir did most of his business.

The advice to plead for a transfer could also be seen as strategic. If such a petition was made and heard, it may well have eaten into Judge Shyam Lal's time—after all, if the Talwars were able to stall proceedings for a month, Judge Shyam Lal would be gone. If a transfer petition failed, the Talwars would no doubt have to come back to an angrier version of Judge Shyam Lal. The chances of failure were high. The Supreme Court's response when the Talwars petitioned for transfer of the case out of Ghaziabad following the attack on Rajesh was to warn the Talwars of impertinence and reject their petition. The Talwars would have to carry the burden of that order into any attempt they made to seek transfer out of Ghaziabad. Had they approached the Allahabad High Court again, the CBI would just have placed the 2012 Supreme Court warning on the table. It is unlikely that a high court judge would differ. The Talwars would have had to crawl back to Judge Shyam Lal.

Singh had made valuable contributions during the trial—he had exposed how Kaul illegally broke the CFSL's seal to try to coerce Umesh, the Talwars' driver, into identifying two specific golf clubs—but Mir was now the new lead counsel, and though his style of functioning was pleasant, it was also direct. The Delhi lawyer had come into the trial several months after it commenced, well past the ill-tempered summer of 2012. He was also paid much more for his appearances. This led to rumblings and disagreements in Ghaziabad.

Mir's cross-examinations reflected the view that the 'blank pages' in the CBI's case would raise reasonable doubt. Every day he was in court, he did his best to keep them blank by not allowing witnesses 'to spin a yarn'. But Singh had long been of the view that the CBI had no clue about how the murders had taken place and that the agency had tried to force-fit a motive into an invented scenario.

He felt it was best for his clients that the improbability and incoherence of the CBI story was exposed.

Mir and Singh took their differences into the courtroom.

***

Dr Mohinder Singh Dahiya made his much-awaited appearance in Ghaziabad in early April 2013. This was as much his case as Kaul's. The story of the murders had been laid out during the trial just as Dahiya had told it in his report in late 2009.

The Talwars considered Dahiya the author of their doom, writing out their conviction sitting hundreds of miles away in Gandhinagar, Gujarat. They had never seen the man. I asked Nupur about her first impression of him. What did he look like to her?

'Like death,' she replied.

The prosecution would never use the phrase 'honour killing', but the narrative pointed there every step of the way, because the case was no more than an extension of the tale told by Dahiya, and he had said that the murders were the work of people interested in the Talwars' family honour.

The fundamental flaw was Dahiya's assumption that Hemraj's blood was found in Aarushi's room. It wasn't, and this had not just been admitted by the CBI in several instances, it had also been established in the court where Dahiya was about to testify. Without that 'fact', the story of the honour killing fell apart. So did Dahiya's confident assertion that Aarushi and Hemraj were attacked in the teenager's bedroom. But would the man admit that he was in error?

Dahiya's testimony opened with a brief description of the decades of work he had done in forensics, the honours conferred upon him and the book he had written. Then, it moved to the more substantive parts. There were three: his theories on the weapons, the motive and the 'dressing up' of the crime scene. In each of these areas, Dahiya's voice had been the most authoritative.

Mir rose to challenge this authority every minute of the way. Screaming that Dahiya's report was 'unscientific and subjective' and had no place in the court's record, Mir said, 'The witness cannot be allowed to give expert testimony! How can he solve a murder by just looking at photographs? How can the word "findings" be used for what he has written?'

The judge allowed Dahiya to continue.

He told the court that he had received photographs, documents, a summary of the case and a questionnaire from the CBI on 13 October 2009. On the basis of these, he submitted his report 13 days later describing in some detail how and why the murders took place. When he took the stand, that document, Document 79, was 'proved' by its author for the purpose of the trial. Dahiya said he stood by every word he had written in it.

The summary wasn't read out, but Dahiya was more explicit in court than he was in his report and actually named the Talwars.

Mir jumped in again, objecting furiously at this. The judge sustained the objection, and Dahiya had to rephrase. He was forced to return to the language of exclusion: that 'no outsider' could have committed the crimes.

Dahiya's testimony also showed that his involvement in the case had begun even before he received the materials for his report—a fact that had not been put on record earlier. On 10 October 2009 he went to survey the scene of the crime along with CBI officials. He told the trial court he saw 'the location and situation of the flat . . . [and found] the walls had been painted'. He later came back to the CBI headquarters in Delhi and had 'detailed discussions with the investigating officer A.G.L. Kaul'.

(Two days later, on 12 October, in a statement before A.G.L. Kaul, Dr Raj would introduce the idea of a scalpel and a surgically trained person; the very next day, Dahiya received his questionnaire, and some documents, including Dr Raj's latest statement.)

Dahiya described to the judge what he had deduced:

Two weapons had been used . . . [but] the necks of Aarushi and Hemraj were cut after both of them were dead.

If the person was living, upon cutting the carotid artery there would be a spurt that could go 10 to 15 feet. In my opinion there was a spurt, but it didn't reach 9 or 10 feet. There was no spurt on the terrace either. Both the victims had their necks slit while they were in a horizontal position. There were also no signs of resistance from either Aarushi or Hemraj.

I found that both the victims were bearing injuries on their head and that these injuries were caused by a golf stick . . . According to my opinion the necks of both the deceased have been cut by a surgical scalpel . . . The head injuries [golf club] caused to both the deceased.

Hemraj's body was taken to the roof after his death and his neck was cut there . . . the bedcover wrapped in which he was taken to the roof was pulled from beneath him . . . The murderer who had cut Hemraj's neck somehow got trapped in the pipes on the roof because of which the blood spattered palm print got embossed on the wall adjoining the door of the roof . . . I found in these circumstances that there could have been no involvement of any outsiders.

Because of Mir's constant heckling, Dahiya's examination by Saini was very short—the transcript is just one page. This is the way Mir wanted it.

Mir began his cross-examination. Had Dahiya examined any of the alleged murder weapons?

'The IO never sent me or showed me any golf club.'

Had he investigated a similar case during his career?

'I have never examined any case where injuries were caused by a golf club.'

How then could he be so sure that the fatal injuries on the heads of the victims were triangular in shape?

Dahiya fell back on 'materials supplied': 'It is correct that in the post-mortem reports it is nowhere written that the injuries were triangular in shape, but the IO had mentioned in the questionnaire supplied to me that the injury on Aarushi's head was triangular. I have made this the basis to say that it was caused by a golf club . . . Such an injury could also have been caused by a hockey stick.'

What about the scalpel then?

'I was never sent a scalpel for examination by the investigating authorities,' said Dahiya, but added: 'It is incorrect to suggest that the injuries on the necks of the deceased were not caused by a surgical knife.'

In the material provided to Dahiya were Dr Raj's opinion that a surgical instrument had been used, and A.G.L. Kaul's opinion that the shape of the injuries to the head were 'triangular'.

In his report Dahiya had said: 'The presence of two distinct impact splatters [from the blunt blows] on the wall behind the headrest of Ms Aarushi's bed also goes to prove the contention of Mr Hemraj having been caused head injuries in the room of Ms Aarushi itself . . . He must have been shifted to the rooftop in a fatally injured condition.'

Mir avoided asking Dahiya about this deduction that Hemraj was bludgeoned in Aarushi's room. He asked him about the splatter patterns instead. Had Dahiya been given scaled photographs?

'Such photographs are not required,' said Dahiya coolly.

'And did you measure the stains?'

'No, I did not.'

Now Mir directed him instead towards his conclusion that there wasn't enough of a blood splatter as a result of the neck injury to Aarushi, and this suggested her neck was slit later as part of an elaborate plan to frame the Nepali servants—to make it look like a 'Gurkha-style' killing.

'Did you see the crime scene inspection report of the CFSL that mentions that the bloodstains on the walls behind Aarushi's bed reached 9 feet 4 inches?' asked Mir.

'I was not sent such a report,' replied Dahiya.

But where was the challenge to the error about Hemraj's blood being found in Aarushi's room?

It would not come from Mir.

He felt that the error had been established in court already, during Dr B.K. Mohapatra's testimony, when the tags from the original seizure were displayed which showed that Hemraj's pillow had been seized from the servant's room on 1 June 2008, more than two weeks after the murders.

Dahiya had said he stood by his report 'one hundred per cent', but the evidence rendered the story he had spun false. And Mir wasn't about to allow him to offer any explanations, or worse, tell another story. He had confined Dahiya to questions on the weapons and the scene based on hard evidence on record. He had repeatedly suggested that Dahiya's findings weren't based on science or fact. He assumed the court heard him. He was done with the witness.

Satyaketu Singh rose to do his part. 'Where had the murders taken place?'

Dr Dahiya now warmed to his theme:

'Both the deceased were attacked in Aarushi's room . . . Both were assaulted on Aarushi's bed . . .'

The CBI counsel R.K. Saini could not contain his excitement. 'What were they doing? The court should record what they were doing! They were having intercourse! *Likho* *"sambhog! sambhog!"*' he screamed.

The Talwars looked on in dismay.

The judge made a mild intervention: asking Saini to tone down the language, he told the witness to continue. For the record, Dahiya calmly said: 'The murders were committed because both the deceased were found in a compromising position, having sexual intercourse in her room.'

Dahiya was steadfast in his defence of his report. He had gone by what he was told. Not by what he wasn't. Like the fact that Hemraj's blood was never found in Aarushi's room. Or that a number of witnesses had contradicted the view that bloodstains had been wiped. Or that Hemraj was found on the roof with his slippers still on. All these facts were available to Kaul when the CBI asked Dahiya to write his thesis.

In conclusion, Dahiya said: 'It is incorrect to say that my report is unscientific and has been made in connivance with CBI officials.' He left the court having placed his expert opinion that Aarushi and Hemraj were having sex. In doing so, he had prepared the ground for the next witness: A.G.L. Kaul.

\*\*\*

On 16 April, exactly a month short of the fifth anniversary of the murders, A.G.L. Kaul walked into the Ghaziabad court to depose. Kaul had turned up in court several times before, to check on progress and hold his informal meetings with reporters. It was time now to reveal the full story—to say out loud what he had only whispered in the courtyard outside.

The final conclusion of Kaul's 2010 closure report was that there wasn't enough evidence to convict the Talwars. He would now have to explain why the CBI sought a conviction.

Kaul began by talking about when he took over the investigation, and said, 'As on date, I am testifying before this honourable court that I fully and firmly stand by my final report dated 19.12.2010.'

This wasn't a mere formality. It was a statement loaded with significance. Because the final report said:

- There is no evidence to prove that Hemraj was killed in Aarushi's room.
- Scientific tests on the Talwars have not conclusively indicated their involvement.
- There is absence of a clear-cut motive and incomplete understanding of the sequence of events and non-recovery of one weapon of offence.

But the same report also said that, in the locked flat, the parents were the only people who could have committed the crimes.

Kaul's testimony tried to explain why. In a rambling deposition, he talked about the evidence he had gathered from the statements of the two post-mortem doctors; the recreation of the events on the roof; the recovery of a murder weapon; and, of course, the conduct of the Talwars: Rajesh's refusal to identify Hemraj's body immediately, and the hiding and cleaning of the missing golf club.

Early in the piece, he made an admission. He had 'created the email ID hemraj.jalvayuvihar@gmail.com during the course of the investigation'.

The Talwars had, according to him, attempted an elaborate cover-up: 'The scene of the crime had been dressed up. The bed on which Aarushi's body was found did not have creases on it. There was no stream of blood from the cut on Aarushi's neck, and there was a spot of wetness on the sheet. Hemraj's body was covered with a panel on the terrace and the terrace door was locked.'

Also, he said, 'no outsider' could have entered the flat, even though the Talwars had tried to create the impression that someone had locked them in from the outside: 'One door to Hemraj's room opened in the passage between the main door and the metal door, while the other door to his room opened inside the house. If one were to exit Hemraj's room from the door in the passage, one could lock the metal door from outside, and then enter the house from the door which was inside the house.'

Much of what Kaul told the court was in the closure report, but in court, Kaul stated categorically what he and the CBI had only insinuated: 'These murders were committed by Dr Rajesh Talwar and Dr Nupur Talwar.' The press contingent on that day was significantly larger than on others, and the news that the 'parents are the killers' was broadcast almost as soon as Kaul had uttered the words.

\*\*\*

Tanveer Ahmed Mir had worked out his line of attack on Kaul. His argument was that the investigations had been completed in 2010 and the CBI had concluded there wasn't enough evidence to convict the Talwars. No new evidence had come in since, so how could the Talwars be suddenly found guilty? This would be a running theme in his cross-examination: from the weapons to the forensic tests and the expert opinions, Mir would challenge Kaul by asking him what in his testimony went beyond his closure report.

Mir would also try to establish the dubious nature of investigations under Kaul: the tampering of evidence and the manipulation of witnesses.

There was a third, subtler, part to Mir's strategy. By limiting what he asked Kaul to the closure report and his conduct, Mir would effectively allow the gaps in the investigation to go unexplained. The law on circumstantial evidence cases was clear: every link in the chain of evidence would have to hold firm for a conviction. Every aspect of the prosecution's story had to, therefore, be clear, logical and backed by an irrefutable circumstance. It wasn't good enough, for instance, for the CBI to say that the entry of outsiders was improbable—the agency had to prove that it was impossible.

Kaul's deposition had left many questions unanswered. The key question was: 'So how exactly did the murders take place?' This was another way of wording the admission in the closure report: that the sequence of events between midnight of 15 May and 6 a.m. on 16th, when the maid Bharti Mandal turned up for work, was unclear.

Nothing that Kaul had said so far had made it any clearer—he hadn't even speculated about how the actual assaults took place. Mir wanted to keep it that way. He went at Kaul from different angles.

Kaul had told the court that a report from the CFSL:

> indicated that two golf sticks were cleaner than the others. Out of these two golf sticks, the dimensions of one golf stick was matching with the blunt injuries . . .
>
> Experts had examined the golf club bearing no. 5 and measured the size of the striking surface as 8 cm and on this basis, I had stated in my report that the injuries on the heads of both the deceased had been caused by golf club no. 5.

The testimonies of the post-mortem doctors had already established that Kaul hadn't sent the clubs to them for an opinion on whether one of them could have caused an injury and he admitted that it was 'nowhere mentioned by the post-mortem doctor [in the post-mortem report] that the injury was V-shaped or U-shaped [triangular]'.

The CFSL hadn't offered any opinion on the matter either: the lab's report merely measured the clubs, and, in the process of looking for DNA or blood, found that two—a wood and a 4 iron—appeared to have less dirt than the others.

But all along, and even during his testimony, Kaul had pointed to the 'cleaner' 5 iron as the murder weapon. Mir wanted him to confirm this yet again; he suggested Kaul had been wrong about both the number and the physical state of the specific golf club that was the purported murder weapon. Kaul replied: 'It is incorrect to suggest that in my final report I had wrongly written that scientists after examination found that golf stick no. 3 [the wood] and golf stick no. 5 were cleaned completely and because of this compared to the other golf clubs they looked very different.'

The sum of this was: if at all a golf club was used as a weapon, it wasn't the one that was allegedly cleaned.

Kaul faced more questions about the golf clubs. In the July 2008 AIIMS report, both post-mortem doctors had endorsed a khukri as a murder weapon in writing. In September 2009, Aarushi's post-mortem doctor, Sunil Dohare—without having seen the clubs—had told Kaul that Aarushi's head injuries were V- or U-shaped, and that a golf club was capable of inflicting them.

Mir asked Kaul why he hadn't placed the doctors' July 2008 opinion on court record: 'Is it because you knew that it favoured the accused? And why didn't you ask Dr Dohare about this report as you recorded his statement?'

Kaul's reply set the tone for what was to come. He denied the suggestion that he had suppressed the report because it favoured the Talwars. 'When I wrote Dr Dohare's statement I did not have knowledge of the opinion.'

'And did you confront him after you learned about it?'

'I did not record any statement of Dr Dohare's in regard to the opinion even after I knew about the report.'

It was the defence's job to suggest Kaul had been manipulative and malicious. It was Kaul's job to deny this. And it was the court's job to look at attendant circumstances—to, in this instance, evaluate whether he was telling the truth. The subject of the 'non-recovered' murder weapon had to come up. Kaul admitted that he had never asked for the Talwars' surgical instruments. Had he seen one? Bought one from a shop?

'It is correct that I did not even procure a dental scalpel from the market.' Kaul admitted that he had interviewed two doctors from Delhi's Maulana Azad Medical College. But that only one of them, Dr Dinesh Kumar, was called as a witness. Dr Chandra Bhushan Singh was dropped. Mir tried to extract why this was the case—after all, Dr Singh was more qualified to speak on the subject of dental surgery.

'It is correct that Dr Dinesh Kumar does not teach dental surgery but Dr Chandra Bhushan Singh in fact teaches dental surgery.'

'Had Dr Singh described the kind of scalpels dentists used?'

'He had stated to me which kind of scalpel is used in dental surgery.'

The no. 15 scalpel that dentists generally use has a cutting edge of 1 cm, and has to be held between the fingers, Mir pointed out. 'It isn't possible to cause the kind of neck injuries in question.'

As if by rote, and with customary authority, Kaul replied: 'It is incorrect to suggest that due to the shape and small size of the dental scalpel it is not possible to cause the neck injuries.'

As pages upon pages of documents were referred to, Mir kept up the pressure on Kaul. As in the case of the scalpel and the golf club, he suggested that the CBI had tampered with evidence, and deliberately withheld information that pointed to the Talwars' innocence. Kaul routinely denied all of this.

If he had been so certain about the guilt of the Talwars, then why hadn't he charge-sheeted them? And why had he not listed Nupur Talwar as an accused? 'I had wanted to charge them, but my senior Neelabh Kishore prevented me from doing so,' he said. Kaul, who had said he stood by his report, was now telling the court—and of course the media—that his seniors hadn't stood by him. Predictably, this made all the headlines the next day.

The most substantive part of the cross-examination was, however, under-reported. And this was the charge of tampering that the defence brought against the CBI: the alleged swapping of the pillow covers and the manipulation of the CDFD. Evidence that these exhibits had been tampered with also existed.

Mir was ready with his questions. Had Kaul seen the CDFD report on the pillow covers? What did it say? 'I had perused this report. In this report it has been stated that the purple colour pillow cover that had been seized from Krishna's room had yielded the DNA of Hemraj.'

And when did he discover that there was a mistake in it?

'I had noticed this mistake during the course of the investigation, but I do not remember at what point of time I noticed the mistake.'

'Did you make a note of it in your case diary?' asked Mir.

'I did not mention this in the case diary.'

'Did you inform anyone when you discovered the mistake?'

'I did not enter into any correspondence with anybody.'

'Why?'

'Because I thought that when the expert [the CDFD scientist Prasad] testifies before this honourable court, he will himself talk about the error. He could have been briefed about it in his examination in chief.'

Mir returned to Kaul's claim that he had realized the error well before he wrote to the CDFD. Could he give a reason why he felt there was an error? Or was there none?

'It isn't correct to say that from the descriptions of the pillow covers no material was yielded on the basis of which it could be concluded that there had been a typographical error.'

In other words, Kaul was saying there were things in the report that led him to believe that a typo had been introduced. Like many of the answers provided by witnesses, it was convoluted, but this was the way of the court. Still, there were some questions to which direct answers were unavoidable.

'Could you give one reason on the basis of which you felt there was a typographical error?' asked Mir.

'I cannot state one reason specifically,' said Kaul.

'I suggest you are deliberately not telling the court the reasons.'

'It is incorrect to suggest that.'

Mir moved on. Had Kaul written to the CDFD about the error?

'On 17.03.2011, I had written a letter to the director CDFD to the extent that it seems to me that the purple colour pillow cover seized from Krishna's room and the pillow and pillow cover seized from Hemraj's room have got interchanged as far as their descriptions are concerned. Therefore, the situation may be clarified.'

This letter was marked 'camp Hyderabad'. Had he visited the lab?

'I had gone to the CDFD for a discussion but there the receptionist told me that no scientist will meet you and whatever you have to ask, give it in writing.'

Why did Kaul have to go through all of this?

'The accused persons had raised the issue with the Allahabad High Court; therefore I had to take a clarification.'

But hadn't the Allahabad High Court already been shown the photographs of the exhibits and told there had been a typographical error before any clarification was sought?

Kaul agreed: 'Before taking any clarifications [from the CDFD], orally, the honourable high court had been given this clarification.'

So the court was shown the photographs?

'I do not know whether the photographs of the purple-coloured pillow cover seized from Krishna's room and that of the pillow and pillow cover seized from the room of Hemraj had been shown to the Allahabad High Court.'

Wasn't it really the case, said Mir, 'that the stickers were changed on the purple pillow cover and pillow and, thereafter, their photographs were taken and shown to the Allahabad High Court?'

'It is incorrect to suggest that,' said Kaul.

And wasn't all this done, Mir continued, 'as a cover-up exercise, and the clarification obtained from CDFD Hyderabad in connivance, in order to conceal the tampering that had been done?'

'It is incorrect to suggest that,' said Kaul.

Mir had bitten into something meaty. He asked Kaul who took the pictures of the sealed items and on whose authority.

'The exhibits that had been returned by the CDFD had been photographed by the CFSL because I had asked them to do so. I needed the photographs for my investigation, but I did not place any of them on record . . . They were not relied-upon documents.'

Now that Kaul had admitted that the photographs were taken on his orders, it was time for Mir to bring on the heavy artillery. He produced a certified copy of the counter-affidavit that the CBI had filed before the Supreme Court. In its annexures were copies of the photographs, in colour.

Mir asked Kaul whether he had filed the affidavit and the photographs.

'I had filed my counter-affidavit . . . Without seeing the original photographs, I cannot say whether their copies had been filed by me along with it.'

Kaul simply refused to answer any questions about the affidavit or the photographs he had attached. The court recorded:

> Counsel for the accused has specifically sought attention of the witness to the copies of the photographs which had been supplied to the accused along with the counter affidavit and upon seeing the same, witness states that he can say nothing about the coloured photographs at all.

Mir moved forward for a final thrust: 'The photographs that were placed on record before the Supreme Court were not placed on record before this honourable court because upon doing so, the tampering done by the CBI would have been caught!'

Kaul said: 'It is incorrect to suggest this.'

\*\*\*

Tanveer Ahmed Mir was pretty satisfied with his cross-examination. It had taken the best part of four days, but he believed he had done enough. He thought he had succeeded in challenging not just the facts that the CBI had presented. He felt he had, through the evasiveness that he was able to elicit from Kaul, made a good case for sinister intent. The motives for this intent were never his concern. These may have exercised the mind of the observer, but the only person who really knew them was Kaul himself. Why would he be silent on the photographs of the pillow covers? Why wouldn't he say exactly when he figured out there was a typo? Why would he say his seniors had tried to prevent him from going the distance in this case?

But these questions were irrelevant to the issue at hand: the guilt or innocence of the Talwars. The proof of guilt, in a court adjudicating on the basis of circumstantial evidence, could only be arrived at if the *whole* story was told. No gaps. Of the five days that Kaul had been in court, he had had the chance to tell that story—the story of the time just past midnight on 15–16 May 2008—on the first day. He had not done so. And Mir, with his relentless questioning of Kaul's methods and intent, had prevented him from doing so over the best part of the next four days.

The 'gaps' remained. The big one was: 'How did the attack(s) actually take place?'

A description of this had to have verbs, words that described actions. Kaul had provided none about the assault.

At the time, Mir thought that a conviction was virtually impossible if these pages in the CBI's story remained blank. To him, blank pages were better material to mount a defence. If Kaul said nothing, it followed that he didn't know. If he didn't know, how could the judge? It was important for Mir not to allow Kaul an 'entry'. The speculative sequence that Kaul had would waste away in his hand if he couldn't play it. So far, Kaul hadn't been afforded the opportunity.

So far.

\*\*\*

As Mir's supporting act, Satyaketu Singh rose to ask a 'few more questions' to complete Kaul's cross-examination. In very little time, on 24 April, the final day of Kaul's cross-examination, he got to the question that he had most often talked about during the trial. The one question that Mir did not want asked: 'How did the murders actually take place? What was the sequence of events on that night?'

The standing suit of low clubs had gained entry.

Kaul told the story as if he was an eyewitness. '[Sometime after midnight] Dr Rajesh Talwar heard a sound. He got up and went to the servant's room and found that no one was there . . .'

The rest of the story was faithfully retold where it mattered most—in the mainstream media. This is how the *India Today* website narrated it, with graphics to go:

'There were two golf sticks lying in Hemraj's room one of which Rajesh Talwar picked up. He heard a noise from the room of Aarushi. The room door was not locked and was just shut. He opened the door and found Aarushi and Hemraj were in objectionable position on the bed of Aarushi,' Kaul said in his testimony.

Kaul said finding them in such a position, Rajesh Talwar hit on Hemraj's head with golf stick. By the time he gave a second blow the servant's head moved from the position and the stick hit Aarushi on her forehead . . .

The officer said the noise generated in the process awoke Nupur Talwar who rushed to Aarushi's room.

'By the time the injured Hemraj had fallen from the bed. Both checked the pulse of Aarushi and found her near-dead which scared them and planned that the servant should be executed so that no one comes to know about the incident,' Kaul said before the court.

He said both decided to hide the body of Hemraj and dispose it of on getting suitable opportunity.

The duo wrapped Hemraj's body in a bed-sheet and dragged him to terrace where they slit his throat, covering the body with a cooler panel, Kaul said.

He said after coming to the room, they dressed up the crime scene by arranging the bed sheet and toys.

They slit Aarushi's throat, to ensure that wounds on Hemraj and their daughter look similar, and Nupur cleaned her private parts, he said.

Giving details of his findings, the officer said the dentist couple cleaned blood stains, disturbed the router, collected all the clothes which were used to clean blood and also the small sharp edged weapon used in the killing with an intention to dispose them off.

'They cleaned the golf stick which was used in the murder and hid it in the loft of Aarushi's bedroom. They locked the door of Aarushi's room from outside. They locked the outermost door from inside and wooden door from outside and entered the flat through Hemraj's room, the door of which opened between these two entry doors,' he said.

Both waited for their maid Bharti to come while Rajesh kept drinking liquor all this time.

\*\*\*

How did Kaul know exactly when Hemraj fell off the bed? Or that his head had moved which is why Aarushi was struck? Or that both parents checked Aarushi's pulse to ascertain that she was dead?

These were questions that the court had to deal with. Plausible or not, Kaul used this opportunity to tell the court his theory. For the electronic media it was more than that, it was a script crying out for visual recreation. The various renditions weren't necessarily more 'true', but they certainly made Kaul's story more 'real'.

\*\*\*

Tanveer Ahmed Mir was beside himself with what I can only describe as grief at this turn of events. His case—that the CBI had no evidence, not even an idea, about how the murders actually took place—had just disintegrated. However outlandish the story might have been to those who followed the case, it had been told.

It was for the judge to now decide whether it was possible to explain how Kaul knew that the parents took Aarushi's pulse. Or why Rajesh's DNA wasn't found on the whisky bottle even though he drank directly from it and his sputum was bound to leave traces. Or why Hemraj, supposedly in the midst of coitus, would eventually be found fully clothed, wearing his slippers, with no traces of Aarushi's blood on him, even though the fatal blow to her was allegedly struck while he was on top of her.

Following his narration, Kaul faced some final suggestions from the defence. That Aarushi and Hemraj were not in the teenager's bedroom together at all. That the question of Rajesh Talwar attacking them there didn't therefore arise at all. That he had concealed material that may have helped acquit the Talwars and deliberately not investigated the real culprits. For each of these suggestions, Kaul had the same five words at the beginning of his response: 'It is incorrect to suggest . . .'

And with that, the prosecution had closed its evidence. It had nothing more to say.

The investigating officer is usually the final witness for the prosecution. When Kaul had stepped in to testify, it was obvious that the CBI wouldn't call any more witnesses. Only 39 of the 141 witnesses relied upon by the prosecution had deposed, but the agency felt that they were enough to make the case.

There was a context to this. It was the end of April 2013, and Judge Shyam Lal was due to retire in November. Several things remained to be done before the judge could pronounce a verdict. The Talwars would have to go through a process under Section 313 of the CrPC where the judge recorded their responses to what each prosecution witness had said: he had a list of 800 questions for them. Defence witnesses would then be summoned, their statements and cross-examinations recorded. The last stage was that of final arguments.

Each of these was a time-consuming procedure—the examination of the prosecution's witnesses itself had taken close to a year. Not the least because of the unpredictable nature of working days in Ghaziabad, with all its 'condolences' and strikes. But the CBI felt that all pending procedures would have to be compressed into that time—the prosecution stood its best chance with Judge Shyam Lal presiding. In part, the shortening of the list of witnesses had to do with the need for speed. In part, it was strategy. There were several witnesses on the CBI's list whose testimony would have favoured the Talwars.

Sushil Choudhry, the eye doctor K.K. Gautam had claimed had asked him to ensure the word rape wasn't mentioned in the post-mortem. Choudhry had denied vehemently that he said such a thing, but not in court, because he was never summoned. Sunita Rana, the lady constable on the scene, could be used to establish the fact that the flat was cleaned in the presence of police personnel while the Talwars were away at the crematorium.

Witnesses for the CBI had routinely changed their statements. What they had told investigators earlier, especially to those from Arun Kumar's team, was often characterized as something they had either no recollection of saying or not said at all. When the defence challenged them on the new 'facts' they had revealed to Kaul's team, they regularly said they had told the CBI this earlier too. They did not know why people on the earlier team had chosen to omit these facts.

One instance of this is the testimony of the Talwars' friend Rohit Kochar. In a statement made to Subinspector Yatish Sharma in October 2008, Kochar said he had gone to the Talwars' flat, but said nothing about observing 'wiped bloodstains' on the stairs leading up to the terrace. In June 2010, in a statement recorded by Kaul, Kochar's memory of the bloodstains was vivid.

The defence felt it had to be given the opportunity to confront the officers with this: Did they really leave crucial details out? Or had the witnesses been pressured into 'recalling' them after more than two years?

And then, there was Arun Kumar, Kaul's predecessor. It was Kumar who had pointed to the guilt of the servants before he was replaced. What were his reasons? Within a week of Kaul's deposition, the Talwars made a list of witnesses the CBI had dropped and applied to Judge Shyam Lal seeking he summon them as court witnesses—that is, neither for nor against any side. They argued that these people could not be reasonably called to testify for the defence because nine of them were serving police officers, and there was no way they could be persuaded to testify against the CBI.

Judge Shyam Lal rejected the application summarily and told the Talwars that he would begin their '313' right away. Without the evidence of the additional witnesses, the Talwars felt their responses to the judge's questions in the 313 would be considerably weakened. They knew that going to Allahabad was pointless—by the time they were heard, the 313 would be over. That court was notorious for its backlog.

Not for the first time, Rajesh and Nupur Talwar approached the Supreme Court directly. They prayed for direction to the lower court to summon additional witnesses, quoting an order in the 2002 Gujarat riots Best Bakery case:

> The Learned Trial Court and its obligation in a criminal trial is to take steps for discovery, vindication and establishment of truth and hence the trial should be a search for truth and not a bout over technicalities, the presiding judge must cease to be a spectator and a mere recording machine . . . In case the prosecution or the defence has failed to produce material witnesses and material evidence, which is necessary for just & proper disposal of the case and to uphold the truth

then it is a duty enjoined upon the trial court to . . .
call all such witnesses whose testimony can be an aid
to uphold the truth and in order to impart justice with
fairness and impartiality.

The Talwars' plea slipped under the news radar that day
because the media was focused on the Supreme Court's
decision in the actor Sanjay Dutt's case (related to the 1993
Mumbai blasts). But it was a busy Friday even otherwise.
The Talwars' petition was listed for 2 p.m., but at the 'end
of the board'—meaning it would be one of the last things
entertained by Justices Patnaik and Sikri. In the event, it came
up at 4 p.m., minutes before the closing for the day—and the
summer. The bench had had to deal with 73 matters. Another
half a dozen urgent ones (like the Talwars') came up after. In
one case, a demolition supposed to take place on Friday was
stayed. The Talwars and the CBI got under 60 seconds.

Just enough time for the defence's K.V. Vishwanathan
and Tanveer Ahmed Mir to tell the court their matter was
really urgent, and for the prosecution's Sidharth Luthra to
mumble something about why they hadn't approached the
Allahabad High Court first. But the judges had had a long
day. They moved the application to a vacation bench. When
this bench met the following week, it told the Talwars they
had to go to Allahabad with their grievance, and made the
accommodation of requesting the high court to hear the
matter out of turn.

Their 313 was in progress, so they went back to the trial
court to plead with Judge Shyam Lal to grant them leave
to approach the high court along with Dinesh Talwar who
had assisted them every step of the way. Saini sprang up to
object, and resorted to the language of the street: 'Kabhi yeh
bhai ko bhejte hain, to kabhi baap ko! [Sometimes he sends
his brother, sometimes his father!] They are just trying to
delay the trial.'

Rajesh Talwar had hot tears of anger in his eyes: he had been very close to his father, an eminent doctor who had passed away a decade ago. Judge Shyam Lal ignored Saini's remark. He was furious at the Talwars, and let this be known in his order on 14 May. It began: 'Undaunted by their unsuccess in the Supreme Court . . . they have now approached the Allahabad High Court . . .'

He gave the Talwars two days' leave. If they failed to appear after that, he would cancel their bail.

And when the Talwars' plea came up in Allahabad, it was rejected on the grounds that it was the prosecution's prerogative who it wanted to call, and the trial judge's discretion to summon witnesses to his court.

All of this was happening while the 313 was in progress. Most of the questions in the process were routine, but Nupur Talwar answered one tricky one for the record. This concerned the keys to Aarushi's room. In their 2011 protest petition filed in response to the closure report, the Talwars had said the keys were kept in the bedroom that night, as they usually were. The policeman Mahesh Mishra had confirmed they had said this in the trial court.

To the judge, Nupur said that she had used the key to enter Aarushi's room sometime after 11 p.m. Rajesh had complained the Internet was slow, and the router kept in Aarushi's room needed to be switched off and turned on again. Nupur told the judge that she may have inadvertently left the key in the keyhole as she returned to her bedroom.

She had obviously changed the Talwars' stand: they had initially said the keys were in their bedroom; at the trial Nupur Talwar claimed she may have left them in the door after she returned to her bedroom having switched the router on and off. That they could not remember this worked heavily against them.

\*\*\*

As the 313 process drew to a close, it was time for the defence to seek the court's permission to call its witnesses. But before that, it needed material placed on record before the court, and permission for its witnesses to examine exhibits. The narco reports of the servants and the raw data from the forensic tests were essential. The servants' scientific test reports would give the defence the opportunity to present a narrative that was more plausible than the one the CBI had offered.

The raw data from the forensic tests would offer them the opportunity to have the reports of the CBI's forensic labs scrutinized by independent experts. The raw data was important because forensics is a science of interpretation: a scientist's report is his view of the data, and depends on a number of factors including competence and protocols followed. This is why, even in this case, there were a number of instances where the same sample threw up two different results in two different labs.

The witnesses for the defence needed this material as well. The Talwars intended to call a former AIIMS department head of forensic science, Dr R.K. Sharma. And a London-based DNA expert, Andrei Semikhodskii, director of Medical Genomics Ltd, a private research company. Also on their list was Dahiya's colleague Dr S.L. Vaya, whose department had conducted the narco tests on Rajkumar, Nupur and Rajesh. Dr Vaya also had access to Krishna's and Vijay Mandal's tests, and she and her colleagues had written the most comprehensive reports on the subject.

The prosecution had used 39, the defence wanted to call a third of that number, but no sooner had they filed their list of 13 in mid-June 2013 than the CBI responded by saying that not one of the 13 was of any use to the trial. Two examples: A year earlier, the CBI had approached the Supreme Court saying it had to get the pathologist Richa Saxena's testimony while Nupur Talwar remained in jail—or else she would influence the witness. It then said

Dr Saxena, who had examined Aarushi's vaginal smears, could not be found and so could not depose. Now it told the court that she was abroad and it would waste everyone's time if she was summoned. And since the narco reports were not relied upon, Dr Vaya was of no use either.

The court chopped the Talwars' list down to seven. Their lawyers were not happy with this. Dr Vaya and Dr Saxena were among the casualties. The Talwars didn't challenge Judge Shyam Lal's order. The pruning of their witness list was a mild setback. The Talwars' pariah status, thanks to the stories about them, made it difficult to find anyone to speak on their behalf. Dinesh Talwar told me, 'No one wants to get involved . . .'

But Rajesh and Nupur's bigger problem was that Judge Shyam Lal had also rejected the application for placing on record the narco test reports of the servants and the raw data of the DNA examination, holding that the CBI was right when it said this was yet another attempt by the Talwars to delay 'the justice'.

Everyone was looking at the calendar. It was June. Judge Shyam Lal retired in November.

***

For the next two months, two stories ran parallel. One was taking place in Ghaziabad, where defence witnesses were being examined. The other, in Allahabad, where the Talwars were compelled to go—once again—because of Judge Shyam Lal's latest rejection.

The first witnesses for the defence appeared on 20 June. Rajendra Kaul, a friend of the Talwars, told the court that he found the parents grieving when he arrived at their flat on the morning after the murders.

The second witness, Dr Amulya Chaddha, carried the answer to an extremely relevant question in his pocket.

The question was: Why weren't the Talwars ever asked to hand over their surgical scalpels? The object told the answer best, and Dr Chaddha, a veteran dentist, produced two dental scalpels. They had tiny cutting surfaces (1 cm and 3 cm): incisions could be made with the instruments using the strength of only the fingers and the hand. It was hard to visualize them as weapons that could slash a victim from ear to ear, cutting through all the tough tissue in the neck.

The no. 15 scalpel (1 cm edge) was the standard instrument for dentists, explained Dr Chaddha. Its use was mainly in cutting through the gums.

'Can they cause cuts in other parts of the body?' asked Saini.

'Yes,' replied Dr Chaddha.

The impeccably mannered and graceful octogenarian Dr Urmila Sharma was next. She was a gynaecologist who had known the Talwars for about a decade and, even though she wasn't close to them, she had agreed to testify on their behalf. Her aged legs, Dr Sharma said, wouldn't be able to take the strain of standing through her deposition. Judge Shyam Lal immediately ordered a chair.

Dr Sharma's deposition was meant to counter Dr Dohare. She explained the normal discharges in girls that age. And that these wouldn't stick to the walls of the vagina unless it was infected. Finding traces of the discharge at the mouth of the vagina and not in its walls was not, therefore, 'strange', as Dohare had put it.

In his final statement to Kaul, Dohare had gone as far as to say that Aarushi's vagina was so dilated that her cervix was visible. At the trial he retracted the cervix bit, but the rest remained.

Dr Sharma countered Dohare's observation, saying that after death the vaginal canal could not be seen unless an examiner used an instrument.

'And what if the girl's hymen is ruptured and she is used to sexual intercourse and her vagina is cleaned after her death? Will it not remain open?' asked Saini.

'The mouth of the vagina will still not remain open,' said Dr Sharma.

'And what if force is used after rigor mortis has set in?'

'It may remain open but there will be injury marks.'

The day the gynaecologist deposed, the Talwars also submitted a report compiled by Dr R.K. Sharma, the former AIIMS forensic scientist. Dr Sharma's report focused on the alleged murder weapons. He had studied golf club injuries reported from all over the world, the kind of swings which caused them and the space required. The fractures that were found on the victims and the nature of the cuts to the neck were impossible to inflict with a golf club and a scalpel, he said. And there wasn't enough space in Aarushi's room to swing a club to inflict the fatal blows. He also weighed in to buttress the gynaecologist's view.

In his testimony Dr R.K. Sharma said that Dohare had no business writing 'no abnormality detected' in the post-mortem report. And that if the vaginal cavity is interfered with after death then 'one is bound to see bruises, lacerations, tears which would be clearly visible during the post-mortem'.

At the end of June, Dr R.K. Sharma's testimony came to an abrupt halt due to events in Allahabad. The Talwars had gone to the high court to challenge Judge Shyam Lal's order refusing them access to the servants' narco reports and any additional DNA data. Mir would later tell me that this was the first time during the trial that he sensed he was getting a fair hearing. This probably had something to do with the immediate outcome. On 28 June, the high court stayed proceedings in Ghaziabad, till it adjudicated on what was to be done about the documents.

Within a week, and much to the relief of the prosecution, the high court decided that it would not allow the narco reports. It held that, as a general principle, narco reports could be used by the accused to help establish innocence, but as the servants were not the accused, their examinations couldn't be admitted. The raw DNA data and other material, however, had to be made available to the defence. The order was detailed, and quoted the best practices followed in the UK. Its central point was that the defence had the same rights of scrutiny and examination of evidence as the prosecution. It ordered Judge Shyam Lal to direct the CBI to provide the material.

The high court order was specific, but the matter was technical. This could have been resolved if the spirit of the order—the principle of reciprocity—was kept in focus. Instead, it became an argument about what constituted 'raw data'. The CBI interpreted it in a way that it had to part with the least amount of information, and provided what it claimed was all it had. The Talwars demanded more. Over the following months an exchange of applications, rebuttals and correspondence ensued.

Meanwhile, the trial moved on. Dr R.K. Sharma was back in court. But the tone of what had started out as scrutiny of a serious scientific report by an expert had now changed. Sharma had said he had studied both the khukri and the golf club to understand how each might cause injury.

Saini asked: 'How do you know so much about the khukri? Were you trained to use it?'

And: 'You have studied injuries due to golf swings, but have you studied swingless injuries?'

This was a court, so Dr Sharma had to reply to every question, but he couldn't help the odd ironic laugh.

There was more to come from Saini:

'Was it not true that you were denied promotion at AIIMS because of poor character and because you indulged in stock market activities?'

'Is it not true that this is why you had to take early retirement?'

'Is it not true that nobody would hire you and that is why you took a job at a "ghatiya" institution like Saraswati Institute?'

'Is it not true that you write favourable reports for your clients in return for money?'

Dr R.K. Sharma managed to maintain his composure through all this and denied each suggestion. But Saini had set the prosecution's tone for the rest of the trial.

\*\*\*

That tone would be reflected not just in arguments in court, but also in applications filed. A formal order to hand over DNA documents to the accused came in mid-July. The high court had said: 'The right of accused to put his best evidence can/should not be defeated in the name of expeditious trial.'

In a week, Dr B.K. Mohapatra had sent in whatever materials he claimed he had and these were passed on to the Talwars. But when the Talwars sent the documents to Dr Semikhodskii, he found serious gaps in them. Data was missing for two key items: the khukri recovered from Krishna's room which had yielded no DNA and mysterious 'non-human' blood; and the controversial purple-coloured pillow cover.

The pillow cover had been tested at the CFSL before it was sent to Hyderabad. But Dr Mohapatra at the Delhi lab had found no DNA. The khukri hadn't yielded DNA at the CFSL either, but was never sent to Hyderabad. These were only two of a bunch of items on which the CBI said it had no information; the Sula wine and Sprite bottles found in Hemraj's room were also in the list.

On 6 July, the Talwars asked Judge Shyam Lal to direct the CBI to hand over the data on these items.

Inspector Arvind Jaitley replied promptly: 'The accused only in the garb of sending documents to a so called foreign expert want to delay the trial . . . In India more sophisticated and advanced kit is being used as compared to be available with so called expert of the accused which further strengthens the belief that the laboratory claimed by the accused is not a well-equipped one but is a shop opened by someone to please their clients after getting money . . .'

On the issue of the missing data, Jaitley wrote: 'When . . . DNA is not available, a blank genotype plot [a graph of peaks and valleys, each peak is a genetic marker] is generated without any peaks. In such a case this is of no use . . . hence unnecessary record is not maintained by the experts.' It was a 'waste of paper', contended the CBI.

The Talwars responded the next day, and made the point that this was a new branch of science which most members of the bar and the bench weren't conversant with. They attached a letter from Dr Semikhodskii that explained the defence's requirements to the judge in layman's terms:

> Mr Jaitley is, obviously, not a DNA expert and does not fully understand that when a sample does not have DNA, there will still be some 'noise' and not a 'blank' . . . at a particular magnification . . .
>
> By refusing to release this information . . . the CBI prevents me to form an opinion on whether there was no DNA found in the samples or [whether] prosecution scientists could have missed evidence of DNA being present.
>
> Without this evidence it is impossible to say whether the samples were actually analysed.

This was clear enough, but Semikhodskii also raised some serious concerns about the way testing had been done, and the way records were maintained—or not maintained.

'It is suspicious that no DNA profiles were generated from items like underwear, blood stained threads, t-shirt, wrist watch and others. These samples are usually in close contact with the wearer and should have his/her biological material on them.' Again, there were no records.

As for Jaitley's numerous remarks on his competence and motives, Semikhodskii clarified that he had helped the Talwars for the last five years, and done it for free. He concluded: 'I leave the words Mr Jaitley used to him. I have attached my CV to this letter.'

Four days later, Judge Shyam Lal rejected the Talwars' plea for the data. 'No useful purpose' would be served by directing the CBI to provide the information Semikhodskii had asked for.

The London expert had written that 'even with the scarce information provided' he could 'explain the issues I have with the evidence'. In his order Judge Shyam Lal understood this to mean: 'Andrei Semikhodskii is ready and prepared to explain with the DNA evidence adduced.' If the expert was ready, what was the problem?

This 12 August order was unique for one other reason. It carried a tailpiece from Judge Shyam Lal: 'Fix 16.08. 2013 for filing expert report of defence and examination of Dr Andre Semikhodskii peremptorily. Dasti summons may be taken by the accused for service on witness.'

'Dasti' literally means 'by hand' in Persian, and is a relic from the time Farsi was the court language in India. Dasti summons are served to confirm that a witness will definitely appear, and on the appointed date.

The calendar said 12 August. Judge Shyam Lal retired in November.

\*\*\*

Andrei Semikhodskii had flown to Delhi in late July and he spent the third week of August in court, mainly being cross-examined. He maintained throughout what he had said in his letter to Judge Shyam Lal: that he was unable to provide a professional scientific opinion given the lack of materials provided by the CBI. He also maintained his composure as allegations of incompetence and avarice were hurled at him.

Even though all seven of their witnesses had come and gone, the Talwars weren't giving up the fight. They approached the Allahabad High Court yet again, taking to it the grievance that, despite its orders, the CBI hadn't provided the defence all the documents it held, and that the lower court had rejected an application for more material. Could the high court clarify its order? Make it more explicit?

In early September, the high court said that its order had to be read and complied with fully, but it was clear enough. No further clarification was required. Plea rejected. The Talwars were now in a bind. If they wanted the DNA data that was withheld, they would have to go back to Allahabad and file for non-compliance against the CBI and Judge Shyam Lal. Could they afford to anger the trial judge further? They chose not to pursue this line.

Their best bet was to try to get the narco reports of the servants on record. Soon after the Allahabad High Court had turned down this plea in July, Tanveer Ahmed Mir had prepared a detailed SLP, or special leave petition. In India, the Supreme Court has the power to adjudicate on any judgement or order by a lower court, where a gross injustice may have been committed. Mir had made the case that by suppressing the narco reports of the servants, the Talwars' defence had been grossly harmed. The reports clearly indicated the involvement of others in the murders, and had even resulted in recoveries.

But though that petition was ready, it wasn't filed. The prime reason was that the Talwars were hunting for a big-name lawyer to represent them. Those whom they approached were willing to do it for free, but schedules were a problem. After more than two months of dithering by the defence, Mir briefed Senior Advocate U. Lalit. In the first week of October, the SLP was finally before the Supreme Court. On 7 October, in a packed courtroom, Lalit pleaded that the reports be brought on record. The court seemed to agree. The bench of Justices Chauhan and Bobde expressed their thoughts aloud: there was no reason why the reports should not be allowed.

The CBI's Sidharth Luthra and R.K. Saini were shaken. Just as proceedings were about to close for the day, they submitted an affidavit that alleged the Talwars had been employing all manner of tactics to delay the trial. The defence had anticipated this and was ready with a written reply which it asked to submit, but the bench felt this was unnecessary. Given that the mind of the court had been made plain to the close to hundred people present, the Talwars did not think much of this.

On the next day, however, came the ruling. There was hardly a mention of the merit of the Talwars' plea, an order on which might have been precedent-setting for many criminal cases. Instead, and not for the first time, the Talwars were censured. It was evident, the bench concluded, that the 'Talwars were adopting dilatory tactics'. The bench commented on the filing of the SLP at this late stage as well. The hunt for the 'big-name' lawyer had come back to bite the Talwars. There was shock in the Supreme Court premises at the ruling.

The outrage about the Supreme Court's turnaround was restricted to the social media. The mainstream went with the 'Talwars Rapped by SC' type of headlines. But had the Talwars really caused the delays? In the reply the Supreme Court never saw was a detailed account of the proceedings of the previous four months. Five weeks had been lost to strikes in Ghaziabad. The

Allahabad High Court had stayed proceedings for a week. Three weeks were taken in CBI cross-examinations of defence witnesses. The Talwars hadn't asked for a single adjournment.

The calendar said 8 October. Sidharth Luthra, the CBI's Supreme Court counsel, said: 'They are delaying because the judge retires in November.'

\*\*\*

The Supreme Court's rejection on the narcos revived a story that had been buried for six years. The journalist Nalini Singh came forward with it. Singh ran a Nepali television channel in 2008, and said that she had received a telephone call from a CBI officer called Anuj Arya a few months after the murders. Arya, who worked under Arun Kumar, had asked Singh to provide a very curious piece of information: What was the playlist on her channel on the night of 15–16 May 2008?

Singh provided the information, and wanted to know why the CBI was concerned with Nepali television programming. Arya told her that the servants in the Aarushi–Hemraj murder case had revealed under narco analysis that they were watching specific songs that night in Hemraj's room. The fact that the details, such as the specific songs, matched led to the inference that the servants had been together that night in Hemraj's room. A fact that each of them had denied.

Down, desperate and exhausted, the Talwars tried one last time to have this story told in the trial court. They pleaded with Judge Shyam Lal to allow two additional witnesses: Nalini Singh and Anuj Arya. Application rejected, begin final arguments, said Judge Shyam Lal.

\*\*\*

On 24 October 2013, as Mir walked towards the court to make his final attempt for his clients' acquittal, one of the Ghaziabad regulars greeted him. Mir's arguments had become something of an attraction for local lawyers, several of whom would drop in at the courtroom to listen.

This gentleman told Mir, *'Pata hai na aap ko, Saza Lalji ka birthday 6 November ko hai?'* Mir was amused. *'Dekh lo, Mir sahab. Saat saal poora ho jayega unka. Kheench logey na aap 6 ke aage? Beech mein ek application file kar dena overage wala'* (You know, right, that Saza Lalji's birthday is on 6 November? He'll turn 60. Can you drag it beyond then? And file an application about his having retired).

The canny lawyer was talking about a technicality. Judges officially retire the day they turn 60, but service rules allow them the remainder of the month's pay and privileges. Technically, according to the lawyer, it could be argued that Judge Shyam Lal should not rule on the case beyond 6 November.

Mir burst out laughing. *'Waise hi mar raha hoon, sahab!'* (I'm getting killed already!)

A few minutes after two in the afternoon, Mir began his final arguments in the Aarushi–Hemraj murder trial.

In court, the Talwars usually sat next to each other, on a bench farthest from the judge, their view blocked by a human wall of black and khaki—lawyers and policemen. Today, though, Rajesh Talwar remained outside, at the courtroom door, watching over duffel bags of documents that lay on the floor—in case one of them helped in an acquittal he was prepared to rush inside with it.

Even before he could begin, Judge Shyam Lal asked Mir how long he would take. Mir told him that he had about 20 circumstances to argue that pointed to his clients' innocence. Of these, the important ones were:

- The circumstance of grave and sudden provocation
- The circumstance of the golf club as a murder weapon
- The circumstance of the scalpel having been used
- The circumstance of continuous Internet activity
- The circumstance of the wiped bloodstains
- Bharti Mandal's arrival

Mir and Nupur Talwar had worked day and night over the past weeks to bring their case to a coherent, convincing close. Its complexity was staggering: there were ten thousand or so pages of documents. Each had a story. Now, it was Mir's job to bring it all together and tell these stories in a way that they were more credible than what the CBI wanted the court to believe. This would take more than two weeks.

Mir started by telling the court that the three pillars of the prosecution's case of grave and sudden provocation were Dahiya, Dohare and Raj. The trial had exposed that the testimonies of the two post-mortem doctors were unworthy of consideration. They had changed their reports a number of times, and said patently absurd things.

As for Dahiya, Mir now offered a full explanation why his 'findings' were false. He reminded Judge Shyam Lal that it had been established in the same courtroom that Hemraj's blood wasn't found in Aarushi's bedroom. Yet Dahiya had continued to maintain that he stood a hundred per cent by his report.

Most of what Mir said that day and through the first week of his arguments was already on record. From what had been heard in court, it was clear that neither the golf club nor the scalpel could have been the murder weapon. It was also clear that they had been foisted on the accused because of the story that Dahiya, Dohare and Raj had written under Kaul's direction. The golf clubs were tampered with in Kaul's office, and the scalpel was never produced.

Mir pointed out that the experts who had testified for the prosecution could not explain why the odd Internet activity that occurred on the night of the murders had continued through the next day when the house was full of people and no one was using the computer. Again, Mir pointed out, Kaul had deliberately not seized the Talwars' router because an examination of this would reveal the truth about what happened. The experts the CBI brought in to testify also admitted that the Internet logs were incomplete and that there could be at least seven reasons why start/stop activity could take place. Not just the one that the CBI was arguing: that the Talwars were awake and physically switched the router on and off as they used the Internet.

He also argued that the bloodstains on the staircase, which implied that Hemraj's body had been taken upstairs from Aarushi's bedroom, were an invention by Kaul, who pressured Rajesh Talwar's friends to testify against him. The testimonies of Dr Varshney and Dr Kochar were countered by nine other prosecution witnesses, including the highest-ranking police officer on the scene. And the one mysterious police officer, Inspector Akhilesh, who was allegedly told about the stains by the two friends, was never called to testify. How could the court know for sure that Kochar and Varshney were telling the truth or just repeating what Kaul asked them to?

And what reliance could be placed on the testimony of a witness who begins by saying she is telling the court what 'has been taught/explained' to her? Bharti Mandal's simple statement that she 'touched the outermost door and it would not open' as she arrived at the flat, and that it opened once she had returned with the keys Nupur Talwar had thrown down, was at the heart of this case. If the Talwars' outermost door was locked from the inside, then no outsider could have committed the murders. But Bharti Mandal had been 'taught' to say this, argued Mir.

While the judge appeared to listen intently to Mir's arguments, he would periodically ask: '*Aur kitna baaki, Mir sahab, khatam keejiye . . .*' (How much more to go, Mir sahab, finish it off).

Mir felt pressure from the judge to move things faster while his anxious clients wanted every possible avenue of acquittal explored. He would speak continuously for about four hours every day, a punishing schedule set by the court with an eye on the calendar. But Mir's passion was unflagging. In the face of everything he had gone through in this case—the pile of rejections from various courts, the sordid environment of Ghaziabad—he always gave the impression that he really, dearly, wanted to win this case.

Mir had made his point that the weapons alleged to have been used were improbable, to say the least, and the actual sequence of the assaults offered by the CBI was absurd. He now moved on to the question of tampering with the evidence. For these, the examples were numerous: the most blatant, said Mir, was the swapping of the pillow covers and the subsequent typo clarification. He submitted a chart that compared the original labels with what was scribbled on scraps of paper over photographs of the exhibits and passed off as genuine. The discrepancies were obvious. Pictures taken at the crime scene were tampered with to such an extent that events from the future could be seen in some photographs. It wasn't the Talwars' conduct that was suspect, argued Mir, it was the CBI's.

Through the first part of his arguments Mir had tried to establish that his clients had not committed the murders. But ask anyone who's heard anything about the case, and they will ask: Well, if not the parents, then who? Although Mir maintained that the burden wasn't upon him to prove who might have committed the murders if his clients had not, the question hung in the courtroom every day. Deep into his final arguments, Mir chose to answer it.

To establish his alternative hypothesis, Mir had to go back to the records of the initial days of the investigation: the closely held case diaries and the more accessible court records. He argued that the CBI had found enough evidence against Krishna and then Rajkumar and Vijay Mandal in 2008.

Mir read out the magistrate's order of 17 June to extend Krishna's remand: 'CBI has produced the case diary, which has been perused by this court, the statements contained in the case diaries have also been perused . . . Accused Krishna has admitted and confessed to be involved in the double murders . . . In the night of 15.05.2008, at around 12.00 he had gone to meet Hemraj. He has also admitted that he can get recovered the mobile phone of Aarushi.'

Mir also read out the magistrate's order of 27 June regarding Rajkumar's arrest: 'Case diary has been perused. The statement of accused [Rajkumar] has also been perused, in which he confessed that he switched off Aarushi's mobile phone, broke it and concealed it, which he can get recovered. He can also get recovered Hemraj's mobile.'

Mir now turned to Saini. On 11 July 2008, the day Vijay Mandal was arrested, Saini had made an appearance in court to argue for the CBI that Rajesh Talwar should be released. Under Section 169 of the CrPC, if an investigating agency does not find evidence against a suspect it has in custody, it can apply for his release.

'Vijay Kumar and special prosecutor R.K. Saini . . . mentioned that during the course of the investigation and upon examination of scientific evidence, fingerprints, shoe prints, footprints, clothes, palm prints etc., the aforesaid evidence could not connect Rajesh Talwar with the crime, therefore his immediate release from custody is sought.'

The magistrate had agreed fully, said Mir.

The CBI had the evidence, said Mir, they didn't do anything about it: they did not even bother to find out what clothes these men were wearing. When the forensic reports came in, they failed to see the evidence. And to hide their connivance and incompetence, they victimized the Talwars.

*\*\*\**

When Mir closed his arguments on 12 November, he had pointed to the involvement of others, but the question of how the assault took place if others were responsible remained open.

Mir didn't go into this for two reasons: it was the defence's job to raise reasonable doubt, and point to the strong possibility of others being involved; second, painting a picture of the assault as if he was an eyewitness never crossed his mind. That was Dahiya's and Kaul's territory, uncharted where most of the population is concerned.

Usually, the prosecution rebuts every argument made by the defence and submits counterarguments. R.K. Saini was looking at 212 pages of final arguments from Mir, and he was looking at the judge. And everyone was looking at the calendar: 12 November. Judge Shyam Lal would be in court till the 30th.

The judge told Saini a written rebuttal was not necessary. Saini spoke for 20 minutes to counter Mir. By the end reporters had poured into the courtroom, climbing over each other, and anyone else who was in the way, to get to Saini. Saini was telling them the last part of the story: '*Aur Rajesh Talwar peeta raha aur saath saath DNA dhulta raha . . . uske baad poori raat yeh dono pornographic films dekhte rahe . . .*' (And Rajesh Talwar kept drinking, and the dripping whisky wiped off traces of DNA from the bottle . . . after that the two of them watched porn all night).

*\*\*\**

The whole truth is a luxury. In case you are looking for it, a courtroom isn't the place to either start or end the search.

All that a court does is reduce the number of ways a story can be told to two: plausible or implausible. The choice is made easier by these limits, the truth is not.

On Monday, 25 November a huge press contingent arrived early at the Ghaziabad court to finally relay the truth to their expectant audiences. The other big story at the time was the Tarun Tejpal sexual assault case, but for that day the electronic media looked away from it.

Cameras, lined up like horses chomping at the bit, were restrained by a thick rope usually meant for convicts that the UP police had thoughtfully carried with them. Journalists climbed on to every available tree for better vantage, booked their slots on the top of every strategic wall. And waited at a distance. For that day, the walled courtyard which houses the special CBI court was out of bounds even for reporters like me who only took notes.

I wandered about slightly aimlessly, and finally climbed on to the deserted roof of the empty court building opposite where the action was. As I looked down from there, the crowd appeared to me like a single animal. It had hundreds of eyes and appendages, all of which periodically reached out in the same direction as the animal grunted and roared.

Television reporting, in the circumstances that most of India's visual journalists find themselves in, is punishing physical work in an environment of intense competition. The pressure is unrelenting: even the long periods of waiting demand alertness. And then, there are the bosses back at the studio, who not only expect you to scythe through the crowd to get the byte, but also 'cut through the clutter' as you tell the story.

Through that day, by accosting just about anyone who emerged through the narrow gate of the courtyard, the byte was available. But there was no story. As the day wore on, patience was running low.

Sometime after 3.30 p.m., there was a sudden chorus that echoed off every wall in the Ghaziabad premises: 'Doshi karaar! Saza kal!' (Guilty! Sentence tomorrow!) The verdict was supposed to have come in the first half of the day, so there were many false alarms: bouts of whooping, running, climbing down from trees—and climbing back up. Now, Judge Shyam Lal had finally spoken.

On every important day through the trial, Advocate Naresh Yadav ensured he got out of the court first and ran towards the cameras. Yadav was a willing 'accostee', and was on television more often than any other lawyer in the trial. But his connection with it was tenuous: he claimed to represent Hemraj's family, who played no part in the case before Judge Shyam Lal. Yadav usually walked confidently into the mouth of the media, but on important days, and today was as important as it got, he would be caromed around like a billiard ball disobeying the laws of physics. As he struggled to find standing room, his black lawyer's jacket was almost pulled off him. He might even have lost some hair. 'Doshi karaar! Saza kal!' he manfully kept screaming for the cameras.

I found myself wondering why anyone would subject themselves to frequent assaults the way Yadav did. I had met him, in the sweltering heat of his chamber, early in the trial. His shirt unbuttoned, he was leaning forward to let the sweat drip while explaining to a hanger-on that the secret of his fair complexion was a daily dose of dry fruits and milk. Above his chamber, opposite the court post office, hung a large signboard with a portrait of his. It described him as a 'nationally renowned advocate'.

Others emerged. Lawyers for each side. Lawyers for no side, court staff and policemen. On the faces of the Talwar family—Nupur's aged parents, Rajesh's brother Dinesh and many others who had negotiated their way through the deep wall of reporters at the court's entrance—there was bewilderment. Inside the court, the Talwars had broken down as they heard the judge. They were taken into custody immediately. They released a brief statement saying they were disappointed—and innocent. The sentence would be announced the next day. The CBI had asked for the death penalty.

Judge Shyam Lal's 210-page judgement would also be made public on the 26th. This was an eagerly awaited document, because it was expected to have the 'whole truth'.

\*\*\*

Tanveer Ahmed Mir had argued that there were at least 19 circumstances that pointed to the Talwars' innocence; Judge Shyam Lal listed 26 that confirmed their guilt.

With its Latin, French and a version of English, the text was difficult to decipher, but as I read it on the evening of the 26th, I thought it was, first and foremost, perverse.

Judge Shyam Lal said his court had reached the 'irresistible and impeccable conclusion' that only the Talwars could have committed the ghastly murders because of his 26 reasons.

1. 'That irrefragably, on that fateful night . . .' the Talwars were last seen by their driver Umesh Sharma at 9.30 p.m.
2. That Aarushi's bedroom was separated from her parents' bedroom only by a partition wall.
3. That Hemraj's body was found on the terrace, whose door was locked from 'inside'.
4. The intervening time between when the Talwars were last seen and when the murders took place was too brief for anyone but them to be the authors of the crime.
5. That the click-shut lock on the door to Aarushi's bedroom could only be opened from the outside with a key. That Rajesh Talwar had told the police the key was with him when he had gone to sleep around 11.30 after locking the door.

6. The Internet was active through the night, which meant at least one of the accused was awake.

7. That there is nothing to show that an outsider(s) came into the house after 9.30 p.m.

8. There was no disruption in the power supply that night.

9. That no person was seen loitering suspiciously near the flat.

10. There is no evidence of forcible entry into the flat.

11. There is no evidence of any larcenous act in the flat.

12. Nupur Talwar gave Bharti Mandal the false impression the door was locked from outside by Hemraj although 'it was not locked or latched' from the outside.

13. That 'Bharti Mandal has nowhere stated that when she came inside the flat both accused were found weeping'.

14. That Nupur Talwar did not tell Bharti Mandal about the murders when she reached the flat, and deliberately told her that Hemraj had gone to fetch milk . . . 'This lack of spontaneity is relevant . . .'

15. That the clothes of the accused were not found soaked in blood.

16. That no outsider will dare take Hemraj to the terrace in a severely injured condition and then try and find a lock to be placed on the door.

17. 'It is not possible that any outsider(s) after committing the murders will muster the courage to take Scotch whisky knowing that the parents of the deceased Aarushi are in the nearby room . . . his top priority will be to run away . . .'

18. No outsider will bother to take Hemraj's body to the terrace. Moreover, a single person cannot take the body to the terrace.

19. 'The door to the terrace was never locked prior to

the occurrence . . . the accused did not give any key . . . to the police despite being asked.'

20. That the Talwars had told the court Hemraj had started locking the terrace 8–10 days before because workers had started taking water from the tank, and that the key remained with him. 'If it was so then it was easily possible for an outsider to find out the key of the lock . . .'

21. That if outsiders had left the flat after committing the crime 'then the outermost door or the middle mesh door must have been found latched'.

22. The motive of the commission of the crime has been established.

23. That it is not possible that after the commission of the crime outsiders will dress up the crime scene.

24. That golf club no. 5 was thrown in the loft after the crime was committed and produced many months later.

25. The nature of injuries on both victims is similar, and can be caused by a golf club and a scalpel.

26. That accused Rajesh Talwar was a member of the Golf Club, Noida, and golf clubs were produced by him before the CBI and scalpel is used by the dentists and both the accused are dentists by profession.

In the list that Judge Shyam Lal had presented, there was just one circumstance where the explanation of the defence was open to doubt. This concerned the key to Aarushi's room, which the Talwars first said was kept in their bedroom, and which Nupur at the trial claimed she might have left in the door. Their memory on this was fuzzy, and in the circumstances suspicious.

The rest of Judge Shyam Lal's hypothesis had cogent alternative explanations. The wall between Aarushi's bedroom and her parents' wasn't a mere partition as Judge Shyam Lal had said. His court had recorded that it was brick overlaid with wooden laminates. The judge had been under the impression that there was only a partition, and I remember him being surprised the day he learned that it wasn't. This fact was part of the sound-test report presented during the trial.

Bharti Mandal, found Judge Shyam Lal, had 'nowhere stated' that she found her employers weeping.

This is an excerpt from Bharti Mandal's testimony before the judge: 'I felt some thief had entered the house and that is why uncle and aunty are crying . . . Aunty threw her arms around me and started crying, when I asked her why are you crying so much . . .'

From Bharti's evidence, Judge Shyam Lal had deduced another critical circumstance pointing to the Talwars' guilt. That if outsiders were involved, then at least one of the two outer doors leading into the flat needed to have been latched. Neither the outermost grill door nor the middle mesh door was either locked or latched, so the Talwars had not been confined by any outside assailant, concluded Judge Shyam Lal.

Bharti had told his court: 'I opened the latch of the inner mesh door and stood in the flat . . .'

In the context of Bharti Mandal's testimony Judge Shyam Lal also did something that appeared unprecedented. One of the first things Bharti had said was that she was 'taught' to say the things she was telling the court.

While considering this admission of schooling, Judge Shyam Lal observed:

One must not forget that Bharti Mandal is totally illiterate and bucolic lady from a lower strata of the society and hails from Malda district of West Bengal who came to Noida to perform menial jobs to sustain herself and family and therefore, if she has stated that she has given her statement on the basis of tutoring, her evidence cannot be rejected.

What Judge Shyam Lal was saying was that it was acceptable to tutor witnesses, provided they were from a low background.

The apparently simple finding that the motive of the crime had been established perhaps hid behind it the grossest perversion. To establish that Rajesh Talwar had killed Aarushi and Hemraj because he saw them having sex in her room, one had to first prove that Hemraj was there.

The source of this 'motive' was M.S. Dahiya's report, with its flawed assumption that Hemraj's blood was found on Aarushi's pillow. Dahiya and Kaul had stubbornly insisted that in a forwarding letter written by an officer called Dhankar, three days after its recovery on 1 June 2008, the pillow cover was described as being found in Aarushi's room.

Tanveer Ahmed Mir had allowed Dahiya to stand by his report and not challenged it on its premise. The source of the pillow cover bearing Hemraj's blood was proved in court over a year ago: the exhibit was displayed and its original tag, signed by CBI officers, read out. It was found on Hemraj's bed, in the servant's room. Not in Aarushi's bedroom.

This was perhaps the most critical piece of evidence in the prosecution's case, the missing keystone. If Hemraj's pillow cover had indeed been found in Aarushi's room, the case against the Talwars was solid. But it wasn't.

Judge Shyam Lal had watched these dramatic events unfold in his courtroom keenly the previous summer. In his judgement, while evaluating the forensic report on the pillow cover, Judge Shyam Lal added this line: '. . . it becomes abundantly clear that Hemraj's DNA has been found on the pillow cover which was recovered from the room of Aarushi as per letter dated 04.06.2008 of SP CBI.'

If you read just the judgement, and not the dozens of references to the true source of the pillow cover in the pile of papers on Judge Shyam Lal's table, you would think he was right because of that line: Aarushi and Hemraj were having sex in her room. The motive had indeed been established.

If this was an error of omission, then it was a grave one. But was it plausible that Judge Shyam Lal was unaware of all that went on around this important piece of evidence in his court?

That question is best asked of Judge Shyam Lal, among several others that his judgement threw up.

The judge's summary dismissal of every defence witness as either biased (by their friendship with the Talwars) or unreliable is his prerogative. The forensic expert Dr R.K. Sharma, DW-4 (defence witness 4), is dismissed out of hand, but then, Judge Shyam Lal writes:

> DW-4 has admitted in his cross-examination that in the shop of his father mobile sets are being sold and mobile set of Ms Aarushi was pre-paid and used to get it recharged at the instance of Dr Rajesh Talwar. He also admitted that his father's sister lives in Punjab. A specific suggestion has been thrown before this witness that data of mobiles of Ms Aarushi and Hemraj were deleted by him and mobile set of Hemraj must have got sent to Punjab . . .

Dr R.K. Sharma's weeklong testimony made no reference to his father, or to any deletion of data or an aunt in Punjab to whom the phone was sent. Where had Judge Shyam Lal got all this from? Perhaps it was an honest mistake; maybe the DW-4 is a typographical error.

But the following passage suffers from no such handicap. Judge Shyam Lal describes how the post-mortem doctor Sunil Dohare was being pressured by the Talwars through Dr Sushil Choudhry and K.K. Gautam. Not just that, Dr Dinesh Talwar handed him his phone to speak to Dr T.D. Dogra of AIIMS, just as Dohare was about to begin Aarushi's autopsy.

Judge Shyam Lal writes:

> Although Dr Dohare had only stated that Dr T.D. Dogra had told him that blood samples of deceased Aarushi be taken but it appears that Dr Dogra had asked him not to mention in the post-mortem examination report about the evidence of sexual intercourse and this fact has been deliberately suppressed by Dr Dohare.

Dr Dohare never told the court this. Dr Dogra never testified, so the question of his telling the court didn't arise. The conversation was never recorded.

This is what Judge Shyam Lal believed:

> The accused persons disposed off/destroyed the scalpel, blood stained clothes worn by them during the commission of the offence, dressed up the crime scene, cleaned private parts of Ms Aarushi, covered the dead body of Ms Aarushi with a flannel blanket and that of Hemraj with a cooler panel, placed a bed sheet on grill dividing two roofs, locked the door to the terrace, concealed or destroyed the key of the terrace which has not been found till yet, wiped the blood stains on stairs, secretly hid the murder weapon—one golf stick in the loft, cleaned the two golf sticks, concealed and threw away the mobile sets of both deceased.

A few pages after that paragraph came Judge Shyam Lal's 26 circumstances—his summing up of why the Talwars were guilty. And finally:

> Now is the time to say omega in this case. To preorate, it is proved beyond reasonable doubt that the accused

are the perpetrators of the crime in question. The
parents are the best protectors of their own children—
that is the order of human nature but there have been
freaks in the history of mankind when the father and
mother became the killer of their own progeny. They
have extirpated their own daughter who had hardly
seen 14 summers of her life and the servant without
compunction from terrestrial terrain in breach of
Commandment 'Thou shalt not kill . . .'

Judge Shyam Lal made no mention in his 200-plus-page
judgement of Satyaketu Singh's demonstration, before
the judge, of how Aarushi's room was too small for the
kind of fatal swings of the golf club that were alleged. He
demonstrated it by swinging a golf club in the courtroom.

Satyaketu Singh responded by sending the by then
retired judge a legal notice alleging mala fide intent and
deliberate suppression. Nothing eventually came of the
notice, but it was clear that Singh felt personally affronted
by Judge Shyam Lal's attitude towards his arguments.

For him it was final proof of what he had been telling
the Talwars for several months leading up to the verdict:
seek a transfer out of Judge Shyam Lal's court, you will
never get justice there.

The decision to seek a transfer or not wasn't an easy one.
But it was Mir's line—of not antagonizing Judge Shyam Lal
any further—that was taken. The result wasn't pretty, but
could there have been, given all that had taken place, any
other outcome?

Privately, the Ghaziabad lawyers—and some people
close to the Talwars—saw the failure to stretch the trial
beyond Judge Shyam Lal's tenure as Mir's greatest failing.
They felt this is what denied the Talwars a fair trial. The
casual remark to Mir about Judge Shyam Lal's birthday thus
wasn't that casual at all. It may have seemed mischievous, a

dodgy tactic, but the point was it was one way of preventing this judge from pronouncing the Talwars guilty.

In the end, the judge did just that. The Talwars were sentenced to life imprisonment. Judge Shyam Lal retired four days later.

# Part 3
# The Dasna Diaries

Several months after the conviction I was bound for Ghaziabad once again. But this time I went past the town, down the highway for another half-hour, crossed the railway tracks to the left, and arrived at Dasna jail, the main prison serving the Meerut–Muzaffarnagar range in western UP.

On the short road before the high walls and large gate was the customary shop that sold shirts, handicrafts and condiments made by Dasna's inmates. There were no customers, just a bored salesman who must wonder constantly about the wisdom of a store in the fields that surround Dasna's walls. Its purpose seemed to be to tell visiting VIPs that inmates were being useful. Dasna had many 'VIP' visitors.

Once let in, I was led to the visitors' area to the left of the gate. The part of it that was used for visits had the look of a narrow junior school classroom. It had the standard bench-cum-desks, where inmates and visitors sat. A 'sardar' (a supervisor from among the inmates) was around, but seldom interfered.

Vikas Sethi, an employee of the Talwars, had taken me to Dasna. Although the rest of the family did their best to visit once a week, Vikas was Rajesh and Nupur's only regular visitor. It was important that he went. He took with him small supplies of food, books and, of course, money. This trickle of money and goods was the accepted system in Dasna—and the Talwars were grateful for it.

Nupur Talwar greeted me with a smile, and before I could even finish saying 'how are you', laughed and said with her customary irony: 'We are veterans here now. We're experienced! We are doing fine . . .'

Rajesh was quieter. 'We have to make do . . . what choice do we have? I am trying to understand why we are here, trying to understand destiny,' he said, as Vikas slipped him a few 500-rupee notes.

Nupur matter-of-factly explained that small comforts were all for sale in Dasna. There were inmates who washed clothes and dishes and cooked. 'You just need to pay,' she said. That's how they always were, the Talwars: Rajesh, emotional, his anger and despair scarcely hidden; Nupur, getting on with life—giving it a good fight.

The Talwars had become Dasna celebrities. Once Rajesh set up a dental chair in the prison clinic, many VIPs in the area—police officers, magistrates—drove down for dental work. They were also brought out and exhibited before VIP visitors to the jail.

As I was leaving, Rajesh Talwar told me he was keeping a diary to pass his time and express his thoughts because the atmosphere in jail was choking his spirit out of him. I wanted to read his diary and, a week later, I received a brown spiral notebook with a plastic cover about the first two months of Rajesh's sentence. I sat down to read it immediately. Afterwards, I decided that the prison diary should speak for itself, and so I will share some excerpts here. Midway through the diary Rajesh lists several of his inmates. For the sake of clarity here is this list, as it appears in the diary, at the very beginning.

Mantriji (Mr Khushwaha): He's been here almost two years, caught in a political web, and may get bail now in a few days. He's a very good person and it is probably because of him that all of us are in this barrack. Most are worried that if he gets bail then what happens to us? Do we move from here or do we stay here?

Faujis: Vijay and Vivek: They came in due to a bank robbery. And an armyman in a bank robbery becomes a very serious thing. They operate both the kitchens in the jail.

Birbal: He's from Bihar and misses home a lot. He's in for smuggling of drugs. He's what's called a numberdaar and looks after Mantriji and also some of the other inmates of the barrack like me, Dr Verma, Guptaji and Shashikant.

Jagdish: He looks after everyone's clothes and the dishes and is paid 2500 a month along with food for the duties.

Sundarji: Also an ex-armyman he is the superintendent numberdaar. A powerful man as far as inmates go due to his connection with the authorities.

The builders: They have just come. Some problem with the society they were making. UP has a lot of land problems. Out here one realizes how much lawlessness there is in UP.

Rakesh: Also a numberdaar. Doesn't talk at all. Haven't heard him talk at all unless spoken to.

Shashikant: He's a customs officer in for corruption. Will probably get bail soon.

Mr Gupta: He's a businessman who was caught along with Shashikant for giving a bribe.

Dr Verma: Part of the NRHM scam, will probably get bail by next week.

Dr Rajesh Talwar: That's me. Convicted for the murder of my own child and servant. It seems so strange and unreal, but that's what it is.

The diary begins on 25 November 2013, the day of the verdict.

We could not believe what was being said. He was saying we were guilty of murdering our own child and Hemraj. Had everyone gone mad? For the media, excellent news.

**27 Nov:** Met Nupur at about 1 pm. She was looking very ragged and tired. Wanted to meet someone from home, she was worried about her dad. But the place is so far . . . how can they come every day? I knew once both of us go in less people will visit, maybe not more than once a week. No one can stop this world.

Hope we can meet someone together tomorrow. The things that one takes for granted outside . . .

Want to talk very badly with my own people, but can't . . . It's only been three days.

Cold water baths.

Had to put a thumb impression on paper which showed us as convicted prisoners.

**28 Nov:** Came back and played some chess to pass some time and lost to Vivek.

Met the deputy jailer, he is a nice man and is always cracking some joke.

It is Friday, I don't think it's going to be easy. The lawyers and Dinesh will meet on the weekend and if they work like this then we will take a long time.

**29 Nov:** Met the jail superintendent [JS] regarding something to do for Nupur and myself. He really shocked us by saying that the media is asking why we were not being sent to Agra [jail]. That if it happens will completely finish us. Anyway gave an application and hope that does not happen.

**30 Nov:** It's been five days and this is going to be an endless punishment, feeling quite tired already.

Some correspondence regarding shifting [to Agra] and I hope that does not happen. That will be complete death, in fact, worse than death. I just don't understand why our life is going from bad to worse.

**1 Dec:** Where we were last Sunday, and where we are today. Extremely depressed getting up . . .

Met Ajay and Radhika and Nupur all together just now. For some time it felt that we were meeting together somewhere till one comes back to the barrack and reality hits you again.

Supposed to have had some good food today because Dr Yadav is leaving tomorrow.

**3 Dec:** Still can't understand how this happened to us. If only I would have gotten up . . . I could not even save my dear Aaru. Very difficult to live without her.

Met with the JS along with Nupur and Mantriji. He promised he would let us do some work at the hospital.

He was talking about exactly what happened that night. Told him about what the first team had said, about the narco etc. He also found the whole honour killing thing very vague.

**4 Dec:** Ajay and Dinesh will come tomorrow. I hope Dinesh is not too negative. Just can't understand God's ways.

**5 Dec:** I should be able to start the dental clinic in a day or two but still nothing for Nupur to do. How will she pass the time?

**7 Dec:** Went off to the hospital to arrange for a few things there. Got X-ray installed and meanwhile got a call for meeting Nupur. Waited for at least one hour before she came.

Met Mantriji and saw the place where table tennis is played. Maybe I'll play tomorrow. Could not play anywhere, now playing in jail.

After I came back, everyone got a rude shock. Two new inmates were unceremoniously thrown out of the barracks. That's to remind us that we are in jail and nothing can be taken for granted. Your ego should be thrown out of the window.

**8 Dec:** Will try and meet Nupur. Wonder what happened with the appeal. The complete lack of information and knowing that this can be endless leaves one with a very bad feeling.

**6.10 pm** [the same day] Seems as if the lawyers are not doing anything. Tanveer also seems busy with himself and so does Rebecca. Don't know what to do.

**9 Dec:** It's been two weeks in jail. Tanveer has still not worked out the appeal. Not even started. He's obviously in no hurry to get us out or he thinks that it is now not possible.

Miss Aaru so much and that time and our life. People talk about their children and what they are doing. They come and meet them in jail. But for us, nothing.

**10 Dec:** Met Nupur in the afternoon. It's really strange what life has dealt us. But this is what it is. Just thank God for what he is giving us in this situation.

**12 Dec:** Went to the hospital and checked out all the stuff. Met with the law mantri since deputy jailer had called me there. Felt like some sort of an animal in a zoo whom people want to see.

**13 Dec:** Did the composite fillings of the deputy jailer.

Sapna, bhaiya and Vibha didi had come. Sat with them for a while. They were encouraging and said that by April we should be out.

Came back to the barracks at about 5.30 and sat with the docs, Yadav and Verma. Dr Yadav was wearing a langot and we had a laugh about that. Laughed after quite a while. It's so strange, I'm laughing even in jail.

**16 Dec:** Very cold today. Lot of fog. It will be difficult to have a bath again, but have to. Hope someone comes to meet.

**18 Dec:** This is the 25th year of our marriage and we will celebrate 25 years on the 19th of January. Could anybody imagine where we would be on our 25th anniversary? No Aaru, no house, no clinic, no money, and sitting in jail for something we haven't done.

Nupur said they were getting food from the bhandara and food from the canteen had been stopped because of some fighting. She looked hungry and it's really a shame what God is making us go through. Even looking forward to some food now.

**19 Dec:** Just kept daydreaming of what would happen if the incident had not happened. Miss Aaru so much. Wonder where she is, and what she would feel if she saw us like this. Just no way to prove innocence. No one has proved anything in this case. Just that they are not satisfied by our reply.

**21 Dec:** When I look at the paper there are so many things that Aaru would have liked, so much that she would have done. She left even without saying goodbye.

**24 Dec:** Last night there was some issue regarding Sudhir and Jagdish. Never imagined we would be in such surroundings. Completely unbelievable.

Met Nupur after about 12 pm for a while in the garden and then met the two lawyers Sisodia and Satyaketu. Now they talk about not doing it in front of Shyam Lal, when everything is done. They never put their foot down earlier. That's the problem with lawyers. They put all decisions on the client and then say, we told you so.

**25 Dec:** Nupur was supposed to come in the afternoon but it was not allowed. Hope she manages to eat.

Today there is a special dinner of aloo mattar, zeera rice, methi aloo, kaddu and puri, and after that sweet dish (kheer). Trying to make the jail clinic into a good clinic.

**26 Dec:** Everyone has just disappeared, enjoying the New Year. Not one has the time to see us.

**28 Dec:** Nupur was looking okay today. It's really strange how she bears Aaru's loss. She used to constantly be with her.

**30 Dec:** Met Nupur's dad and mom today after meeting Nupur. Both were looking quite down. Dad was looking old, and didn't look like he was comprehending much. What this has done to our family. We are destroyed. We were destroyed by Aaru's loss and he has completely destroyed us by this kind of verdict.

**31 Dec:** Shashikantji and Guptaji are still relaxing in bed. Birbal is doing exercise, while Mantriji is walking vigorously. The day, as usual, has started.

**1 Jan 2014:** I got up to 2014. Aaru never even saw 2009.

Today is Papa's birthday. Also wonder what he would say to what we are going through. I am thankful that he's not there to see this, but I miss his presence.

**3 Jan:** Sapna came and saw how Nupur stayed, and was shocked. She came to arrange for a satsang.

I hope the lawyers work on the appeal with unity. No one is affected by this except us.

**4 Jan:** Everybody is spending time in this barrack, but they will all go free before me. But doesn't matter, have the strength of mind to face any situation, and must give the same to Nupur also.

Dinesh is expected tomorrow, so I hope for some information. At least we know that there is someone outside to take care of our interests and who cares.

**5 Jan:** Some people and Parminder Awana, the cricketer [of the IPL's Kings XI Punjab], came. They were made to meet me, really don't know why. How am I supposed to react? Obviously some of them think I'm a criminal. This is such a strange situation.

**10 Jan:** Very cold, fog entering barracks.

By the time I get up Dr Verma is up and Mr Gupta is taking a walk, he's diabetic so it is essential to do that. Mantriji is sleeping.

(Evening)

Miss Aaru so much. Can't imagine she's no more. She braved a lot. And she had to suffer so much. I can feel the pain that she must have felt, and it leaves me helpless. I couldn't help her at all.

\*\*\*

## Shyam Lal, Advocate

I met Shyam Lal three and a half months after the verdict, in his chamber in the Allahabad High Court. In Ghaziabad, Lal would be dwarfed by his chair, and hidden by the large desk in front of him. Here in the Allahabad High Court, he just sat across an ordinary table, the kind that could be found in every chamber down the crowded corridor, its legs stained with betel juice, with a man in a black coat sitting behind it.

Shyam Lal smiled. What did I want with him? 'The bail hearing is tomorrow,' he said, 'why don't you just attend that? That will be enough.' I explained to him that I was writing a book and that it was vital that I interviewed him. In the end, he agreed to meet me and be interviewed that evening, in his house in Jhalwa, a poorly lit part of Allahabad that is being rapidly taken over by new housing with charmingly descriptive names. Shyam Lal lived with his family in a part designated 'mini HIG' (high income group), as though galloping real estate prices had cut 'high' income down to size.

A smog of suspended concrete dust from half-constructed homes hung in the air, lighting up only bits of the streets. Addresses were difficult to find.

The house was new, and close to a street light. Shyam Lal stepped out on to the small porch to welcome me. We sat in the first room: the lawyers' chambers he shared with his son Ashutosh, whose mainstay was also criminal law. Its shelves were lined with bound Supreme Court case records, but weren't full. Many of the volumes were still sealed in plastic covers—the classic signs of a practice that was yet to take off.

\*\*\*

In the days after the verdict on 25 November 2013, Judge Shyam Lal exiled himself from the media. He turned down every request to appear on television or be interviewed for print. Having met him on some occasions in his office, and observed him in the courtroom he presided over, I had formed some opinions about the man. He was someone who worked very hard, took pride in what he did.

Lal was born in a village 18 kilometres from Chitrakoot. 'This is the place where Lord Rama was in exile. This is also the place of Tulsidas. My village name is Sarayna.'

He attended the primary school there. It was like any other subdivisional primary school. The medium of instruction was, of course, Hindi. 'But I have command in both the languages, English, Hindi.' He would keep reminding me of this through the conversation, but now he reached for a paper on his desk and pushed it towards me.

It was a court order. He had just secured bail for a client in an attempt-to-murder case; he appeared pleased with his day's work.

I was just beginning to ask him how different it was for him to start practising post-retirement when his phone rang. It was a client, but one with whom Shyam Lal shared a familiarity. I could hear only one side of the conversation, and it sounded like a man boasting of his connections.

'*Aisa hai, brother, isi Holi mein jaoonga Justice S.K. Singh ke paas jaoonga . . .*'

There was concern at the other end. Holi was a week away: it would be too late to approach Chief Justice Singh, as the 'matter' would already have been decided upon.

Shyam Lal, who had been in the system long enough, wasn't convinced: '*Tab tak kanhaan taye ho jayega?*'

'Brother' informed him that an order would come in a day or two—the meeting would have to be sooner.

'*Theek hai, kal main lunch mein milta hoon, Justice S.K. Singh se . . .* He will be seized of every fact. I will convey him. *Mil ke shyam ko aap ko batata . . . theek hai, brother?*' (Okay, I'll meet Justice S.K. Singh for lunch tomorrow and then tell you . . . okay, brother?)

Chief Justice S.K. Singh was in fact a Patna judge. He had been transferred to Allahabad, before being elevated to the Supreme Court.

We returned to the topic of our conversation: him. His elder brother was already in Allahabad when he arrived in 1971. Their father was a 'simple farmer, 8th pass' but always inspired his sons, said Shyam Lal, instilling in them the importance of hard work. He read English literature, Hindi literature and Hindi for his bachelor's degree, continuing on to a master's in English literature. By 1975, this was done, and he began studying law.

Law was his thing; he became animated as he spoke about completing his degree: 'Mean-the-while, mean-the-while I started my practice in Allahabad, but fortunately I got the government job, as upper division assistant in the civil secretariat. I continued there for six years.'

And through these years, he repeatedly applied for competitive government jobs of higher station. In 1978, he got through the written exam, but stumbled at the interview stage. This would happen again.

'In 1983 I topped in the written exam, but in the interview, not very good marks were given. So I did not get the post of deputy collector. Rather I was given job like inspector of jails, district inspector of schools, etc. I wanted deputy collector.

'In the same year I also got my selection in the munsib . . . you know munsib? Munsib means one who does justice. Then my guru was Mr R.K. Agarwal, since deceased . . . he advised me to join judicial service. Because of my temperament. He was knowing it very well. That I cannot succumb to any person, whosoever he may be.

'Even if the God will say me . . . *ki* you do this, if my conscience does not permit I will never do, whatever the consequences may be.

'Nineteen eighty-five, 5th August, I joined up judicial service having secured 4th position. I was sent for training to administrative training institute, Nainital . . . you see the photograph there . . . this one, it has got faded now . . .'

The photograph was indeed faded, and scabs on it obliterated some of Shyam Lal's coursemates. It was placed above a high bookshelf behind him. I looked at it blankly, my mind summing up this man's entry into the judicial services: the clerk burning the proverbial midnight oil to rise above his station. The repeated failures at the interview stage where, to a discerning selection panel, a single 'mean-the-while' would mean the end of prospects, specially if it was preceded, as I suspected it was, by the pathological need to say he had command over English. After three months' training, he entered the judiciary, where his 'temperament' found its vessel.

The Aarushi case gave Shyam Lal the opportunity to write a judgement which would be widely read, one that he would be remembered for. And one that, most crucially, would be in English. The opening lines of the most awaited murder trial judgement in modern India were:

> The cynosure of judicial determination is the fluctuating fortunes of the dentist couple Dr. Rajesh Talwar and Dr. Nupur Talwar, who have been arraigned for committing and secreting as also deracinating the evidence of commission of the murder of their own adolescent daughter—a beaut damsel and sole heiress Ms. Aarushi and hapless domestic aide Hemraj, who had migrated to India from neighbouring Nepal to eke out living and attended routinely to the chores of domestic drudgery at the house of their masters.

The high colour style continued through the text. The victims were 'jugulated'. (At one time, jugulated did indeed mean killing by cutting the throat, but this was about 400 years ago.) The crime was 'fiendish and flagitious'. On the morning of the discovery of Aarushi's body, neighbours heard 'ululation' and 'boohoo'. And though Rajesh Talwar was wearing a T-shirt and 'half pant', Nupur Talwar wasn't merely in a nightdress, she 'was wearing peignoir', as the 'bucolic' maid Bharti arrived on the scene that morning.

An entire document seemed to have been written with Shyam Lal's favourite refrain playing in the background: 'I have command in English.' At times this became ridiculous: there were phrases like 'warp and whoof'; Aarushi's bag was filled with 'whim wams'. And, believe it or not: 'to repeat at the cost of repetition'.

Then there were my favourites: synonyms for penis.

Hemraj's 'willy was turgid'; his 'pecker was swollen'.

'What were you thinking when you used words like willy and pecker in your judgement?'

Lal betrayed a little discomfort, and then smiled and had a question of his own: 'Do you think it was not proper?'

'I just want to understand why you would use these words in a judgement . . .'

'There was no special reason.'

'But you once told me that you think about every word you write, for appropriateness . . . so you must have thought about this.'

'Yes, yes, certainly.'

'So why did you use those words?'

'Was it not proper?'

'I found it odd . . .'

'This is your perception . . .'

'Yes, it is. You didn't find it odd to be using these words?'

'No.'

'Have you seen it used in any other judgements?'

'Look, this is very difficult . . . how can I say, where I might have seen this . . . *kahin na kahin to padha . . . dekha isko . . .*'

'But synonyms for penis aren't exactly common in judgements . . . do you use these words in your daily dealings?'

'Why not! *Dekhiye* . . . I told you that I have done my MA in English literature . . . I know many words like this . . .'

I realized, talking to him that night, that this wasn't about semantics, or about the correct use or otherwise of the language. Profound as the consequences of that can be (we have only to look at the Supreme Court's poorly drafted Hindutva judgements of 1994), there was something deeper at play. And 'command in English' was a big part of it.

Shyam Lal was excluded from the 'privilege' of English early on in life. But he believed he had overcome this handicap. This was reflected in his repeated assertions that he had command over English.

To those, like the Talwars, who he felt were more equal than he would like them to be, he had 'English' reactions. These were expressed in scathing (if often incomprehensible) attacks in orders he passed through the trial.

Beneath all this, there were two things about Shyam Lal which became clear in interactions outside his court. The first was his celebration of his eccentricities—some of which have been mentioned earlier—and his belief that all of them were virtues, that they made him, somehow, 'better' than everyone else. That night in Allahabad, he reeled off a few:

'I have hardly seen four or five films in my whole life . . . My entertainment, my joy is in law journals . . . I have never been on an aircraft . . . I have not been to any metro except Delhi. I have never gone to Kolkata, Mumbai, Madras. Abroad, no question, I don't even have a passport.

'I have taken no holidays . . . my father had said "work is worship". I have not taken medical leave in entire service life.'

But there were underlying aspirations. As Shyam Lal repeated his biodata to me, telling me about postings in Farrukhabad, Kanauj, Bareilly, Ghaziabad and so on, he made a special mention of his shortest posting. It was in Mohammedabad, Ghazipur district. 'I stayed only one and half months.'

'Why?'

'I applied for transfer on ground that there was no English medium school, for my children.' Shyam Lal's request was granted.

Lal's obsession with English remained the theme of our conversation.

'*High court ka judgements nahin padhta hoon . . . dekhiye . . . saare Supreme Court ke cases hain . . . Mere paas Hindi ke kitaabein shayad hi koi mile . . . saare English ke honge . . .*' (I don't read high court judgements . . . see . . . there are so many Supreme Court cases . . . you might not find books in Hindi here . . . all are in English).

'What are you reading now?' I asked.

'*Time kahan hai?*' He pointed to a small pile of papers. '*Jab time milta sirf law hi padhta hoon.*'

'But your vocabulary . . .'

'I have read Shakespeare, *Merchant of Venice*, *Tale of Two Cities*, *Two Gentlemen of Verona*, Milton, Dryden, Shelley, Keats.'

'So you liked the Romantic poets? Who was your favourite?'

'I am giving the reply what you want to elicit from me . . . I have studied *Rape of the Lock* . . . that is a mock epic, written by Dryden, it is a very good novel . . . He had said "coffee makes a politician wiser".'

'What is the last book you have read?'

Shyam Lal contemplated for a while, and said, 'Last book . . . was at the time of my MA. That time.' This would be 1975.

'But newspapers I read regularly.'

He then pointed me to his collection in one of the lower racks of his book case. 'Chambers, Oxford . . . Father

Camille Bulcke . . . has done a tremendous job . . . English
to Hindi . . . here is Law Lexicon.'

Shyam Lal was enjoying showing me his books, but
he wasn't saying much. He was chewing paan, emitting
sounds and smiling each time he pointed to a title. There
were books by Fali Nariman, Justice Krishna Iyer, more
law books and, then suddenly, a book definitely post-
1975, Chetan Bhagat's *Five Point Someone* tucked in
between.

'Have you read it?'

There was no real answer. Just more nodding and more
smiling.

I now asked the retired judge about his writing: 'How
long does it take you to write a page?'

'One page? Ten minutes, maximum. Only ten minutes.'

His lawyer son Ashutosh, who had joined us, spoke:
'But the situation was different in the Aarushi case . . . We
had to use some good words in the judgement . . . We have
to go through that page again and again, so there is no
mistake. So it took some time.

'The difficulty was finding a typist. Because, you know,
in Ghaziabad all typists are for Hindi language only. Only
one or two stenos are there who can type the judgements
in English. We had to make special arrangements. In fact I
was the one who typed the beginning personally. First ten
pages.'

The judgement was 210 pages, and although much of
it was cut and pasted off other judgements, I was interested
in how long it took to write. Ashutosh Yadav, who was
extremely happy to have made his own contributions to the
document, unwittingly let a secret out:

'It took more than one month,' he said.

'So you had gone to Ghaziabad more than a month
before to help out . . . ?'

'Yes, I was there,' said Ashutosh.

I took this information in, and did my best to appear deadpan. Because the facts were these: Judge Shyam Lal pronounced his judgement on 25 November 2013. Tanveer Ahmed Mir, counsel for the defence, began his final arguments on 24 October. Over the next two weeks he would argue on a total of 24 circumstances that he felt should lead to acquittal. Seven of these were major points. As Judge Shyam Lal and his son sat down to write the judgement, Mir had not even begun.

The Talwars and Mir had their own stenographer-related problems and would submit the arguments in writing only around 10 November. (Their typist was also a kabab seller who had got busy with his food business in the festive season.)

At each hearing Judge Shyam Lal would urge Mir to do two things: wrap up quickly and submit the written arguments. As Mir soldiered on, neither he nor the Talwars would have known the fruitlessness of their exercise. Ashutosh was right, the guilty verdict was already being worked on.

Shyam Lal after a brief while mumbled: 'No, no . . . about a fortnight, not a month.' But by then, his son had given too many details away: his trip to Ghaziabad, that he typed out the first ten pages himself as they tried to make special arrangements for a typist, the requirement for 'good words' which took time.

\*\*\*

As I sat across him in his Allahabad home, I asked Shyam Lal whether he remembered the day in court when the CBI had to admit they had lied about Hemraj's pillowcase being found in Aarushi's room.

'Yes, yes . . .'

'But in the judgement you returned a finding that the pillow cover was recovered from Aarushi's room . . .'

Shyam Lal stiffened up slightly: '*Dekhiye*, I cannot remember . . . *har ek chhoti cheez aise* . . .' (every small thing).

'But it was a very major thing,' I went on.

'*Nahin*, but what is the point of some controversy? I cannot remember . . . *iss time pe* . . .'

'Sir, I find it very hard to believe that . . .'

'I cannot remember, I will not give you some hypothetical answer . . . *Dekhiye*, let bygones be bygones . . .'

I returned to whether he was satisfied with the judgement, whether it was, indeed, the best work of his career. A smile of contentment came over his face.

'I have given *badhiya badhiya* judgements . . . *yeh* highlighted case *thaa* . . .'

'Were you in some kind of hurry? You were about to retire . . .'

'Supreme Court asked that we expedite the hearing. It was incumbent upon me to comply.'

In fact, the Supreme Court had refused to rule on a petition by the Talwars asking for a direction to the trial judge to allow them to cross-examine witnesses, asking them to apply to the Allahabad High Court instead. When the Talwars sought a week's time to do so, Judge Shyam Lal only granted them two days, threatening to cancel their bail if they didn't comply.

On 17 May 2013, he passed what was considered in Ghaziabad a 'strong' order filled with 'good words', including this gem:

Undaunted by their unsuccess in the Supreme Court, they have now approached the High Court. The application has been oppugnated by CBI tooth and nail on the fulcrum of putting unwarranted road blocks in the surge of an urge for expeditious trial as mandated by the Supreme Court.

There was more:

> Procrastination is the thief of time. Now the time
> has come to see that the syndrome of delay does
> not erode the concept of expeditious justice which
> is a constitutional demand. Sir Francis Bacon in his
> aphoristic style said 'hope is a good breakfast, but it is
> a bad supper'.

Apart from Bacon and breakfast, I was particularly struck
by the phrase 'surge of an urge'. So I asked Shyam Lal about
it. Where had he come across that phrase?

'I have done so much study . . . I can't say where I
have read, I have read so much, which newspaper, which
magazine, which journal . . . but this is very difficult to
remember . . .'

The press, including the English press, was utterly
impressed with the 17 May order. 'This judge can write,'
one of them told me, nodding in appreciation.

***

In both style and content, Judge Shyam Lal had provided
a glimpse in May of what was to come in November.
The Talwars, by repeatedly challenging his orders (and
repeatedly being rejected), had helped him. Tanveer Ahmed
Mir told me that he had taken too long to understand Judge
Shyam Lal's temperament: by the time he did, it was too
late. He had had enough of piling up rejections from Judge
Shyam Lal, and perhaps the defence would have been better
served if they had challenged him less.

But Judge Shyam Lal's reputation would have to be
dealt with regardless. After all, they called him 'Saza Lal'.

I asked him, 'Do you know what they call you in
Ghaziabad?'

He smiled a smile that was at once smug and bashful. 'Yes.'

'You like the name Saza Lal?'

He let out a short laugh. 'I take it lightly. It was given to me when I was posted in Bulandshahr . . . by the lawyers of Bulandshahr.'

'Why?'

'Because of conviction in certain cases . . . I did not spare anyone.'

'Do you remember acquitting anyone?'

'So many cases. I don't have any personal animosity.'

'Give me an example . . .'

'So many cases.'

'Tell me about one.'

'This is very difficult . . .'

I believed Shyam Lal. Judges tend to convict in high-profile cases because they don't want to open themselves up to any controversy. It almost makes sense for a man in that position to convict. In case there is a miscarriage of justice, it becomes a higher court's responsibility to correct it. Meanwhile, one can at least retire in peace.

But what of the process of a lower court trial itself? The Talwars repeatedly challenged Judge Shyam Lal's orders, and were repeatedly thwarted. For instance when they went to the high court and won an order giving them access to vital DNA analysis, the CBI simply decided not to provide the material. They told the trial court they had already given the Talwars all they had, and Judge Shyam Lal accepted this. The Talwars had the option to go back to the high court to force compliance, but they didn't. They knew they would be accused once again of trying to delay proceedings. By now, they also knew they would be angering Judge Shyam Lal.

Why don't the higher courts intervene? They are overworked and often use their discretion to send the matter back instead of examining the merits themselves.

There were more than a dozen orders Judge Shyam Lal passed through the Talwars' trial that could have been overturned by a higher court. Even if a few had been, the complexion of the case may have altered dramatically. As things stood on the evening in March 2014 when I met the trial judge, the Talwars were bracing themselves to join the queue in the appeals process. Their turn would come in four or five years, at the earliest.

'Mean-the-while', as Judge Shyam Lal would say, Dasna jail would be their home.

## The Appeal

I had travelled to Allahabad to get a sense of the appeal court. The Talwars had been there often enough. During the trial, a harrowed Dinesh Talwar would often be booking multiple tickets for himself and lawyers travelling up and down. The Talwars were never quite sure when there would be a date, or how long they would have to stay.

The Prayagraj Express (named after the holy confluence of the Ganga and the Yamuna) was dependable, but sometimes schedules demanded a flight to Varanasi airport, a rough four-hour-drive away. Arranging all this was a logistical nightmare, but it had to be suffered: two people were in jail for life.

Dinesh Talwar would check into Hotel Ravisha, a mid-range property close to the court. Saini and Co. stayed at another hotel a few hundred yards away.

The court was an impressive nineteenth-century colonial building: one of those that confirmed the belief that the British didn't really want to leave India (ironically, it was built by an Indian satrap). Allahabad remains an important cultural centre. But in that area, it appears to be living on interest on fixed deposits. It was Premchand's home town, and the hub of Indian language publishing in the first half of the twentieth century. Most of Rabindranath Tagore's works, for instance, were printed out of presses in Allahabad. (Yes, there were a few other Allahabad notables: the Nehrus—and Amitabh Bachchan.)

The hearing in the Aarushi–Hemraj case had been postponed, so I spent the day exploring the city with an acquaintance. He knew Anurag Khanna, the local CBI counsel for the Aarushi–Hemraj case. Khanna had been a classmate of his, so we dropped in at Khanna's bungalow in the evening. I saw a police vehicle outside—and knew instantly who the other visitors were.

Khanna was a man in his late thirties or early forties, the kind of age where successful people begin to look distinguished. He was very much a part of the Allahabad upper class. Seated across him in his office were R.K. Saini and Arvind Jaitley.

I was just introduced to Khanna as a journalist, when Saini interrupted, as if by training. (In the context, this was amusing.)

'He is not a journalist, he is no less than a counsel for the accused,' Saini told Khanna. Tea, and Allahabad's famed samosas, arrived as Saini continued: 'He is such a person, he will write anything and everything!'

I put in a mild interjection: 'Did you have any issues with the facts I reported?'

Saini's brow was twitching wildly now. 'I don't read your reports,' he said with a wave of his hand. He turned to Khanna: 'I will give you an example. One day I had been ill and had not come to court. The next day, in the courtyard, Rajesh Talwar asked me how I was and what I had been prescribed. I showed him the medicines. And this man was standing there and wrote all this!'

I remembered the day well. 'The incident happened, didn't it?' I asked.

Saini ignored this. Addressing Khanna, he said, 'I can tell you that we are sitting here with him and this fellow will now go and write everything about this. He will say Saini said this and Saini said that.'

On the evidence adduced above, I can verily say that this cannot be classified as a hollow claim.

\*\*\*

In his diary, Rajesh Talwar had expressed the hope that he and Nupur would be out of jail by April. But he was going by what he was told on visits. The hopes of Dasna and the realities of Delhi were utterly different.

The first step was a plea for a suspension of sentence (the same thing as bail, except that it concerns those convicted and appealing). The preparation for this was taking its time because of disagreements between the defence's lawyers rooted in their collective fear of rejection.

Rebecca John, senior advocate of the Supreme Court, who had worked for the Talwars pro bono since 2011 was to be the lead counsel; Tanveer Ahmed Mir would assist. Mir's involvement in the case meant that he knew it backwards and was ready to go at any stage. Rebecca was more circumspect, and needed time to study the best options.

It wasn't until mid-May that the high court finally heard the prayer.

This was only a plea to release the Talwars from custody and allow them the opportunity for appeal, but the case made out resembled an appeal. It was in four thick volumes, most of which concerned why Judge Shyam Lal's judgement was flawed.

The basic grounds for a suspension of sentence are that those convicted get a fair chance to go in appeal. For instance, unfettered access to their lawyers, which isn't possible in jail. Or the life-destroying wait in the appeal process: in 2014, Allahabad was still hearing appeals from 1982–83. Other grounds included the convict's track record. Would he or she be a menace to society if let out of jail?

The Talwars' four-volume submission went much further, but not necessarily to their advantage.

In the high court, before Justices Agarwal and Tiwari, Rebecca John, whom the bench for some reason addressed as 'Robert', laid out most of the defence's arguments. Mir followed, saying his clients had been model citizens with no hint of a prior conviction, who had turned up in court every time they were required. There was no danger of them running away or repeating the crime they were supposed to have committed.

Judge Tiwari said, 'Mr Mir, your clients cannot repeat the crime because they do not have another daughter to murder.'

The Talwars' lawyers were stunned. That evening they argued passionately about whether they should seek a transfer out of the court on the grounds of prejudice. Mir was of the view that the case was strong: the remark was made in public, and conformed to no standards of propriety, leave alone a high court's.

In the end, they decided to remain silent. They had already been branded compulsive litigants—moving against yet another judge would only fortify this perception. Yet again, they would be cast as people who believed the world was conspiring against them while everyone else thought it was fair.

Perhaps this was a mistake. Because what was handed to them in end-May was about what they might have got had they mooned their lordships.

Judge Tiwari wrote the ruling. Having considered the volume of submissions, he thought it only fair to the Talwars that he go beyond the limited scope of the plea—a suspension of sentence—to the merits of their case for appeal.

He proceeded to agree with every one of Judge Shyam Lal's findings, and added some of his own. Tiwari's ruling said the Talwars had 'dressed up' the crime scene on the terrace as well: they had slipped Hemraj's chappals on him after killing him.

'Prima facie,' concluded the judge, 'no legal infirmity is found in the impugned judgement. We, therefore, do not see any mitigating circumstance why they be granted freedom on bail . . . We may not be misunderstood by any observations made above, as it is only for the purpose of disposal of bail application and are not on merits of appeal.'

The judge took note of the Talwars' concern that appeals are delayed, and set a date for appeal one week later.

That, however, was not enough time for the Talwars to reprepare their appeal in the light of Judge Tiwari's rejection of their plea for a suspension of sentence. There was a difference of opinion within the defence team on strategy and the kind of damage that Tiwari's order might have done to the case.

At the Allahabad High Court, routine reconstitution of benches was also taking place. All of this dragged the case on for the next six months.

\*\*\*

## A.G.L. Kaul

On the morning of 10 October 2014, A.G.L. Kaul passed away. He suffered a sudden heart attack sometime around dawn.

Kaul had been active till the end, and the news came as a shock to everyone who knew him. News reports and obituaries all mentioned his work in the Aarushi–Hemraj case. It was the investigation he would be remembered for.

His former director, Amar Pratap Singh, under whom the closure report in the case was filed, wrote a touching piece in which he praised Kaul's dedication to his work. Singh mentioned the Aarushi case as an example: despite the shortcomings of the early investigations, and opposition from seniors, Kaul was able to win a conviction, said Singh. He had been proved right.

Others remembered him too. Two months after the Talwars had been convicted, Kaul travelled to the Gandhinagar lab with another case. At what used to be Dr Vaya's department, he met one of her juniors, Dr Amita Shukla.

Dr Shukla had been involved in the tests done on the Talwars and Rajkumar. She told Kaul, 'Why have you come to us? What is the point of doing tests for you if you either dismiss them or twist reports?'

Kaul replied that it was his job as an investigator to use what he needed for prosecution.

'But you had all these tests conducted, why didn't you at least allow them on record? Let the court make up its mind after that.'

Dr Shukla remembers Kaul laughing and saying, 'Madam, if we had placed all your tests on record, the case would have turned upside down.'

About a week before his death, Kaul travelled to Indore to place evidence in the trial of Zahida Parvez, accused in the murder of the Bhopal activist Shehla Masood. The evidence was an audiotape of a conversation between Parvez and an acquaintance in which she purportedly incriminated herself.

Fair enough until then, except that the transcripts of the 17-minute conversation were completely different from what was actually said. Courts rely on the text for ready reference rather than the actual recording, which is stored. The transcripts were incriminating; the recording wasn't. The defence spotted this straight away, and the evidence is being contested.

That isn't all. Irfan, the man who allegedly shot Shehla Masood, had turned state's witness. The shooter's testimony would also implicate Zahida Parvez. But once Kaul passed, Irfan changed his story. He refused to admit that he had shot the activist, and refrained from involving Zahida in any way.

Parvez's husband Asad met Kaul in Indore. Asad told me that the CBI's case was in trouble. The transcripts appeared doctored; the state's witness had backtracked. The main piece of evidence against Zahida, her explicit diary, with which the CBI had tried to establish the jealousy motive was also being reread. Kaul had highlighted only those portions of the diary that suited his case. But when read in its entirety, it suggests Zahida was trapped in a situation she was finding hard to get out of. On the one hand, she enjoyed the physical aspect of the relationship, on the other, she wanted to get out of it—she says this several times in the diary.

But the biggest blow to the prosecution's case was Kaul's death. 'The evidence is weak,' Asad told me, 'and now Kaul is no more. He was the main man. He was fixing everything.'

## Vijay Shanker

Vijay Shanker lives in Noida, plays golf, and employs a Nepali servant, whom, typically, he calls 'Bahadur'. An Uttar Pradesh cadre IPS officer, he headed the CBI for three years from 2005 to 2008, and retired exactly two months after the Aarushi–Hemraj case was handed over to the CBI.

'The way the two directors [who followed him] took so much of time not deciding the matter, and the way this matter has been decided by CBI and consequently by the court, I would say that this is one of the most unfortunate cases. One in which the cause of justice has not been served as yet. I'll say that,' he told me when I caught up with him in October 2014.

'This is a classic example. This is a case where everything had gone awry right from the beginning.

'There are crimes that are quite simple to open up. There are crimes that are difficult to open up, and there are crimes that are in between that never get opened even if they are simple cases. This is one of those.

'In this case, two things were happening . . . That girl, who didn't even know what was happening to her body, is being accused of all kinds of things. She was just 13–14! I'm the father of a daughter . . .

'What are we talking about? We are talking about the dignity of the dead. We are talking about two parents. We are talking about the criminal justice system. We are not talking about a P.D. James novel.

'I would also say this: I wish I had more time. This case would have been decided if I had had more time. And I wish that my successors hadn't shown this much insensitivity in this case which has drawn so much attention from society. Shouting Eureka! Eureka! We've got it! Even the magistrate . . . Oh my god! This is my personal anguish,' he said.

'There was both a lack of sensitivity and a lack of responsibility. What is applicable to the media became applicable, at a given point of time, to the CBI as well. I have these very very unfortunate conclusions.

'If a police officer volunteers to give me a leak, it is my responsibility to verify. In this country, journalism and bureaucracy have gone much beyond accountability.

'Do you remember the hawala case? In that case the person through whom the hawala was done [hawala is the illegal transfer of money from one country to another, to fund activities as varied as campaign finance, film production and terrorism], this man was met by one of my officers along with his lawyer, and that officer when he declared at the end of the meeting that he was a CBI officer, the man said . . . "Sahab, I'm so lucky to have met a CBI officer because I want to ask a question."

'The officer asked him to go ahead. So he said, "Sahab, this hawala business has been going on in my family for four generations. Now tell me, what wrong have I suddenly done?"

'It was a great example of how times change. And the law changes.'

## Arun Kumar

After spending an eventful five years in Uttar Pradesh, Arun Kumar was recalled to New Delhi as inspector general of the Central Reserve Police Force (CRPF) in September 2014. His new job involves dealing with one of India's biggest internal threats: the Naxalite problem.

We met at the CRPF's Lajpat Nagar guest house one evening. Kumar liked his new assignment. As a student in Bihar, he had been involved in left politics and had an awareness of the movement's history. The work was interesting.

But the Aarushi case still haunted him. 'At the time, the media pressure was immense. It was like the Nithari case, only worse. In Nithari, everybody wanted to see Pandher convicted. It was impossible to explain that he had nothing to do with it. In the end we had to charge him under 201 IPC [destruction of evidence; giving false statements to protect an accused], because otherwise people would say he has just been let off. And then look at what the court did . . . it convicted him of murder. It took years for this to be overturned.

'Aarushi was even worse. All the whole sex and wife-swapping stories. No evidence, but everybody thought they were true. Everybody thought the Talwars were guilty.

'And even later, it didn't let up. The way it was played out when the case was cracked, even my children would ask me, "Is this what happened? What went wrong?" I would tell them that some things are best left to destiny.

'Kaul was far too junior to me for me to have anything personal against him. Yes, I had warned him on more than one occasion about his conduct, but it is difficult to believe that this is all it took to turn the case. There must have been other factors involved . . .'

'Like what?'

'I don't know. And I don't understand how, after a decision has been taken to file a closure report which says there isn't enough evidence to charge anyone, a report is written out like a charge sheet. Kaul wrote the report, but his seniors were silent about its contents.'

I told Kumar that the investigation his team had conducted was disregarded and dismissed on a daily basis during the trial.

'I had a lot to say about this. The least they could have done is call me as a witness. I would have said everything I knew. But I was never given that opportunity. I don't see what harm it would have done.'

Perhaps he knew too much. Like witnesses being pressured, for instance.

'I can tell you that Gautam wasn't the only one who called me for help . . .'

'And what about the forensic evidence your team missed: Hemraj's blood on Krishna's pillow cover. That report from the Hyderabad lab came in November 2008, when you were in charge.'

'Look, there could have been mistakes or omissions in investigation. I have investigated a thousand cases, it would be foolish to say I have not made mistakes. I was ready to go in for touch DNA [a forensic method that requires only a few cells from the outer layer of the skin, not blood samples, etc.], everything would have become clear after that. But then I moved out.

'But even before that, we were close. We were very close. Vijay Mandal had agreed to turn approver; his family had been spoken to. But we didn't get the go-ahead from the director.'

'Why?'

'You have to ask him. What I know is that the director's refusal to grant permission is clearly noted on the file.'

The then director, Ashwani Kumar, did not want to comment on anything related to the Aarushi case.

## Bharti Mandal

Bharti Mandal's testimony may have changed the lives of her former employers, but after her day in court in 2012 her own life went back to being exactly as it had been. Rise by five, to make her way to Jalvayu Vihar; do chores in multiple homes; return to the tiny room deep inside the Baans Balli slum to cook the afternoon meal for her family; go back to work for her evening shift; return by 6.30 or so, to cook dinner; and if luck wasn't on her side that day of the week, suffer a beating at the hands of her husband Bhishu. Bhishu was a daily-wage worker whose employment was erratic. He was also fond of alcohol—the rest followed a script familiar to many households in the slum.

Bharti described her life as an 'existence', something she was doing to bring up her children. This is why she would turn up at work every morning, often bearing the bruises from the night before. She lived in Noida out of the basest necessity, not to 'make a life'. Even after more than a decade in the city, her Hindi was poor.

She was talking sitting in her tiny, dark room in the slum. The bed dominated the space, and Bhishu was on it, relaxed, reclined. Bharti Mandal wasn't a complex human being, and it was her simplicity that probably saw her through life. She had agreed to meet earlier, but couldn't: 'There was tension at home,' she said laughing, looking at Bhishu. 'I was really upset . . .'

This passed. As it did on a weekly basis. Bharti began her story:

'On the 15th [May 2008] I was on leave.

'When I went, Hemraj would always open the door after just one bell. That day he wouldn't come out.'

She rang the bell again, and saw Nupur Talwar standing at the last door to the flat. After this, there was the exchange about the key. She told me she hurried down to fetch the key that Nupur threw from the balcony, and hurried back up. 'I was getting late,' she said.

'I wasn't paying attention to anything, so I didn't notice whether the middle door was latched when I was ringing the bell. When I came up after collecting the keys Aunty had thrown down, I pushed through the outer door and found the middle door latched. I undid the latch and I saw them crying.'

The scene inside Aarushi's room was beyond Bharti's comprehension. 'Her throat was cut the way they cut the throats of goats. Aunty just held me and cried and when I asked her what had happened she said she didn't know.'

Bharti didn't really know what to feel. She didn't know the Talwars that well; she had been with them for just a week.

'I would hardly get to see the family. They would all be asleep at the time I came, only Hemraj would be awake. And Aunty would wake when I started doing the sweeping.'

Bhishu, who had been mostly silent, spoke: 'Just after the incident, one policeman came and picked me up, and forcibly took me to the Sector 42 police station. They asked me some questions. But they may have confused me with one of the other servants. I told them I am a daily-wage construction labourer. They gave me some tea and matthi and let me off.'

It was Bharti the police were interested in. 'I would never know when they would pick Bharti up,' said Bhishu.

'I wouldn't know when they would come either,' said Bharti.

She doesn't remember exactly how many times she was picked up by the police or the CBI, but it was more than half a dozen times.

Three or four policemen would wait at the Jalvayu Vihar gate. As she made her way home after work, she would be accosted and bundled into a police vehicle and taken to one of the police stations, usually the one near Nithari village. Sometimes, she says, it would be in the afternoons, and sometimes, in the evening.

'They would keep me there for about an hour. They would always say the same thing: say as much as you know. This is all they would say, and make me repeat the story over and over.

'I would tell them that I have kids at home, or that I have work, so they would sometimes show consideration, not make me wait.

'Four days or so before the summons came [in 2012], two policemen came here. They knew this place. They came and they asked me the same thing once again. To tell the story once again. It was a little irritating, but what could I do? So I repeated the story. A couple of days later, they came to serve the summons.'

By then, after repeated rehearsals, Bharti knew what she had to say by heart. There was no real need to 'coach' her, and besides, her poor Hindi would have made this very frustrating.

Bharti told me: 'That morning, I did exactly what I would do on the other days, and in other homes. I rang the bell, and when no one opened, I rang again. I never touched the door.'

'Are you sure?'

'Yes. I never touched the door.'

'You didn't try to open it?'

'No. I just stood there and waited, and then aunty came to the inner door.'

'You remember this clearly?'

'Yes. I didn't touch the door. I did what I would do on other days. I rang the bell and stood there, waiting for Hemraj to open the door.'

'Like every other day?'

'Yes. Servants don't just barge into people's homes. We have to wait to be let in.'

That morning Bharti Mandal had done at L-32 exactly what she did every other day, at every other home. She rang the bell and waited. She made no attempt to open the outer door.

Why then did she say she touched the door at the trial?

The reason the record shows what it does isn't hard to see. It came down to how the clerk sitting to Judge Shyam Lal's right typed out transcripts.

In Ghaziabad, as in many other lower courts, the record doesn't reflect what lawyers say. The questions or propositions put to witnesses are not recorded. What is put down is only the response of the witness, not a Q&A.

In one long sentence, the CBI counsel R.K. Saini gave his slightly awestruck witness a grocery list of facts she had to verify about her arrival at the Talwars' flat.

'Touched the door' was one subclause in the narrative of the first events of the morning. It was part of a longer story of Bharti arriving at six, ringing the bell, waiting, ringing the bell again, fetching the bucket from the stairs and finally finding not Hemraj, but Nupur Talwar at the innermost door.

Almost all parts of this sentence were undisputed, but one, about her 'touching the door', was not. To Bharti, most of the sentence was true, and the gravity of the small falsehood in its midst was beyond her. She said it was all true.

R.K. Saini at her side, she either agreed with what he said, or repeated it. The noise the defence made about this isn't part of the record, but that Bharti 'touched the door' and it did not open, is.

This is the fact that Judge Shyam Lal would use in his judgement. This is the fact that shifted the burden of proof entirely on to the Talwars: they had locked the flat from the inside, it was up to them to explain how their daughter and servant were killed.

But a year and a half after her testimony, Bharti was telling me that she made no attempt to open that door. She had no idea that this detail had sent two people to jail for the murder of their daughter.

She went back to her 'existence'. She told me that a film crew had recently come to shoot at the slum. It was a film about the murders, and some of her neighbours pointed her out to the film-makers. 'There is the real Bharti! they said. I ran away from there.'

## K.K. Gautam

One afternoon in October 2014, I met K.K. Gautam at his office in congested Karol Bagh, near Sir Ganga Ram Hospital. This was Gautam's base in Delhi, the place from where he managed his interests in education and social work. 'I am retired, one must remain occupied,' he told me.

He was a fairly big man, in his mid- to late sixties, but looked younger. He was initially reluctant to speak with me, saying the CBI counsel R.K. Saini had advised against it. This told me I should get to the point right away.

I asked him first of all why he had changed his initial statement to what he told A.G.L. Kaul. Gautam responded by asking blandly whether there was a change at all. I told him both of us knew that there were substantial changes, crucially, the introduction of the phone call from his eye doctor, and the angle of a rape cover-up which counted so heavily against the Talwars in the trial.

'Sushil Choudhry called me and said a girl has died, the family's reputation may be affected. I said nothing can be done about that, the doctors will write what they have to write. I just said whatever they think is right, they will do.'

'What were the actual words he used? Did he use the word rape?'

Gautam gazed at me for a few seconds and, after giving the question some thought, said: 'Yes.'

'What were his actual words?'

'He said the girl has died. If rape is mentioned in the post-mortem the family name will suffer. I said now the girl is dead, how does it matter what happens to the family name? Whatever the doctors find, they will write. Leave it. The girl has died, why are you talking about these minor things?'

'The post-mortem said nothing about rape, assault or anything of that kind. So it was correct?'

'Look, I have not seen it. And I don't know about it . . . But when this whole matter is settled, in the high court and Supreme Court, we can sit down and talk about many things.'

A young boy came in, Gautam asked for tea for me, coffee for himself. It seemed to me he had become more comfortable talking.

'Look, I said what Dr Choudhry told me. Now he got irritated. He said he would have nothing to do with me. He was just an eye doctor. It is not as if he was treating me free.'

Gautam let out a short laugh, and continued, 'There are many eye doctors, I go to someone else.'

I said, 'Your first statement was very detailed, it talked about how you noticed the impressions on Hemraj's bed, indicating several people had sat on it, the toilet appeared used by many people, there were glasses. You went back on all of this in your testimony . . .'

'I don't remember.'

'Remember what?'

'Remember what I said when.'

'So what did you see when you arrived at the scene and had the terrace lock broken? What was the scene like? Did you know anyone there?'

'Look, the fact is that I did not know Dr Talwar or anyone in his family. The CBI has used the call records from the day to say this, but the fact is I did not know any of them. I did not know whether they were good or bad. How could I? I had nothing to do with them.

'I went there because Dr Choudhry asked me to. Even then, I told him, I don't know these people, it isn't as if there is a feast there that I have been invited to. But he insisted, so I went along.

'I saw Dr Rajesh Talwar for the first time the day I went to court to testify [in 2012].'

I asked, 'But what did you see at the scene on the morning of the 17th?'

'There was a big crowd there when we reached. Dr Sushil Choudhry started talking to Dr Dinesh Talwar. I left them alone and began looking around and talking to people. I noticed that on the railing outside [of the stairs to the terrace] there were bloodstains. On the railing, not on the stairs. I saw no stains on the stairs.

'The press all reported there was lots of blood on the stairs. But I'm telling you, there was none.

'Now, see. There are blood spots on the railing, but nothing on the stairs. But the prints of these stains were not taken. So I saw three or four stains like this and I asked, why haven't prints been taken, there are so many policemen, officers, on the spot?

'Slowly, I climbed up the stairs. Then I saw the terrace door was locked. They had not tried to open it. There were bloodstains there too. Means: the murderer had gone up. And I thought, this was great evidence, why weren't prints taken? There were so many officers there!

'From there I called up the SP City, Mahesh Mishra. I told him, you had come here, and you had also told me to help out, but what have you done so far? You don't deserve my help.

'He said, "*Arre bhaisahab*, I had told the SHO, he must have forgotten." Then he came over, and Dataram Nanoria, the first IO, was also there. We asked him, why didn't you open the door yesterday? He said, "Sir, we could not find the key." And I said *"Saale, yeh koi State Bank ka taala hai?"* That you cannot open it without a key, you need permission from headquarters? He was a duffer, that Nanoria.

'And right there, he brought a brick, and in one blow, the lock broke. I had a feeling that perhaps the murderer had hidden the weapon on the terrace. It happens that way in villages, knives and things they hide in the fields.

'Nobody had imagined that there would be a dead body there! And the blood. Just all over the terrace.

'Now I will tell you the real story. Pay attention. Now where a murder takes place, that is where you find a pool of blood. That is where most of the blood is released. Now if we take a body and dump it on a road or in a jungle, there won't be much blood there. The blood flows out at the spot where the murder takes place. Right?

'Now this body was on the terrace. There was blood all over the terrace. Even under the body there was a lot of blood. It had been lying for 36 hours in the heat.

'Hemraj's throat was slit. And every few seconds, there were bubbles and liquid escaping from the wound.'

Gautam now used his palms to show me how swollen Hemraj's face was. 'It was huge, nobody was able to recognize him. Then more policemen arrived on the scene, and I was asking them, what investigation have you done in the last 36 hours? There were palm prints on the walls. It meant a scuffle must have taken place. Hemraj must have struggled with his assailants there.'

'So, according to you, Hemraj was definitely killed on the terrace.'

'I'll tell you. Then these people got a bed sheet from downstairs, and they placed the body in it. So much blood just went on to the bed sheet. It was soaked in blood. Four policemen picked the body up, two on each side, he was a healthy, heavy man. And they rested on each stair as they took the corpse down.

'And now they say the Talwars killed him downstairs and took the body up. So where was he killed? Where is Hemraj's blood downstairs?'

Gautam's words were filled with regret: no one seemed to value experienced policemen any more. 'The things we can see, people who have been around for five years or ten cannot. But they do not realize this.'

'But what was the motivation of the CBI to twist the case the way it did?' I asked.

'There was no motivation, whether it was UP police or CBI. Just that these people had crossed all the limits of stupidity.

'In the beginning, when I saw them [the Talwars] on TV, I may have felt their behaviour was abnormal. Then the investigators started saying no one saw them crying. But to base a conclusion on this? That way, no one saw Indira Gandhi cry when Sanjay died!

'Now, look. What is the story you read? That Aarushi was in her room. Dr Rajesh went there. What did he see? Now, whatever he saw, what would a normal person do? Suppose he had found out about some illicit relations. Would he not simply sack the servant and deal with his daughter? Say he was very angry, would he kill the servant there? In the house? In the same room? Wouldn't he just get him killed outside and dump the body in drain?'

Gautam had by now made it clear that he did not believe a word of the CBI's story. Yet he had helped the CBI. I asked him about the police officers he knew on the case, and what he thought of them. He had the highest regard for Arun Kumar, he said, while suggesting that many of the younger IPS officers on the case were incompetent. He emphasized that he fraternized only with people of 'highest, spotless reputation'.

'What about Gurdarshan Singh? Did you know him?'

'He was a very senior officer.'

'What was his reputation like?'

Gautam gave me a sly smile, thought for some time, and said, 'Medium.'

I turned to a far more serious subject, his interactions with A.G.L. Kaul. I told Gautam that I knew he had called Arun Kumar for help. Why did he need help?

'It was more advice.'

'That is not what I heard.'

'What did you hear?'

I asked him whether he was under pressure from Kaul to change his testimony because Kaul had some personal information on him.

Gautam gave me another long look. 'It is best we don't discuss this.'

'So were you put under pressure?'

'Why not drop this subject?'

'It is important that I know from you.'

'You know everything already. Please let us not discuss this any more.'

### M.S. Dahiya

It was November 2014. A thin, stooped man ambled through the gate of the Forensic Science Laboratory building in Gandhinagar. This was Mohinder Singh Dahiya, who had retired from his position of deputy director, Directorate of Forensic Studies, that very week.

Dr Dahiya took me to the first-floor foyer, in one corner of which was a well-used sofa. As we talked his former colleagues walked past, each one greeting him respectfully.

I began by saying he must be looking forward to some rest after a 35-year career.

'No, no. I continue as director of the Institute of Forensics, at the Forensic Science University [next door].

And I will be reinstated here as deputy director very soon. Government has taken a decision. Formally, communication may come later.'

'But you know you will be back?'

'Yes, yes. They have indicated to me that I will continue to hold both positions.'

Dahiya was in his late sixties, and this would be his eighth extension—very unusual for a government servant, but so were most of the seven he had been offered in previous years.

'You must be highly valued by the state,' I said.

'Yes. Because I have solved many mysteries. Like Godhra, recently Goa, then Aarushi murder case, so many mysteries. Police were confused, but I was able to solve.'

'Yes, Aarushi . . .'

'That was only one. But it was a major one, whole country wanted to know. All police, CBI, everyone had failed, but I succeeded.'

Mohinder Dahiya was a success. He was born in the village of Didlan, in Sonepat district, Haryana, the son of a farmer. He grew up in a joint family that depended solely on agriculture and went to the village primary school till standard eight, and then to secondary school in Sonepat, about 20 kilometres from his village.

Thereafter, he travelled to Sagar University in Madhya Pradesh, where he remained until he completed his PhD. And from then began his seemingly interminable career in forensic science.

Dahiya told me solving crimes started with getting a plausible idea. This, he said, comes from experience and study. 'I have many books in my house. I study. Here I work during office hours, and then at home another two or three hours, I study and work.'

How did he get his ideas?

'It is not that I have to go to a quiet place by the river and sit down to think. If you study, ideas come.

'Like in the Aarushi case. I saw the pictures of the deceased and their head injuries, and I thought these could be caused by a golf stick. And Talwar was a golfer. Similarly, for scalpel. Nature of cut and easy availability. Have you read my report? It is all detailed over there.'

'I have, and I had a question about it. Your report is a theory that is based on the finding of Hemraj's blood on a pillow cover in Aarushi's room. The whole story follows from there. But that information is false.'

'Really?'

'Yes, it was established during the trial that the pillow cover in question was seized from Hemraj's room, not Aarushi's.'

'I am not aware.'

'So who gave you that piece of false information?'

'I was given all information by Mr Kaul, the IO. All the documents. What the post-mortem doctors were saying, we discussed.'

'But that particular piece of information . . .'

'Whatever was given to me, I went by that.'

'Had you worked with Mr Kaul before?'

'No, this was the first time. But we enjoyed good rapport.'

'And he never told you at any later stage that the pillow cover was not found in Aarushi's room?'

'No, after I submitted my report, my job was done. I was only called by the court in the trial.'

'So you did not know that in the closure report itself, this issue was clarified, and thereafter in submissions even to the Supreme Court. That it was clear there was no physical evidence of Hemraj's blood in Aarushi's room.'

'I am not aware.'

'Would your theory have been different if you knew this?'

'No, no. It was a very clear-cut case of honour killing. I have said in my report. Also there is physical evidence. From the photographs it is clear that there are two impact splatters, two people were killed in Aarushi's room.'

'You could tell this from photographs?'

'Yes. Very clearly.'

'How come there was no scientific evidence of Hemraj's blood then? Or anything else.'

'May have been cleaning. I have said that in my opinion this was the case.'

'There was no hard evidence then.'

'I was asked to give my opinion. Now court also has accepted my opinion.'

Two cases don't establish a pattern, but this is exactly what happened with Dahiya's other famous theory—on how the fire was started on the Sabarmati Express in Godhra. Dahiya had arrived on that crime scene two months after the event. In his reconstruction he proposed that the mob had boarded the S6 coach having failed to set fire to the train from the outside. They did this by cutting through the vestibules that connected coaches, breaking the door to the coach and then unloading cans of petrol in the compartment.

The trial Judge P.R. Patel agreed with Dahiya's reconstruction in his judgement, just as Judge Shyam Lal did in the Aarushi case. And like Judge Shyam Lal, Patel left several inconsistencies unexplained. The most significant of these was that none of the survivors from S6 told the court anything about such a raid at all. No one said they saw anyone cutting through canvas, breaking down the sliding doors, splashing petrol, or any such thing. The witnesses saw none of this, but two months after the event Dahiya did.

Judge Patel offered an explanation as to why none of the survivors saw the events that Dahiya's report was so authoritative about: 'Admittedly, at the time of the incident [around 8 a.m.] all the doors and windows of the entire train were closed because of the tense atmosphere and the passengers were not in a position to see or identify the assailants, and that too, unknown assailants.'

Judge Patel, relying heavily on Dahiya's report, concluded that the ghastly crime was the work of a Muslim mob which was instigated by the announcements from a nearby mosque airing its encouragement live through its loudspeakers.

In Gujarat, the Godhra judgement established Dahiya's reputation as a forensic scientist of rare ability. He acquired the reputation of a man who was able to see things no one else could see or had seen.

'How did you work out that this was an honour killing?'

'The situation of the bodies. Murders take place in one location, one body is shifted elsewhere. Cleaning is done. All these factors.'

Dr Dahiya was getting a little restless by now, and I knew I did not have much more time with him. I said, 'In your testimony you said that Aarushi and Hemraj were engaged in intercourse.'

'Yes.'

'How did you know this? Were you there?'

'It was my opinion.'

'You stated it as a fact in your testimony.'

'I was asked for my opinion. I gave my opinion. The court accepted it as a fact.'

'When you were saying Aarushi was engaged in intercourse, Dr Dahiya, did you once consider that this was a fourteen-year-old girl you were talking about?'

'I have to go now. People are waiting for me.'

Dr Dahiya disappeared into an office in the corridor in front of us.

I spoke to him over the phone a month later. By then, his extension had been formally confirmed.

## Dr S.L. Vaya

Dr Surabhi Vaya continues to live in Gandhinagar, but she is no longer associated with the Forensic Science Lab. 'After a point it became untenable. I could not stand by and just watch. I have always been outspoken about what is right and what is wrong. But nothing was done to correct the wrongs.'

At the FSL, it is ungrudgingly acknowledged that Dr Vaya built the behavioural science department from almost nothing into one of the best in the country. She started with herself, a toolkit and an assistant. Over two decades, the Gandhinagar lab grew to become one of the best in the country.

What went wrong? In a sentence: She found herself engaged in a power struggle with M.S. Dahiya. Dahiya got his extensions; Dr Vaya left.

The problem, according her, was the kind of attention, acclaim and even money her department was bringing to the institution. 'Egos were hurt. People like Dahiya made it a point to try and belittle behavioural science in general, because it was gaining rapid recognition, and threatened the importance of their stream of work. Their default position was to oppose anything that came out of the department. The Aarushi case is just one example.'

There were underlying cultural differences as well. Dahiya and Vaya came from completely different backgrounds. She had had a middle-class upbringing in Mysore, and had made her way up in her field casting herself as an independent-minded woman. She never says so herself, but it is hard to believe that her gender would not have been a factor in shaping her peers' attitude towards her.

'When Dahiya was submitting his report, we had a meeting, where I said it did not make sense that two diametrically opposite reports are sent from the same institution. His attitude was "you have sent your report, I'll send mine", and let us see whose is accepted.

'Of course it would be easier for the CBI to accept his report at the time. It was unscientific, but it was the position they had taken. I did not want our lab to simply put out reports to please agencies or governments, just to be in their good books. This was happening regularly where Dahiya was concerned. I spoke out against it. We are scientists, not stooges.'

Several years ago, Dr Vaya met the then chief minister of Gujarat Narendra Modi at a function. He asked about the work being done at the Directorate of Forensic Science and appeared keen on the idea of a dedicated forensic science university. Modi asked her how much it might cost, and Vaya replied that she could get one up and running at a fraction of what was being spent on the chief minister's security.

On a plot of land allotted by the Modi government, the Forensic Science University has indeed come up. It is where M.S. Dahiya holds the position of director, Institute of Forensics.

Dr Vaya has moved on as well. She is now director, research and development, at the fledgling Raksha Shakti University. It too is a government institution, founded during Narendra Modi's tenure as chief minister of Gujarat. Its focus is internal security and disciplines related to it. To get to Raksha Shakti University, you have to ask for 'Mental Chowk'—a well-known mental health institute is close by.

Dr Vaya's work continues. She would like to restore the importance of her discipline as a tool in investigation. It suffered a major setback with a 2010 Supreme Court ruling which disallowed the use of scientific tests to incriminate suspects. The court ruled that tests without consent violated an individual's right to privacy, and his right to not give evidence against himself. The court said the test results by themselves were inadmissible because the subject did not have 'conscious control' over his responses when they are undertaken.

This is true of narco analysis, where the truth serum induces a trance. But the same cannot be said about non-invasive procedures such as polygraph or brain-mapping tests. However, the clubbing of all the procedures under one ruling made it appear that way.

In practice, the Supreme Court ruling has allowed investigators the opportunity for selective use. In the Nithari killings, for instance, Surinder Koli's narco narration was accepted in full by both the CBI and the trial court. In the 2014 murder of two girls in UP's Badaun district, the investigating officer A.G.L. Kaul relied on polygraph tests to not charge some of the suspects. In the Aarushi–Hemraj case, the tests were all dismissed as unreliable.

'The problem is not the tests. It is their misuse,' said Dr Vaya. 'Even if you don't want to depend on them to establish guilt, when there is consent, why can't they be used to establish innocence?'

In the Aarushi–Hemraj case, neither the CBI nor the court had any intention of allowing this. Dr Dahiya testified as a star witness for the CBI. Dr Vaya was prevented from appearing for the Talwars. She remains convinced about their innocence to this day.

## Who Did It?

No one, not Gurdarshan Singh or Arun Kumar or Kaul or Dahiya or Dr Vaya or the judge who wrote so authoritatively about the crime, was at the crime scene. I wasn't either. The only people who were there were the assailants and their victims.

But as the story panned out, the Talwars' undisputed presence in the flat that night burdened them with having to not just plead their innocence, but also answer the question 'If you didn't do it, who did?'

They did not know. In fact, investigators knew much more than them—the CBI had enough material to, at the very least, form a plausible alternative hypothesis. This is the material they hid from the Talwars, and prevented from being brought on the record in court.

This material was gathered by investigators in the months of June and July 2008. They are the reports of the scientific tests on the three servants. A few fragments were leaked in 2008, but once A.G.L. Kaul took over, they were just buried.

Sometimes, the methods of concealment were crude—even in situations where the CBI was obliged to furnish the material. In the counter-affidavit the CBI filed in the Supreme Court in 2012, for instance, Krishna's polygraph examination at CFSL Delhi was submitted as an annexure by the CBI. However, what was annexed to an affidavit filed by Kaul were copies of just the first two pages. These contained details of memos and procedures. The actual results were in the pages that followed—and those weren't attached.

Annexed to the same affidavit are the reports of each and every scientific test done on the Talwars. The scientists' conclusions in these reports clear the Talwars, but those parts that Dahiya and Kaul chose to draw their own theory from are highlighted by helpful markings.

The story contained in the scientific reports of the servants has never been told. The documents were buried. Until now.

KRISHNA'S STORY
Excerpted from Krishna's narco analysis narration on 12 June 2008 at Bowring and Lady Curzon Hospital, Bangalore:

During the trance Mr Krishna said that basically he is from Nepal and had come to Noida 10-12 years back. He was staying with his sister in sector 25, Noida. He

said that he was working and has also written 12th
exams . . . He was introduced to Dr Talwar by Vishnu
who was working as compounder in Dr Talwar's clinic.
He said that Vishnu was working both at Dr Talwar's
home and hospital. Vishnu's parents were sick so he
left the job, Vishnu had bought Hemaraj [sic] to Dr
Talwar's house. Hemaraj was Vishnu's relative . . . He
said that he was going to Talwars' house to collect
the keys from Hemraj. He also had the spare keys
but he handed over the keys to Hemraj before going
home. He said that Hemraj was coming to the clinic
sometimes and was doing reception work . . .

He said on the day of the incident he was little
upset about his girlfriend Sujata. Sujata is his friend
and is married now, she is a housewife and stays in
Noida . . . Hemraj was killed on the terrace. He said
that the terrace was not locked. He said that he had
bought kokari [sic, khukri] from Sujata. He said that
he had kokari with him, kokari was very long. Hemraj
did not have any kokari. He said that both Hemraj and
Arushi were killed with the same kokari and he has
seen it himself. He said that he will show the kokari.
The blood stains on kokari was wiped with tissue and
then flushed with water . . .

He said after the murder those people have thrown
the kokari outside to destroy it. He said that Rajkumar
liked Arushi. Rajkumar was Nepali and was working
in Dr Anita Durani's house, was staying in sector
53 and was visiting sector 25 to meet Hemraj . . .
Rajkumar was around 23 years old and if he is
subjected for the test the truth will be revealed . . .

He says the reason for the murder may be sex . . .
He says that Dr Talwar may not be involved in this
murder as Arushi was his only daughter and Hemraj
was innocent. He says that first Arushi was killed,

Hemraj was killed for the reason that he had known about the murderer. Arushi was killed from behind with kokari and Hemraj was hit behind [sic] the back to the head. He says that Rajkumar and his friend Shambu [Vijay Mandal] are responsible for these murders. He does not know about the kokari used by Shambu and Rajkumar, says that tissue used for cleaning have been flushed in the bathroom in Arushi's house and later destroyed. He said that he does not know where the keys of main door and terrace are kept . . .

He said that he is not involved in this murder and Rajkumar has done this murder. He has only witnessed it. He said that Hemraj did not have habit of drinking alcohol and Krishna was drinking whisky, beer. The incident occurred at night between 12-1 am. Hemraj had gone on terrace and is killed. He said that Dr Talwar had not given him money to do the murder. He says that Hemraj saw murdering Arushi so he ran and tried to escape from terrace route and he was caught hold and killed. He said that after the murder he went back through terrace. He says that there is a way from the terrace to his home.

RAJKUMAR'S STORY
Excerpted from Rajkumar's narco analysis, brain-mapping, polygraph and interviews, FSL Gandhinagar, 23–24 June 2008:

Before the trance he said that he was at sector 35 Noida at Dr Durani's house. He said before joining there he had worked at Delhi and Chandigarh . . . He said he had friendship with Hemraj since January/February 2008 . . . He said the distance from his house to Dr Talwar's house was around 20 min drive by cycle . . . He said he was seeing Aarushi from past two years.

During the trance he said he had not seen any relation between Dr Talwar and Dr Anita but knew that they both had friendship and had seen them moving together and their relationship was even known to Aarushi's mother. He said he had met Krishna when he had been to meet Hemraj in his room. He said Aarushi was murdered with a Khukari [sic] but he did not possess any Khukhuri and the same type of Khukhari he said is available at Delhi. He said one day Hemraj had told him that Aarushi was like his daughter and they should not have any type of physical contacts with her. He said he was in love with Aarushi. He said on 15th night Hemraj had called him over phone and asked him to come home. He said he had been to his house 12 o'clock. He said he had come out of the Durani's house opening the lock himself taking the keys which were kept behind the fridge near kitchen. He said that on that day he had gone on a cycle to Talwar's house which was kept in the garage. He said when he reached there he had seen Krishna in Hemraj's room and Vijay was standing outside the room. Krishna and himself had drinks.

He said he was responsible in raping Aarushi first and followed by him Krishna had raped her. When all of them entered the room Aarushi opened the eyes and saw them and she screamed. Krishna then hit her on the head using iron hammer. Rajkumar at that time he was present in the room when he had hit her. He said Aarushi was having a Nokia mobile phone. He said when she was hit she had fallen unconscious. He said after the murder he had taken away the mobile phone and presently it is not with him but had not taken away Hemraj's Tata Indicom mobile. He said he had sold Aarush's mobile phone . . . and Hemraj's phone was taken away by Krishna. He said the blood-stained grey-blue coloured T-shirt was kept by him in his bathroom which is outside the house. He said he had washed the T-shirt using soap and dried it in bright sunlight. He said they had hit Aarushi first and then Hemraj was murdered. He said before the attack he was drunk.

He said after he had returned back to his house he had changed his dress. He said at the time of attack Krishna was wearing black coloured T-shirt. He said Krishna had brought the Khukari for the murder and was a new one. He said the Khukari used to kill them both was not disposed in the drainage. Khukari was thrown in the open area ie ground near Hemraj's house near a park. He said he raped her because he was told by Krishna to rape Aarushi. He said Krishna had asked him to dispose the Khukari after the murder. He said after the murder he went back on his cycle. He said Krishna was drunk before and even after the murder. He said on the day of the incident Dr Talwar and his wife were very much present in the house and when the incident occurred their bedroom door was closed, after the murder they went out keeping the door closed.

Krishna had opened the bedroom door of Aarushi and she was in deep sleep. He said Krishna had hit her on the head with a hammer and she had screamed when she was attacked which was witnessed by him. Later one after the other all three raped Aarushi when she was unconscious. He said after she was hit they went to terrace. Terrace door was opened by Hemraj with the keys which he had with him. On that night Hemraj had fought with Krishna. He said after they had murdered Hemraj on the terrace Krishna had locked the terrace door and they had come down. He said the keys of the terrace were with Krishna after the murder . . . He said Aarushi was murdered because she

might inform the parents about them about rape her
so she was done to death. He said around 4 am they
had left Hemraj's house and had returned back home
after committing the offence.

On the second day of the test, Rajkumar offered further
details:

According to him Krishna went to Hemraj's room.
After having his drink there, he wanted to go to
Aarushi's room, which was prevented by Hemraj. In
the pretext of getting water, he visited dining area from
where he went to Aarushi's room. He tried to impose
himself upon her and she must have got awakened.
Krishna got scared and killed her and when he came
out of her room with blood soaked cloth and weapon,
that time Rajkumar came there and was sitting with
Hemraj in his room. Looking at Krishna's blood
soaked clothes, Hemraj got upset and asked what
you did. Being worried that Dr Talwar and his wife
Dr Nupur Talwar may wake up, he rushed Hemraj
and Rajkumar to terrace to sort out.

As Krishna was unsuccessful in handling Hemraj
to save himself, he hit Hemraj when he was opening
lock of terrace from behind. Then Hemraj fell down
then Krishna took Hemraj on terrace and cut his
throat. Then on the terrace, pulled the dead body
under the cover of cooler, locked the terrace, brought
back the key and left the key in Hemraj's room and
went off.

According to him, he was threatened by Krishna
not to talk of this incident to anyone and if he talks
he will also be killed. This was a possibility he could
think of and he says all this happened in his presence.
After narrating this story, he said he can say this to

police, but what he is worried is they will ask him as to how did he come after Dr Durani locked the house, and then he has to say he had a duplicate key and he will be asked to give the key.

Rajkumar's narco, a post-test observation: In the post-test interview, scientists observed something unusual: Rajkumar was fully aware of what he was saying in his trance state. He remembered what he had said after the effects of the drug wore off.

Rajkumar's polygraph, a post-test observation:

On completion of the test, he was very curious to know on what issues his answers were found to be deceptive. When it was conveyed about the deception to him, it was found that his anxiety was markedly increased. By the evening when he went for medical check-up his blood pressure had increased to 170/100 which caused concern for the medical officers. (His BP was normal when he reported back the next day.)

VIJAY MANDAL'S STORY

Excerpted from Vijay Mandal's polygraph and brain-mapping tests, FSL Mumbai, 30 June, 1 July 2008:

He said he had seen Aarushi moving around in front of his house many a times when she was to return from school and also had seen Dr Talwar when he was to return from the hospital in the afternoon during lunch hours . . . He said he was not that close with Hemraj . . . He said whenever he was to meet Hemraj they were to pass gestures and had formal talks with him . . . He said he would meet Krishna at dhobi's shop. He said he was never called as Shambhu and were to call him by the name of Vijay . . .

He said on the day of the incident Hemraj had called him to come and meet around 12 o'clock in the midnight. He said whenever he was to go their house to meet Hemraj they would sit and discuss on the stairs. He said he was in the habit of washing clothes in the night and on the night of the incident when he was washing around 10-10.15 his friend had come to meet him to his house . . . before meeting Hemraj.

He said when he went to Dr Talwar's house when he rang the call bell Hemraj had come and opened the door and directly had been to Hemraj's room and saw Krishna in the room. He said they all had discussed about Aarushi and said Rajkumar was not present in the discussion. He said after the discussion he had come back to his garage and when he was going to toilet he saw Rajkumar going towards Dr Talwar's house. He said according to him all three i.e. Rajkumar, Hemraj and Krishna were speaking about Aarushi and started to quarrel among themselves. He said he never used to drink and said on the day of the incident Krishna and Rajkumar were drunk. He said he was called on the terrace to meet them.

He said he was not aware as to who has hit Hemraj and he had not hit Hemraj as he had no reason nor enmity to hit him. He said Hemraj was to call him by the name of Vijay and never had called him by the name of Shambhu. He said he had seen a Khukari in the hands of Krishna and that was the first time he had seen Khukari in Hemraj's room. He said before the occurrence of the incident he had returned back home. He said he had seen Hemraj, Krishna and Rajkumar on the terrace. On the day of the incident he had not carried any weapon from his house to give them.

He was aware that Aarushi was raped. He said he is not sure whether all the three might have raped Aarushi. He said Aarushi was murdered first and followed by Hemraj. He said Rajkumar raped her first and then Krishna. He said they have hit Aarushi on the head and she was fallen unconscious. He said he was neither participating in the offense nor witnessed when they were raping her . . .

He said Krishna along with Rajkumar fought with Hemraj on the terrace as they were fully drunk. He said the Khukari used for the murder was made of iron and had seen it in Hemraj's room which belonged to Krishna. He said he was not aware whether the Khukari was old or a new one.

Vijay Mandal was also tested under the Brain Electrical Oscillation Signature (BEOS) profile, also known as brain-mapping, on 1 July 2008. In this he was tested for experiential knowledge (EK) related to his involvement in the double murder. The report states:

Experiential Knowledge (EK) is present on probes related to him talking about Aarushi (with his friends), watching his friend going towards her (Aarushi), and him teasing her (Aarushi). EK is further seen on probes related to watching Aarushi trying to free herself, and him getting scared (after realizing Aarushi is dead). EK is also seen on probes related to him going on the terrace (with others), him watching Hemraj say that he will complain, him cutting Hemraj's neck. EK is further seen on probes about holding the dead body (Hemraj's), pulling the dead body (Hemraj's), and taking Hemraj's mobile.

Who among these men was telling the truth? Or were they all telling only part of what they knew?

Krishna, for instance, gave his interrogators yet another version of what he claimed he had witnessed. In his (inadmissible) confessional statement, he had the order of the murders the other way around.

He told the CBI that Hemraj had gone to the terrace to smoke, and an argument occurred between the men there. Rajkumar killed Hemraj, and then came down because he wanted to have sex with Aarushi. But Rajkumar was nervous about an alarm being raised and killed her.

(Incidentally, the post-mortem and forensic investigation found no evidence of rape; Dr Dohare had eight occasions on which to say so had it happened. It is likely that for the servants 'rape' was an all-encompassing word which included various degrees of molestation and assault.)

Forensic scientists thought Krishna's version was outlandish. They tend to look for a logical sequence of events and, to them, Rajkumar's interviews seem closest to the truth. They were also backed up by Vijay Mandal's brain-mapping results.

The scientists on the case recognized that their work did not provide all the answers. But they also knew that their work raised a disquieting question. Whatever the contradictions, including those related to the admissibility of the evidence, it seemed possible that the three men were at the scene of the crime. If they were innocent why would they even unconsciously place themselves there?

Unless that is how it was.

We will probably never quite know what happened. Aarushi, thirteen years old, was taken by surprise. Suffering from severe laryngitis, she could not even scream.

***

## Revisiting the Talwars

S.P. Yadav, the superintendent, wanted to see me. It was closing on six in the evening on 26 November 2014, and a swarm of mosquitoes had descended on Dasna jail. This was Mr Yadav's primary concern as I sat before him in his neat office. Nupur and Rajesh Talwar sat beside me. That day, they completed a year in jail, and I thought I'd visit.

Mr Yadav was a mild-mannered man. He spoke slowly, softly. But the mosquitoes were really bothering him. The repellant plugged in behind him didn't seem to be working. He called an attendant in. 'This unit looks like it is a fake. So many fakes in the market these days. Go to my quarters and fetch a proper Goodknight,' he said.

He then turned to Nupur Talwar. 'What do you do about the mosquitoes?'

'Sir, when we have a coil, we light it. If not . . .' She smiled wryly. There were no electrical points in the wards. And coils could be brought in, but their flimsy metal stands were considered a security risk—for their possible use as small weapons.

In fact, very little that wasn't sealed was allowed, and anything that could cut was banned. Pickle, or jam, for instance, could not be brought in bottles.

We were sitting in front of Mr Yadav not just because he wanted to see me. He also had a medical problem for which he required the Talwars' help. His prostate was acting up, and he needed to see a specialist. He had asked them to recommend a doctor in Delhi and fix an appointment. Delhi is a long way from Dasna, so it was important that Mr Yadav didn't have to wait. It was also important to the Talwars that he wasn't kept waiting. These things helped you survive in jail.

Mr Yadav was a well-read man, with a special interest in the caste system. He told me that to understand Uttar Pradesh, even India, you needed to understand caste. He opened his new MacBook Air, and said he had an idea for a study: look at the caste of all those sentenced to death in independent India. 'There are very few exceptions who are non-lower caste.'

I told him the idea was interesting and that he had the temperament of an academic. Why did he choose to become a jailor? The prison service was a specialized stream.

He smiled and said, 'I wanted to help. There is work to be done. This jail itself, there are 3400 prisoners, but the capacity is 1700. We have to do something about conditions. There are so many undertrials also.'

About then, a young inmate in the standard bright yellow uniform brought tea for us. He had committed a crime and fled when he was 16. He was caught after he turned 18, but there was no clarity as to how he should be tried: as a juvenile or as an adult. He had spent about nine years in Dasna.

The two inmates sitting by my side were different, but they had experienced two ends of the spectrum of the conditions in Dasna in the year they had been inside. Nupur Talwar lived in a rectangular ward with about 50 other women. Their mattresses lined tight against each other on either side, with a space down the middle filled with footwear, the women in her ward had a personal space that measured about 6 feet by 3 feet. Of this, a foot or so at the head was where personal belongings were stacked. Nupur told me her feet extended out on to the corridor of footwear when she slept. At night, if inmates turned in their sleep and disturbed a neighbour because a leg had crossed an invisible boundary, there were vicious fights.

Nupur Talwar tried to escape the atmosphere of the ward as often as possible. The jailor had given her work at the quaintly named 'English Office'. This is where jail correspondence, a fair amount of it in English, was supposed to be handled by staff. But not many staff knew the language.

Nupur was glad to go there and work. It allowed her to step out of her ward and, on most days, meet Rajesh.

He had set up his dental chair and was seeing all manner of patients. During our meeting, a lady guard walked over, making Nupur nervous. She thought there was a reprimand in store—we had long crossed visiting hours. But the guard just wanted to check with Rajesh about when she should come in for her root canal.

Rajesh's ward was far more comfortable than Nupur's. There were just over a dozen inmates in the same kind of space. This was because Mr Khushwaha, or 'Mantriji', the former Uttar Pradesh minister accused in the medical equipment scam, was housed there whenever he had appearances in Ghaziabad. (His base jail, if you will, was Lucknow.)

Mantriji's visits were eagerly awaited by all inmates of the ward, especially Rajesh Talwar. The minister had taken a liking to the dentist, and shared with Rajesh the home-cooked food that was brought for him daily. Mantriji had a supporter who lived very close to the jail who brought fresh food.

Sometimes, Rajesh's man Friday, Vikas Sethi, bought vegetables and delivered them to this man so these could be cooked and sent to the minister and Rajesh.

The shopping was done in a small market a few hundred metres from the jail. It existed just for the inmates. It was a place where you could find essentials that met jail specifications: sealed packets of condiments or snacks, basic clothing, fruits, vegetables. Also some contraband, such as cigarettes that might be smuggled in. The market's timings matched the jail's visiting hours. By about four in the afternoon, the sellers prepared to head home.

In September, at his little clinic in the jail, Rajesh Talwar had received a patient who made him awkward. It was Bachu Singh, the policeman who claimed he couldn't smell during the trial, and who had some trouble explaining what seemed like obvious forgeries in documents he had written. Rajesh had never acknowledged him when he passed Bachu Singh in the premises, but the policeman turned up at his clinic for treatment anyway. Rajesh gritted his teeth and did what he had to as a dentist.

They ran into each other again shortly after Rajesh read about Kaul's death. This time, Rajesh stopped Bachu Singh and relayed the news. Bachu Singh was surprised, but went on to tell Rajesh of his harrowing experiences with the CBI man. Of being summoned '200 times' to the CBI office. Of being pressured into doing things he should not have done.

'Why don't you speak the truth now?' Rajesh asked. Bachu Singh promised he would. But Rajesh heard little from him thereafter.

In earlier portions of this book, I've given examples of Nupur Talwar's toughness under pressure. I hold these to be true in their contexts. But a year in jail changes things. The Nupur Talwar I saw in November did not have the bearing of the woman I had seen striding into court, the policemen making way for her. She had, instead, the sharp movements of a bird on constant alert for approaching predators. She saw her work at the 'English Office' as a privilege granted to her. She was wary of bending any rules, and deferential to the lowest authority, lest what little she had to look forward to be taken away. Rajesh was more settled, telling her constantly that it was all right. That nothing was going to happen.

The news on the day that I visited wasn't good. Their appeal in Allahabad had been put off indefinitely, their application joining a long waiting list, rather than being treated with urgency, as the same court had instructed earlier in the year. There was no telling when they would be heard. In Allahabad, there are appeals pending from the 1980s.

It was well past six in the evening. As I headed for the exit, Nupur scurried back to her ward clutching a plastic bag of precious supplies, as if committing a felony. I left the jail after a guard checked the entry stamp on my palm with just a little less courtesy than a nightclub bouncer letting you in. Outside, the shopkeepers of the inmates' market had all gone home.

# A Note on Sources

This book has been investigated and reported over a two-and-a-half-year period. It began with my reporting on the trial which I attended every day. Alongside this I have had extensive interviews (both on and off the record) with most people central to the case. An abridged list includes Rajesh Talwar, Nupur Talwar, Shyam Lal, A.G.L. Kaul, R.K. Saini, Tanveer Ahmed Mir, Satyaketu Singh, Arvind Jaitley, Arun Kumar, Vijay Shanker, K.K. Gautam, Bharti Mandal, Kalpana Mandal, Amit Jogi, Dr Sushil Choudhry, Dr M.S. Dahiya, Dr S.L. Vaya, Dr C.N. Bhattacharya, Group Capt. (retd) Bhalachandra Chitnis, Lata Chitnis, Dr Dinesh Talwar, Dr Vandana Talwar, Fiza Jha, Vidushi Durrani and Manini Mathur.

I have relied on the following documents:

1. CBI's LIST OF RELIED UPON DOCUMENTS (RC/(S)2008/SCR-SCR-III/DLI). 101 documents including all FIRs, post-mortem reports, forensic reports, seizure memos, forwarding letters, emails, etc.

2. CBI's LIST OF RELIED UPON WITNESSES (RC/(S)2008/SCR-SCR-III/NDLI). Contains recorded statements of 141 listed prosecution witnesses (only 39 eventually testified). Includes all subsequent 'improvements' that witnesses made, e.g., Dr Sunil Dohare, Aarushi's post-mortem doctor, has four statements (July 2008 to May 2010) improving upon his original post-mortem report; Dr Naresh Raj, Hemraj's post-mortem doctor, and the retired police officer K.K. Gautam have two statements each.

3. Witness testimonies of both prosecution and defence witnesses from court records. (For English translations, I have depended on the written submissions of the defence during final arguments, which were accepted by the trial court.)

4. Judge Shyam Lal's orders through the course of the trial and his judgement of 25 November 2013.

5. Applications moved by the Talwars in the trial court; the CBI's replies.

6. Review petition by the Talwars in the Supreme Court (2012).

7. Counter-affidavit by the CBI in the Supreme Court (2012).

8. Polygraph, brain-mapping and narco analysis reports of tests conducted on Rajesh and Nupur Talwar between June 2008 and January 2010 in New Delhi and Gandhinagar.

9. Polygraph, brain-mapping and narco analysis reports of tests conducted on Krishna, Rajkumar and Vijay Mandal in June and July 2008 in New Delhi, Gandhinagar, Mumbai and Bangalore.

10. Essays and cards that Aarushi had written/made.

11. Rajesh Talwar's jail diaries.

Information gleaned from media reports has, to the best of my knowledge, been acknowledged directly in the text.

# Acknowledgements

There are many people I have to thank for helping me with this book. Rajesh Talwar provided the first pile of documents that I went through. In the Ghaziabad trial court, the Talwars' lawyers Satyaketu Singh and Manoj Sisodia did their best to answer every question I had, as indeed did the CBI's counsel R.K. Saini and Inspector Arvind Jaitley.

Tanveer Ahmed Mir, Shivek Trehan and Dhruv Gupta, all of whom represented the defence, were patient in explaining many points of law. Dr Dinesh Talwar's unflagging energy in seeking justice for his brother was inspiring.

There were several current and former officials who were generous with their time, and added immense value to this book by offering their perspective, and allowing access to documents. Dr S.L. Vaya, who headed forensics at the Gandhinagar Forensic Science Laboratory, and her colleague Dr Amita Shukla provided critical inputs. Former CBI director Vijay Shanker and Arun Kumar, now additional director general of the CRPF, threw light on a number of aspects of the investigation that were in the shadow. Neeraj Kumar, who served in the CBI and was commissioner of police, Delhi, offered insights on policing and the functioning of the CBI that were invaluable.

This book took shape only after a year and a half of reporting on the case for the *Mumbai Mirror* and Sify.com and I must thank Meenal Baghel and Sarita Ravindranath for allowing me both space and freedom.

Chiki Sarkar, my editor at Penguin, offered constant support, but also asked the kind of questions one dreads as a writer. This is a good thing. Without Chiki's interventions, this would not have been half the book it is. My copyeditor Jaishree Ram Mohan felt the book as much as I did, and I was often touched by her commitment to it. Dr Neeru Kanwar's insights into human nature also greatly benefited the book.

The final thing to have happened before this book went to press was the lawyers' read. As a part of this I was ambushed into meeting the legal and literary man Rajeev Dhavan. This book may never have been published had he not gone through the manuscript and seen some merit in it.

Last, and very much the most, I would like to thank my friend and fellow traveller Aditya Sinha. Aditya spent weeks with me on the manuscript.

Thank you, everyone.